J. (James) Greenhill, Frederick James Furnivall

A list of all the songs and passages in Shakspere which have been

set to music

J. (James) Greenhill, Frederick James Furnivall

A list of all the songs and passages in Shakspere which have been set to music

ISBN/EAN: 9783742875129

Manufactured in Europe, USA, Canada, Australia, Japa

Cover: Foto ©Thomas Meinert / pixelio.de

Manufactured and distributed by brebook publishing software
(www.brebook.com)

J. (James) Greenhill, Frederick James Furnivall

A list of all the songs and passages in Shakspere which have been set to music

A LIST OF

ALL THE SONGS & PASSAGES
IN SHAKSPERE

WHICH HAVE BEEN SET TO MUSIC.

COMPILED BY

J. GREENHILL, THE REV. W. A. HARRISON,
AND F. J. FURNIVALL.

THE WORDS IN OLD SPELLING, FROM THE QUARTOS
AND FIRST FOLIO,

EDITED BY

F. J. FURNIVALL AND W. G. STONE.

———◆———

PUBLISHT FOR

𝕿𝖍𝖊 𝕹𝖊𝖜 𝕾𝖍𝖆𝖐𝖘𝖕𝖊𝖗𝖊 𝕾𝖔𝖈𝖎𝖊𝖙𝖞

BY N. TRÜBNER & CO., 57, 59, LUDGATE HILL,
LONDON, 1884.

v

CONTENTS.

CONTENTS.

CONTENTS.

[1] Compare Byron's Poem on attaining his 36th year.—T. Tyler.

FOREWORDS.

AFTER the first 'Musical Evening' of the New Shakspere Society, in May, 1883, several Members exprest the
wish that the Words of the Songs had been put into their
hands, for their memories had sometimes faild them.

As the Musical Evening will, no doubt, be repeated
every May while the Society lasts, the Committee thought
that all Shakspere's Songs and Lines which have been
set to Music, had better be printed, with a List of the
Composers who have set them, and the Voices which are
to sing them, so that the 'Book of the Words' might be a
permanent one, and suit all the changing yearly Programs.

Accordingly, our Conductor, Mr. James Greenhill, compiled,—from Alfred Roffe's *Handbook of Shakspere Music*,
1878, and other sources,—a draft List of the Songs and
Composers, and I added the Words, from the revises of the
Old-Spelling Shakspere edited by Mr. Stone and myself, and
from the Quartos and First Folio.[1] The draft 'List' has
been checkt by the Rev. W. A. Harrison and me with, and
enlarged from the Shakspere entries in the British Museum
Catalog of 'Authors whose words have been set to Music,'
many volumes of music, Chappell's Catalogs, &c.,[2] and has
been revised by Mr. Wm. Chappell and others.[3] Mr. Edward

[1] Some context, or a short statement. has been given, in most cases,
to show how and why each Song was brought in.

[2] In some instances we have been unable to ascertain the exact date
when a piece was composed or published ; and the date given in the List
must be taken as only approximately correct. But in very many more
we have discovered the precise year—and had it been thought necessary
could have added the month and day—when a piece was first given to
the world. Genest's 'Account of the English Stage' (10 vols., 1832),
and Sir G. Grove's excellent 'Dictionary of Music and Musicians' have
been of great service to us in this respect.

[3] Mr. Fry, of Novello and Co., has been good enough to look over
our proofs.

Flügel of Leipzig has **been so** kind as to send **a** list of the German settings. I have also compiled a 'Contents' of such Collections of Shakspere Music as I have been able to get hold of. Tho' still incomplete, the 'List' is no wise so ridiculously imperfect as the entries of Shakspere Music in the British Museum. Whether the Museum has only the Shakspere Music catalogd, **or its** Catalog is desperately behindhand, the result is equally lamentable, **and** does little **credit to** the Museum Authorities.

Readers will note how the Musicians have naturally **found more** material for their art in Shakspere's Comedies, **than in his** Histories, Tragedies, and Poems; how, of these **Comedies, the** *Midsummer Night's Dream* (15), the *Tempest* (13), *Twelfth Night* (9), and *As you like it* (7), have had **most pieces from them set;** and how the following Songs **have proved the most attractive** ones :[1]

    1. Take, oh take those Lips away (*M. for M.*)   ...   **set 30 times.**
    2. Fletcher's 'Orpheus with his Lute' (*Henry VIII.*)   ,, 21   ,,
    3. It was a Lover and his Lass (*As you like it*)   ...   ,, 18   ,,
    4. Who is Sylvia? (*Two Gentlemen*) ...   .   ,, 18   ,,
    5. O Mistris mine (*Twelfth Night*) ...   .   ,, 16   ,,
    6. Marlowe's 'Come liue with me' (*Pass. Pilgr.*,
         including 'To shallow Riuers' (*Merry Wives*) ...   ,, 16   ,,
    7. Sigh no more, Ladies (*Much Ado*) ...   .   ,, 15   ,,

Of **the** Poems, the spurious ones in the *Passionate Pilgrim* have drawn to them more composers than Shakspere's own non-dramatic **work.** Marlowe's 'Come live with me' has been set **16 times,** to the 6 times of Shakspere's 18th Sonnet, " Shall I compare **thee** to **a Summer's** Day ? "

                                                F. J. F.

9 April, 1884.

[1] After writing the above, and correcting the proofs up to the *Merchant*, I turnd to Roffe's book in the British Museum on April 10—Mr. Greenhill has had my copy for the last 18 months—and I was rather shockt to find that Roffe had given the extracts too, so that our book looks like a piracy of his. But my part was done independently; and Mr. Greenhill's compilation from Roffe was a necessity. Every cataloguer must use his foregoers' work, and add to it, so far as he can. Such **merit** and usefulness as are in the present book must therefore be set **down as** flowing from Roffe's example, though we have really workt **hard to** add to his material. Our additions of settings to his list are **stard (*).** But these stars do not represent the fresh dates and details **which we** have inserted in Roffe's entries, or our corrections of his **mistakes.**

THE following is a 'Contents' of the chief Collections of
Shakspere Music. Of Dr. Kemp's 'Musical Illustrations of
Shakspere' and many other books, no fit details are given.
These books are not in the British Museum.—F. J. F.

1660. JOHN WILSON. "Cheerfull Ayres or Ballads. First
composed for one single voice, and since set for three
voices." Contains 69 songs, and among them :

(2. From the faire Lavinian shore).
4. Full fathome five (*Tempest*). R. Johnson[1] [writer of the air].
5. Where the bee sucks (*Tempest*). R. Johnson [writer of the air].
(6. When love with unconfined wings.)
33. Lawne as white as driven snow (*Winter's Tale*). (See the late Dr.
E. F. Rimbault's *Who was Jack Wilson?* 1846, p. 12-14.)

1742. Dr. Thomas Augustine ARNE. The Songs in *As you
like it* . . . To which are added The Songs in *Twelfth
Night* . . . .

1742. Dr. T. A. ARNE. The Songs and Duets in the
Blind Beggar of Bethnal Green[2] . . .

11. The Owl, Written by Shakespear in (*Love's labour lost*), it is a
description of Winter, as the Cuckoo Song is of the Spring.
When Isicles hang on the wall   15

[1] Robert Johnson was a celebrated performer on the lute, and young
Wilson (born, 1594) may have been his pupil. He wrote the music for
Middleton's *Witch*, as well as Shakspere's *Tempest*. Rimbault, p. 9-10.
Tho' John Wilson could not have composed the original music to 'Take,
oh take, those lips away!' (*Meas. for Meas.*) he may have been the 'Boy'
who sang it (p. 25 below). Later in his life, he did set it.—Rimbault,
p. 3-5.
[2] The *Merchant of Venice* Song named in the continuation of the Title
is the spurious 'To keep my gentle Jessy'.

17 .. DR. T. A. ARNE.   The Second Volume of Lyric Harmony . .

PAGE

5. Ariel's Song in the *Tempest.* 'Where the Bee sucks.'[1] Solo 185
14. On Cloe Sleeping, taken from Shakespear.
One of her Hands, one rosy Cheek lay under. (*Rape of Lucrece*. st. 56, 'Her lillie hand, her rosie Cheeke lies vnder.') Solo 197

1745. J. F. LAMPE. *Pyramus and Thisbe;* A Mock-Opera. The Words taken from Shakespeare, as it is Perform'd at the Theatre-Royal in Covent-Garden. Set to Musick by Mr. I. F. Lampe.

3. And thou, O Wall (. . . eyne. *M. N. Dr.*, V. i. 173-5). Solo, T.   8
4. O wicked Wall (. . . me. *M. N. Dr.*, V. i. 176-9)   "   12
6. Not Cephalus to Procris was so true (*M. N. Dr.*, V. i. 196-7). Duetto, S. T.   17
11. Approach, ye Furies fell (*M. N. Dr.*, V. i. 275-8). Solo, T. .. 29
12. Now am I dead (*M. N. Dr.*, V. i. 292-7)   "   32
13. These Lilly Lips (*M. N. Dr.*, V. i. 319—350)   33

1745. THOMAS CHILCOT. Twelve English Songs, with their Symphonies. The Words by Shakespeare and other Celebrated Poets. Set to Musick by Thomas Chilcot, Organist of Bath. London. John Johnson.

1. Pardon, Goddess of the Night. (*Much Ado.*)   1
2. Come, thou Monarch of the Vine. (*Ant. and Cleop.*)   ...   4
3. Hark, hark! the Lark. (*Cymbeline.*)   7
4. On a day, alack the day! (*Love's Lab's Lost.*)   10
5. Take, oh take, those lips away. (*Meas. for Meas.*)   ...   12
(6 Place beneath a Spreading Vine. (Anacreon.)   ...   ...   15)
(7. Come live with me, and be my Love. (*Pass. P.*, by 'Kit. Marlow.')   ...   .   19)
(8. Friends of Play and Mirth and Wine. (Anacreon.)   ...   22)
(9. Fill, kind Females, fill the Bowl. (Anacreon.)   ...   ...   26)
10. Wedding is great Juno's Crown. (*As you like it.*)   31
11. Orpheus with his Lute. (*Henry VIII*, by Fletcher.)   ...   34
(12. The Choir awake! (Euripides.)   39

---

[1] The 'Song from Shakespear's *Cymbeline*, on p. 187, is the spurious ' To fair Fidele's grassy Tomb.'

1755. JN. CHRISTOPHER SMITH. The *Fairies*. An Opera. The words taken from Shakespear, and Set to Music by Mr. Smith.

1756. JN. CHRISTOPHER SMITH. The *Tempest*. An Opera. The Words taken from Shakespear, &c. Set to Music by Mr. Smith.

[1] Theodore Aylward's 'Six Songs in Harlequin's Invasion, Cymbeline, and Midsummer Night's Dream, &c.,' 1770, contains only one genuine song 'Hark, the Lark,' sung by Mr. Vincent.

1807. J. HUTCHINSON. A Collection. (Not in Brit. Mus.)

1812. *Musica* **Antiqua**, 2 vols, ed. J. Stafford Smith.

Willow **Song** in *Othello*, by Pelham Humphrey, Composer to the King,
1673. Solo, S. ii. 171.
Fare-well deere love, (quoted in *Twelfth Night*,) by Robert Jones, 1601.
Song, in 4 Parts. ii. 204.[1]

1814 (?). DR. J. KEMP.   Musical Illustrations of Shakspere.
(Not in Brit. Mus.)

Lady, by yonder blessed Moon. (*Romeo and Juliet.*)   Duet, S.T. ab.
1799.
A Lover's eyes will gaze an Eagle blind. (*L. L. Lost.*)   Solo, T. ab.
1799. Cello accompaniment.
Hamlet's Letter. Doubt thou the **Stars** are fire. (*Hamlet.*) Solo, T.
1814. **Cello** and P. F. accompaniment.
Willow Song. A poor soul sat sighing. (*Othello.*) Solo, S. 1807.

1816. WM. LINLEY. Shakspeare's Dramatic Songs. 2 vols.

[1] In Henry Smith's 'Six Canzonets for the Voice . . . the Words
selected from Shakespeare,' &c., 1816, Congreve's two lines, "Music hath
charms to soothe the savage breast, To soften rocks and bend the knotted
Oak " (*Mourning Bride*, I. i. 1-2) are assigned to Shakspere.

[*Appendix:*] The Music in *Macbeth* as it is now performed on the Stage. Newly arranged in three parts, and a Piano Forte accompaniment by Mr. Samuel Wesley, p. 69—89. (As the words are not Shakspere's, the names of the Songs, &c. are not given here.[1])

[1] The spurious song "O bid your faithful Ariel fly" is included in Linley's Collection. It was composed by Thos. Linley, Junr., 1777. The words are attributed to Dr. Laurence ('Shakspere Vocal Magazine'). The *Tempest* was brought out at Drury Lane in 1777, the year after Garrick retired. Garrick transferred his share of the theatre to Sheridan. Sheridan's wife was the sister of Thos. Linley, who thus became composer of the music for the theatre. Is it not likely that Sheridan may have written these words?—W. A. H.

1820. HENRY R. BISHOP. The Songs, Duetts and Glees,
in Shakspeare's Play of *Twelfth Night* performed at the
Theatre Royal, Covent Garden.

1821. HENRY R. BISHOP. The Overture, Songs, Duetts,
Glees and Chorusses, in Shakspeare's Play of the *Two
Gentlemen of Verona*, as performed at the Theatre Royal,
Covent Garden.

---

[1] No. 4 is ' Come o'er the brook, Bessè, to me ' (*Lear*), with a spurious
continuation, set as a Glee for 4 Voices, S.,A. or S.,2, T.B., p. 22. The
burden, p. 26 and 31, is from Dr. Calcott.

1824. HENRY R. BISHOP. The **Whole of the** Music in
As you like it, as performed **at** the **Theatre** Royal,
Covent Garden [&c.]. The Three Songs composed for
the above Play, by Dr. Arne. The poetry Selected
entirely from the Plays, Poems, and Sonnets **of**
Shakspeare.

---

[1] 'Whilst . . find,' l. 29-34, 6 lines ; then l. 51-2, 'She (*for* He) that is
for,' 8 lines.
[2] O.—Shakspere. **The** last 2 lines of the Sonnet are not set.

1847 (?). Shakspere Songs, edited by Charles Jefferys.
Jefferys and Nelson.

1. Blow, blow thou winter Wind (*As you like it*). Tenor Solo. Dr.
   Arne.
2. Under the Greenwood Tree (*As you like it*). Tenor Solo. Dr.
   Arne.

ab. 1850. J. REEKES. Six Shakspere Songs. (Not in B.
Mus.)

1. O Mistress mine. (*Tw. Night.*) Song.
2. Shall I compare thee to a Summer's day? (*Sonnet* 18, lines 1—3,
   and 9.)
3. Full many a glorious Morning. (*Sonnet* 33.) Solo.
4. Farewell, thou art too dear. (*Sonnet* 87.) Solo.
5. If Love have left you twenty thousand tongues. (*Venus and Ad.* st.
   130.) Solo, A. or B.
6. Wilt thou be gone. (*Romeo and Juliet.*[2]) Solo.

1864. JOHN CAULFIELD. A Collection of the Vocal Music
in Shakespeare's Plays. 2 vols. J. Caulfield.

Vol. I. *The Tempest.*

[3]Come unto these yellow sands. Solo. Purcell 1
Hark, hark! the watch dogs bark. Chorus, S.A.T.B. Purcell ... 3
Full fathom five. Solo. Purcell 4
Sea Nymphs hourly ring his knell. Chorus, S.A.T.B. Purcell ... 6

---

[1] Art.—Shakspere.
[2] J. L. Hatton's 'Overture and Music incidental to Shakspere's Play of
K. Henry VIII.,' 1855, consists of 6 pianoforte pieces; and no. 7, Fletcher's
'Orpheus with his Lute' set as a Duet for Soprano and Contralto.
   B. Isaacson's 'Favorite Airs in Shakespeare's K. Henry V.', 1858, is a
set of 12 pianoforte bits of old airs and new music.
   Bishop's Music to the *Tempest* is the pianoforte score.
[3] Before this, is Garrick's "Thou soft flowing Avon," set by Arne.

[1] Follow, the spurious 'O bid your faithful Ariel fly' (p. 20);
Symphony and Grand Chorus descriptive of a Storm and Shipwreck, composed by Thos. Linley, Junr. (p. 21); Grand Chorus, 'Arise ye Spirits
of the Storm' (S A.T.B.), (p. 30); 'Kind Fortune smiles,' Solo, H. Purcell
(p. 48); 'Dry those eyes,' Solo, H. Purcell (p. 51); 'Where does the
black Fiend,' Solo and Chorus 'In Hell,' H. Purcell (p. 57, 58); 'The
owl is abroad,' Solo, J. Smith (p. 62); Grand Masque, 'Great Neptune,'
H. Purcell, duet (p. 65).

[2] Two spurious songs follow : 'Haste Lorenzo' (p. 110), and 'To keep
my gentle Jessy,' p. 116.

[3] 'The annexed Piece ('Which is the Properest Day to Drink') is at
present performed in the place of the Catch before mentioned,' p. 143-7.

1864.   *Shakspeare Vocal Album (and Magazine[1]).*

[1] This is the Album in separate Songs, but with the same paging.

[1] 'Sweet Anne Page' ('With thee fair summers joys appear') follows, p. 42. Then Wm. Ball's 'Light o' Love,' p. 113.

[2] 'Thou soft flowing Avon,' Garrick's Ode to Shakspere, set by Arne, follows, p. 1.

[3] 'The Warwickshire lad,' Jubilee Music, 1769. Song and Chorus; Dibdin, is on p. 125.

1865.   The Music in Shakspeare's *Tempest*, by Purcell, Arne, Smith and Linley.   New Edition, with additions by Dryden, &c.   London.   C. Lonsdale.   [I give only the genuine pieces, as usual.]

	PAGE
No more Dams I'll make for fish. Solo. J. C. Smith.	25
Come unto these yellow Sands. Solo and Chorus, S.A.T.B. Purcell.	28
Full fathom five. Solo and Chorus, S.A.T.B. Purcell	31
Where the bee sucks. Solo. Dr. Arne	56
„ „ „ „ Quartet, S.C.T.B. Harmonised by W. Jackson of Exeter	59
(Four spurious lines are added, followed by the genuine ' Over park, over pale, Thorough bush, thorough briar ; Over hill, over dale, Thorough flood, thorough fire ' (*M. N. Dream*) ; and then ' Merrily, merrily ' comes in again.)	
While you here do snoring lie. Solo. T. Linley. Appendix	69
Ere you can say ' Come and go.' Solo. T. Linley	71
Honour, riches, marriage, blessing. Duet. W. Linley	77

1866 (?).   Chappell's Musical Magazine.   Edited by E. F. Rimbault.   No. 47. — Thirteen Standard Songs of Shakspeare.   Price 1s.

1. Blow, blow, thou winter wind (*As you like it*). Solo. Dr. Arne.
2. Where the bee sucks (*Tempest*). Solo. Dr. Arne.
3. Under the greenwood tree (*As you like it*). Solo. Dr. Arne.
4. When daises pied (*L. L. Lost*). Solo. Dr. Arne
5. Come unto these yellow sands (*Tempest*). Solo and Chorus.
6. Full fathom five (*Tempest*). Purcell.
(7. Oh : bid your faithful Ariel fly. (Words by Dr. Laurence.) T. Linley.)
8. Sigh no more, ladies (*Much Ado*). Solo. R. J. S. Stevens.
9. Bid me discourse (*Ven. and Ad.*). Solo. Sir H. R. Bishop.
10. Who is Sylvia? (*Two. Gent.*). Solo. F. Schubert.
11. Hark ! the lark. (*Cymbeline*). Solo. F. Schubert.
12. On a day (for two voices) (*L. L. Lost*). Sir H. R. Bishop.
13. The airs sung by Ophelia (*Hamlet*). Traditional. ' How should I '; ' Lady, he is dead ;' ' White his shrowd '; ' Good morrow'; ' They bore him bare-faced '; ' For bonny sweet Robin'; ' And will he not come '.

1864. Choral Songs. (S.A.¹T.B.) ... by G. A. MACFARREN. Novello and Co. (Thirteen of em : the first by Fletcher ; the next 6 by Shakspere.)

No. 1. "Orpheus with his Lute" (by Fletcher). *Henry VIII.*, p. 1.
 „ 2. Song of Winter. "When Icicles hang by the Wall." *Love's Labour's Lost*, p. 5.
 „ 3. "Come away, come away, Death !" *Twelfth Night*, p. 9.
 „ 4. Song of Spring. "When Daisies pied." *Love's Labour's Lost.* (A fresh p. 1—5.)
 „ 5. "Who is Sylvia ?" *Two Gentlemen of Verona*, p. 20.
 „ 6. "Fear no more the Heat o' the Sun." *Cymbeline*, p. 24.
 „ 7. "Blow, blow, thou Winter Wind." *As you like it*, p. 30.

1869. Eight Shakspere Songs, set to Music in Four Parts, by G. A. MACFARREN. Novello's Part-Song Book. Second Series. Book XV. Price 1s. 4d.

No.
124. "Sigh no more, Ladies." *Much Ado.*
125. "You spotted Snakes." *Mids. Night's Dream.*
126. "Take, O take those Lips away." *Meas. for Measure.*
127. "It was a Lover and his Lass." *As you Like it.*
128. "O Mistress mine." *Twelfth Night.*
129. "Under the Greenwood Tree." *As you like it.*
130. "Hark the Lark." *Cymbeline.*
131. "Tell me where is Fancy bred." *Merch. of Venice.*

[In later numbers of this 2nd Series of Novello's Part-Song Book, are two Part-Songs by Richard Reay :]

146. "As it fell upon a Day." *Pass. Pilgrim*, by Richard Barnfield. Treble, A.T.B !
149. "Take, Oh take those Lips away." *Meas. for Measure.* Treble, A.T.B.

18 . . Sir H. R. Bishop's Glees and Choruses. A Selection, publisht by Novello.

7. "Who is Sylvia ?" (*Two Gent. of Verona.*) Key of G. S.A.T.B. 2d.
15. "What shall he have?" (*As you like it.*) Key of E flat. A.T.T.B. 2d.
18. "Come, thou monarch." (*Antony and Cleopatra.*) Key of D. A.T.B. 2d.

¹ Or 2nd Soprano. These Songs also appear in Novello's Part-Song Book, 1st Series.

33. "Good night, good rest." (*Pass. Pilgr.*) Key of C. S.A.T.B. 2*d.*
58. "Blow, blow, thou winter wind." (*As you like it.*) Key of G.
S.A.T.B. 2*d.*

18 .. Novello's Secular Music. Glees, Madrigals, or Part-
Songs, for Four Voices (S.A.T.B. unless otherwise
expressed). 1½*d.* each.

124. "Full Fathom five." (*Tempest.*) S. solo and Chorus. Purcell.
124. "Come unto these yellow sands." (*Tempest.*) Purcell.
67. "Hark, the Lark." (*Cymbeline.*) Dr. Cooke.
81. "Sigh no more, Ladies." (*Much Ado.*) S.S.A.T.B. Stevens.
275. „ „ „ „ „ „ (S.A.T.B.) Macfarren.
254. "Tell me where is Fancy bred." (*Merchant.*) Mrs. M. Bartholomew.
49. "The cloud-capt Towers." (*Tempest.*) Stevens.
246. "Who is Sylvia?" (*Two Gent. of Verona.*) G. A. Macfarren.
64. "Ye spotted Snakes." (*Mids. N. Dream.*) R. J. S. Stevens.

1878. SIMPSON, Richard (the late: Member of the New
Shakspere Society's Committee). *Sonnets of Shakspeare,*
selected[1] from a Complete Setting, *and Miscellaneous
Songs.* London. Stanley Lucas, Weber and C.

SONNETS.

[1] The selection, from a great number of songs submitted to her, has been
kindly made by Mrs. Macfarren, wife of the eminent Professor, and Principal
of the Royal Academy of Music. 'Notice' by Mrs. Simpson. April 1878.

MISCELLANEOUS SONGS.[1]

*   *   *   *   *   *

Of the following books of Shakspere Music given in Bohn's *Lowndes* I can find no copy in the British Museum :

1675.   Choice Ayres and Dialogues . . and . . Songs sung . . in the *Tempest.* C. E. HORN. Shakspere's Seven Ages. Midsummer Night's Dream.

      „   „

1692. Hy. PURCELL. Some Select Songs in the *Fairy Queen,* an adaptation of *M. N. Dream.*

W. BOYCE. Masque in the *Tempest.*

G. NICKS. Ophelia's Airs in *Hamlet,* arranged by . . . Vernon's *Witches ;* Song in *Two Gent. of Verona,* &c.

S. Arnold's *Macbeth* is, I suppose, to spurious words, like the editions of Locke's music to *Macbeth.*

---

[1] I give only the Shakspere ones.

All's Well that Ends Well.

Act I. Scene iii. lines 67—75.

"WAS THIS FAIRE FACE THE CAUSE, . QUOTH SHE?"

[The scene is laid in the palace of Count Bertram, at Rousillon. There are present the Countess, Bertram's mother, her steward, and the clown Lavache.]

Steward. May it pleafe you, Madam, that hee bid *Hellen* come to you : of her I am to fpeake.

Counteffe of Raffillion (to the Clowne, LAVATCH). Sirra! tell my gentlewoman I would fpeake with her; *Hellen,* I meane. 66

Clowne. [sings] *" Was this faire face the caufe," quoth fhe,* 67
     " Why the Grecians facked Troy ?
     Fond done, done fond !
     Was this King Priams ioy ? " 70

     With that fhe fighed as fhe ftood, [*bis.* 71
     And gaue this fentence then :
     " Among nine bad, if one be good,
     Among nine bad, if one be good,
     There's yet **one** *good in ten."* 75

Counteffe. What! "one good in tenne"? you corrupt the fong, firra! 77

Clowne. One good woman in ten, Madam; which is a purifying ath'fong : would God would ferue the world fo all the yeere! wee'd finde no fault with the tithe woman, if I were the Parfon. "One in ten," quoth a! And wee might haue a good woman borne but ore[1] euerie blazing ftarre, or at an earthquake, 'twould mend the Lotterie well : a man may draw his heart out, ere a plucke one. 84

[For the verse (l. 58—61) which comes before the passage quoted above, see p. 2.]
WM. LINLEY, A.D. 1816. Solo : Tenor or Bass. The 'Dramatic Songs of Shakspere,' by Wm. Linley.

[1] ore = over.

B

All's Well, Act I. Scene iii. lines 58—61.

"FOR I THE BALLAD WILL REPEATE."

Counteſſe. Wilt thou euer be a foule-mouth'd and calumnious knaue ?

Clowne. A Prophet I, Madam ; and I ſpeake the truth the next waie :   57

> *For I the Ballad will repeate,*   58
>   *Which men full true ſhall finde ;*
>   *Your marriage comes by deſtinie,*
>   *Your Cuckow ſings by kinde.*   61

Counteſſe. Get you gone, ſir ! He talke with you more anon.

[No setting of this verse is known.]

Anthony and Cleopatra.

Act II. Scene vii. lines 120—125.

SONG.

"COME, THOU MONARCH OF THE VINE."

[The triumvirs, Octavius Cæsar, Mark Antony, and Lepidus, with their followers, have been banqueting with Sextus Pompeius,[1] on board his galley. Before they part, Enobarbus, a friend of Antony, proposes that they should " daunce now the *Egyptian* Backenals, And celebrate our drinke."]

Enobarbus. All take hands !
[*To* Musicians.] Make battery to our eares with the loud Muſicke !
¶ [2] The while He place you : then the Boy shall ſing ;
The holding,[3] euery man shall beare as loud,
As his strong sides can volly.

[*Muſicke Playes.* ENOBARBUS *places them hand in hand.*

The Song.

> *Come, thou Monarch of the Vine,*
> *Plumpie Bacchus with pinke eyne !*   121
> *In thy Fattes our Cares be drown'd,*
> *With thy Grapes our haires be Croun'd !*   123
> *Cup vs, till the world go round,*
> *Cup vs, till the world go round !*   125

THOS. CHILCOT, about 1750. Solo, Tenor, or Bass by transposition.
Chilcot has left out the fifth line. Caulfield's Collection, 1824.

---

[1] Son of Pompey the Great.
[2] '¶' marks that the Speaker addresses some fresh person.
[3] *holding*, burden.

Another. Name unknown, 1759. See Roffe, p. 3.
WM. LINLEY, about 1815. Solo, Boy, with Chorus for Treble (Boy),
Alto, Tenor, and Bass. Linley's 'Dramatic Songs of Shakspere,'
1816.
SCHUBERT (d. 1828). Solo, Tenor or Bass. A verse added in German
and English. 'Shakspere Vocal Album (1864);'[1] and 'Shakspere
Vocal Magazine,' 1864, p. 118.
SIR H. BISHOP, 1837. Chorus for three male voices. Composed for
the *Comedy of Errors*. Novello. Arranged for Soprano, Contralto,
Tenor, and Bass (Lonsdale's 'Shakspere Vocal Album,' 1864,
p. 226, now publisht by Augener and Co., Newgate St.).
Ditto, rearranged by Hatton, 1862. Chorus, S.A.T.B. 'Shakspere
Vocal Album,' 1864, and Ashdown.
WEISS, 1863. Bass Solo.

𝕬𝖘 𝖄𝖔𝖚 𝕷𝖎𝖐𝖊 𝕴𝖋.

Act II. Scene v. lines 1—8, 34—39.

"UNDER THE GREENE WOOD TREE."

[Sung by Amiens to the melancholy Jaques and his mates with
the banisht Duke "in the Forreft of *Arden*, and a many merry
men with him; and there they liue like the old *Rol in Hood* of
England: they fay many yong Gentlemen flocke to him euery day,
and fleet the time carelefly, as they did in the golden world."—
I. ii. 105—109.]

Enter AMYENS, IAQUES, *& others.*

Song.

Amyens. *Vnder the greene wood tree,*
         who loues to lye with mee,   2
       And turne his merrie Note
         vnto the fweet Birds throte,
       Come hither! come hither! come hither:
         Heere fhall he fee
         No enemie,
       But Winter and rough Weather.

       *   *   *   *   *

                    Song.   [*Altogether heere.*

       Who doth ambition fhunne,
         and loues to liue i' th Sunne;   35
       Seeking the food he eates,
         and pleas'd with what he gets,   37
       Come hither! come hither! come hither!
       Heere fhall he fee, &c.

[1] Not the piano-forte folo volume 'The Shakspere Album, or Warwickshire Garland.' London: Lonsdale and Longmans, 1862; 26, Old Bond St.

B 2

Dr. T. A. Arne, 1740.   Solo, Tenor.[1]
Maria Hester Park, about 1790.   Three voices.
Stafford Smith, about 1792.   Glee for four voices.
*Edward Smith Biggs, about 1800.   Three voices.
Wm. Linley, *Shakspere's Dram. Songs*, 1816.   (Chorus **only to Arne's**
      Song.)   Chorus: "Who doth ambition shun?" **for S.S.B., or**
      T.T.B., to follow Dr. Arne's Song.
Sir Henry Bishop, 1824.[2]   Dr. Arne's melody arranged for four male
      voices, and in this form introduced into the *Comedy of Errors*.
*G. A. Macfarren, 1869.   S.A.T.B.   Novello's Part-Song Book.
*H. W. Wareing, 1878.   S.A.T.B.   Part Song.   Novello.

As You Like It, Act II. Scene vii. lines 173—189.

"BLOW, BLOW, THOU WINTER WINDE!"

Duke Senior (to Old Adam, *and his young Master,* Orlando, *at their Meal in the Forrest of* Arden). Welcome! fall to! I wil not
      trouble you
As yet, to quetion you about your fortunes.
⁵¶ Giue vs fome Muficke! ¶ and, good Cozen, fing!   172

Song.

Amyens.   *Blow, blow, thou winter winde!*   173
            Thou art not fo vnkinde
               As mans ingratitude;   175
            Thy tooth is not fo keene,
            Becaufe thou art not feene,
               Although thy breath be rude.   178
         Heigh ho! fing, heigh ho! vnto the greene holly:
         Moft Frendhip is fayning; moft Louing, meere folly: 180
            Then, heigh ho, the holly!
            This Life is moft iolly.   182

            Freize, freize, thou bitter skie!   183
            That doft not bight fo nigh
               As benefitts forgot: 185
            Though thou the waters warpe,
            Thy fling is not fo fharpe
               As freind remembred not.   188
         Heigh ho! fing, &c.

---

    [1] Roffe has, in error, entered as a setting of Shakspere's **words, an old**
ballad in an Ashmole MS., mentioned by Chappell, *Pop. Mus.*, ii. 539, 541.
The words are given by Chappell at p. 541.
    [2] He also arranged Dr. Arne's Melody for Voice and Piano **in his 'The**
whole of the Music in *As you like it*.' 1824.   p. 34--7.
    [3] '¶' marks that the Speaker addresses some fresh person.

DR. T. A. ARNE, 1740. Tenor, or Bass by transposition (ed. 1854, 1856, &c.).

JOHN DANBY, about 1785. Three Tenors and one Bass. Arne's Melody harmonized.

R. J. S. STEVENS, about 1790. Glee, S.A.T.B. Novello.

WM. LINLEY, 1816. "Heigh ho" Chorus, to follow Arne's Song. Linley's 'Dramatic Songs of Shakspere,' 1816.

SIR HENRY BISHOP, 1824.[1] Four male voices, and S.A.T.B. Introduced in the operatized *Comedy of Errors*. Arne's Melody harmonized, and the burthen from Stevens's Glee. Novello; also S.A.T.B. Novello.

SAMUEL WEBBE, about 1830. Glee for five voices.

HON. MRS. DYCE SOMBRE. Contralto or Bass Song, without the burthen 'Heigh ho'.

*MRS. A. S. BARTHOLOMEW (*first* MOUNSEY), 1857. Part Song, S.A.T.B. 'Six four-part Songs,' No. 3. Novello.

AGNES ZIMMERMANN, 1863. Song. Novello.

*G. A. MACFARREN, 1864. Part Song, S.A.T.B. Novello. 'Choral Songs,' No. 7.

R. SCHACHNER, 1865. Part Song. Addison and Lucas.

As You Like It, Act III. Scene ii. lines 81—8.

"FROM THE EAST TO WESTERNE IND.

[Rosalind, drest as a young man, finds stuck on a tree in the Forest of Arden, some verses praising her, written by her lover Orlando. She reads them to the Clown, Touchstone, and the peasant, Corin.]

From the Eaſt to weſterne Inde,
no iewel is like Roſalinde.   82
Hir worth, being mounted on the winde,
through all the world beares Roſalinde.   84
All the pictures faireſt linde,
are but black to Roſalinde.   86
Let no face bee kept in mind,
but the faire of Roſalinde!   88

*SIR ARTHUR S. SULLIVAN, 1865. Solo, Soprano. Called 'Rosalind.' Metzler & Co. He adds a spurious verse :

Rosalind, of many parts,
By heavenly synod was devised ;
Of many faces, eyes, and hearts,
To have the touches dearest prized.
Heaven would that she these gifts should have,
And I to live and die her slave.

[1] He also arranged Dr. Arne's Melody for Voice and Piano in his 'The whole of the Music in *As You Like It*,' 1824. p. 51.

As You Like It, Act IV. Scene ii. lines 10—17.

"WHAT SHALL HE HAVE, THAT KIL'D THE DEARE?"

GLEE OR PART-SONG.

Enter Iaqves *and Lords, like* **Forresters.**

Iaques. Which is he that killed the Deare?
A Lord. Sir, it was I.
Iaques. Let's present him to the Duke, like a *Romane* Conquerour! and it would doe well to set the Deares horns vpon his head, for a branch of victory. ¶ Haue **you no** song, Forrester, for this purpose?   6
A Lord. Yes, Sir.
Iaques. Sing it! 'tis no **matter how it bee in tune, so it make** noyse enough.   9

Musicke.

Song.

A Lord. *What shall he haue, that kild the Deare?*
          His Leather skin, and hornes to weare!   11
              [Then sing him home : the rest shall **beare this burthen.**
          Take thou no scorne to weare the horne!
          It was a crest ere thou wast borne :   13
              Thy fathers father wore it,
              and thy father bore it :   15
          The horne, the horne, the lusty horne,
          Is not a thing to laugh to scorne!   [Exeunt.

JOHN HILTON, about 1652. Round for four Bass voices. **In Charles** Kought's 'Shakspere.'
HENRY CAREY, 1723, or 1730. Solo. In 'Love in a Forest,' known as "The Huntsman's Song."
DR. PHILIP HAYES, about 1780. Three voices.
R. J. S. STEVENS, about 1790. Four male voices.
J. STAFFORD SMITH, about 1792. Glee : One Alto, Two Tenors, One Bass. In Caulfield's Collection.
WM. LINLEY, 1816. Two Sopranos **and One Bass.** An arrangement of J. S. Smith's Glee. Linley.
SIR HENRY BISHOP, 1824. Four male voices. A.T.T.B., in the operatised *Comedy of Errors.* In 'Shakspere Vocal Album' (1864), p. 219 for S.C.T.B. Pub. by Chappell.
*E. EDGAR, 1881. 'The horn, the horn.'

As You Like It, Act V. Scene iii. lines 14—31.

"IT WAS A LOVER, AND HIS LASSE."

[To the Clowne, (Touchstone,) and his country-wench, Audrey, whom he is about to marry.]

Enter two Pages.

1. *Page.* Wel met, honeſt Gentleman!

Clowne. By my troth, well met! Come, fit, fit, and a ſong!

2. *Page.* We are for you : fit i'th' middle ! 8

1. *Page.* Shal we clap into't roundly, without hauking, or ſpitting, or ſaying we are hoarſe? which are the onely prologues to a bad voice.

2. *Page.* I faith, y'faith! and both in a tune, like two gipſies on a horſe. 1

Song.

It was a Louer, and his laſſe,
With a hey, and a ho, and a hey nonino,
That o're the greene corne feild did paſſe, 16
In the ſpring time, the onely pretty ring time,
When Birds do ſing, hey ding a ding, ding :
Sweet Louers loue the ſpring. 19

Betweene the acres of the Rie,
With a hey, and a ho, & a hey nonino,
Theſe prettie Country folks would lie, 22
In ſpring time, &c.

This Carroll they began that houre,
With a hey, and a ho, & a hey nonino,
How that a life was but a Flower 26
In ſpring time, &c.

And therefore take the preſent time !
With a hey, & a ho, and a hey nonino ;
For Loue is crownèd with the prime 30
In ſpring time, &c.

Clowne. Truly, yong Gentlemen, though there vvas no great matter in the dittie, yet yᵉ note was very vntunable. 33

1. *Page.* You are deceiu'd, Sir ; we kept time, we loſt not our time!

Clowne. By my troth, yes ; I count it but time loſt, to heare ſuch a fooliſh ſong. God buy[1] you! and God mend your voices! ¶ Come, *Audrie!* [*Exeunt.* 38

MORLEY, 1600. Solo. In Chappell's ' Music of the Olden Time,' pp. 704 and 704, and C. Knight's ' Shakspere '. (Sung by Mr. Wilbey Cooper at the Crystal Palace, 23 April, 1859.—Roffe.)
R. J. S. STEVENS, 1786. Glee, S.S.A.T.B. Novello.
WM. LINLEY, 1816. Duet, S.C.
SIR HENRY BISHOP, 1824. Soprano Solo. Sung by Miss M. Tree in the operatized *Comedy of Errors.*—Roffe.
S. REAY, 1862. Madrigal. Novello.
EDWARD LODER, 1864. Part Song.
*F STANISLAUS, 1868. Solo. Soprano or Tenor. Ashdown.
*G. A. MACFARREN, 1869. Part Song, S.A.T.B. Novello.

[1] *buy* = be with.

*H. HILES, 1870. S.A.T.B. Novello.
*C. H. HUBERT PARRY, 1874. 'Spring Song.' 'A Garland,' No. 2. Con-
   tralto. Sung by Madame Ant. Sterling. Boosey.
*M. B. FOSTER, 1876. Solo, Contralto. Alfred Phillips. **Kilburn.**
*J. MEISSLER, 1877.
*C. LABUNEYER, 1881. 'In the spring time.'
*D. DAVIES. Part Song. First sung May 7, 1883, at the Highbury
   Philharmonic Society.
*DR. J. C. BRIDGE, Nov. 1883. Part Song, S.A.T.B. Novello.
*B. LUARD SELBY. Part Song. Novello.
*J. BOOTH. Part Song. Novello.
*MICHAEL WATSON. Part Song, S.A.T.B. **Ashdown.**

As You Like It, Act. V. Scene iv. lines 101—8.

"THEN IS THERE MIRTH IN HEAVEN."

[Rosalind is the Duke's daughter, and is to wed Orlando. To the
Duke, Orlando, and their fellows.]

Enter HYMEN, ROSALIND, *and* CELIA.

Still Musicke.

Hymen. *Then is there mirth in heauen,*
When earthly things made euen
   Attone together.   103
Good Duke, receiue thy daughter!
Hymen from Heauen brought her,
   (Yea, brought her hether,)   106
That thou mightst ioyne hir hand with his,
Whose heart within his bosome is.   108

DR. T. A. ARNE, 1740. Song.
SIR HENRY BISHOP, 1824. Song. Sung by Master Longhurst in the
   operatized *As You Like It,* p. 73.
   In his setting of the operatized *Two Gentlemen of Verona,* 1821, Sir
H. Bishop has, at p. 81-91, first a Soprano Solo, of the first four lines
of Sonnet 25, then a Chorus made up of lines 104-5 above, part of the
Hymen song below,[1] and then a duet, one Soprano taking the first four
lines of *Sonnet* 25, the other, the first four of *Sonnet* 97. See *Sonnet* 97,
   below.

As You Like It, Act V. Scene iv. lines 134—9.

"WEDDING IS GREAT JUNO'S CROWNE."

[To the 4 couples about to wed,—Orlando and Rosalind, Oliver
and Celia, the Shepheard and Phebe, and the Clowne Touchstone
and Audrey,—Hymen says:]

----

[1] Good Duke! receive thy Daughter!
Hymen, from heaven brought her.
Such Union is great Juno's crown :
To Hymen, honour and renown!

Here's eight that muſt take hands,
To ioyne in *Hymens* bands,   122

*   *   *   *   *

Whiles a Wedlocke Hymne we ſing,
Feede your ſelues with queſtioning;   131
That reaſon, wonder may diminiſh
How thus we met, and theſe things finiſh!   133

Song.

Wedding is great Iunos *crowne :*   134
  O bleſſ'ed bond of boord and bed!
'Tis Hymen *peoples euerie towne ;*
  High wedlock then be honor'ed!   137
Honor, high honor and renowne,
  To Hymen, *God of euerie Towne!*   139

THOMAS CHILCOT, about 1740. Solo.
WM. LINLEY, 1816. Song. Linley's ' Dram. Songs of Shakspere.'
*B. TOURS, 1882. Part Song. Unpublished.

Comedy of Errors.

Act II. Scene ii. lines 187—191.

"OH, FOR MY BEADS! I CROSSE ME FOR A SINNER."

[This is not a song, but two couplets and a half of rymed verse. The slave Dromio of Syracuse, not able to underſtand how he is mistaken for his twin-brother slave of Ephesus (of whom he has never heard), or how his master—Antipholus of Syracuse—is suppoſed to be that master's twin-brother of Ephesus, of whose existence he has never been told, declares that he and his Master muſt be in ' Fairie-land ' :]

Luciana. Dromio, goe bid the ſeruants ſpred for dinner!

Syr. Dromio. [*aside*] Oh, for my beads! I croſſe me for a ſinner.
  This is the Fairie land : oh, ſpight of ſpights!
  We talke with Goblins, Owles, and Sprights ;   189
  If we obay them not, this will infue :
  They'll ſucke our breath, or pinch vs blacke and blew. 191

DR. KEMP, d. 1824. Solo, Tenor, in Dr. K.'s 'Illustrations of Shakspere.'

Cymbeline.

Act II. Scene iii. lines 21—27.

"HEARKE! HEARKE! THE LARKE AT HEAVEN'S GATE SINGS."

[The foolish lout, Prince Cloten, serenades the perfect Imogen, (wife of Posthumus,) with whom he fancies he is in love.]

Cloten. I would this Muficke would come! I am aduiſed to giue her Muficke a mornings; they fay it will penetrate.

Enter Mofitians.

Come on! tune! If you can penetrate her with your fingering, fo: wee'l try with tongue too: if none will do, let her remaine; but he neuer giue o're. Firſt, a very excellent good conceyted thing; after, a wonderfull fweet aire, with admirable rich words to it; and then let her confider.

Song.

Hearke! hearke! the Larke at Heauens gate fings,   21
and Phœbus 'gins arife,
His Steeds to water at thofe Springs
on chalic'd Flowres that lyes;   24
And winking Mary-buds begin to ope their Golden eyes.
With euery thing that pretty is[1], my Lady fweet, arife!
Arife, arife!   27

THOMAS CHILCOT, about 1750. Solo.
THEODORE AYLWARD, 1770. Solo. (Key of E♭; from lower B to apper A♭.) Sung by Mrs. Vincent.
DR. BENJAMIN COOKE, 1792. Glee for S.A.T.B. Novello.
K. F. CURSCHMAN (d. 1841). Solo. Publ. 1851.
FRANZ SCHUBERT (d. 1828). Solo. Publ. 1842, 1851, 1856, &c. In Chappell's 'Thirteen Standard Songs of Shakspere,' No. 11.
*T. RICKEN. Part Song, S.A.T.B. Novello.
*F. MOCKRING, 1863. 'Horch, horch, die Lerch', in Aether blau.' '6 Gesänge,' No. 4.
*HENRY LESLIE, 1867. An arrangement of Dr. Cooke's Glee for S.S.A.A. Novello.
*G. A. MACFARREN, 1869. Part Song, S.A.T.B. Novello.
*R. EMMERICH, 1814. 'Horch, horch, die Lerch', im Aether **blau.**' 'Funf Gesänge,' &c. Op. 42, No. 1. Ständchen.
*E. H. THORNE. Part Song, S.S.C. Novello.

Cymbeline, Act IV. Scene ii. lines 258–281.

"FEARE NO MORE THE HEATE O' TH' SUN."

[Guiderius and Arviragus—seemingly peasant lads, but really the sons of King Cymbeline—sing over the apparently dead body of their unknown sister Imogen, disguised as a page, the Dirge which they had formerly sung over the corpse of their supposed mother Euriphile.]

Song.

Guiderius. *Feare no more the heate o'th'Sun,*   258
Nor the furious Winters rages!
Thou thy worldly task haft don,
Home art gon, and tane thy wages.   261

---

[1] One of the song-writers, seeing that the plural *bin* (hen) would ryme with ' begin ' in l. 25, has, in spite of grammar, put *bin* here.

DR. T. A. ARNE, (? ab. 1740). Solo. Sung by Mr. Lowe.
Name unknown. ? 1746. See Geneste, vol. iv. p. 193. Solo. In G
    major. Caulfield's Collection.
DR. BOYCE, 1758. (? Solo, or Glee. See Warren's 'Life of Boyce.')
    Called 'The Dirge in *Cymbeline.*'
DR. NARES, d. 1783, and W. LINLEY, 1816. Trio for equal voices.
*G. A. MACFARREN, 1864. S.A.T.B. Choral Songs, No. 6. Novello.
*F. M. HAYES, 1881. 'The Dirge of Fidele.'
*JAMES GREENHILL, 1884. Part Song. S.C.T.B. *In Memoriam* Miss
    TEENA ROCHFORT SMITH, died Sept. 4, 1883.

Hamlet, Prince of Denmark.

Act II. Sc. ii. ll. 116—119. (Qo. 2, sig. E 4.)

"DOUBT THOU THE STARRES ARE FIRE."

[Hamlet's Letter to Ophelia.]

Letter.

Doubt thou the Starres are fire ;	116
Doubt that the Sunne doth moue ;	
Doubt Truth to be a lyer ;	
But neuer doubt I loue!	119

W. TINDAL, 1736. Op. 5. Solo Tenor. With an accompaniment
    for Flute, Violin, and Violoncello. 'Eight Ancient Ballads,' No. 8.
    (A 2nd verse added, not by Shakspere.)

R. J. S. STEVENS, 1790. Solo. With an accompaniment for two **Flutes,** two Violins, and one Bass.
Ditto. The same melody harmonized as a Glee.
J. FISIN, 1800 (?). Solo. 'Ten Songs,' No. 3. With an added verse.
C. DIGNUM, ab. 1800. Solo Tenor. (With a 2nd verse by Dr. Moore.)
M. KELLY, ab. 1800. Soprano Solo. Composed for Miss Abrams. 'Shakspere Vocal Album,' p. 56. (The lines are enlarged, and a verse is added. Line 1 is, ' Doubt, *O most beautified,* that the stars are fire,' &c. &c.)
WM. RUSSELL, ab. 1806 (1808, **B. Mus. Cat.**). **Solo Tenor.** Dedicated to Mr. J. P. Kemble.
DR. J. KEMP, 1814. Tenor. Accomp. for Violoncello **and Piano.** 'Musical Illustrations of Shakspere,' by Dr. Kemp.
EDMUND KEAN. See Proctor's Life of E. Kean.—Roffe, p. 26.
SIR JOHN STEVENSON. Glee for two Tenors and one Bass.
J. DAVY, 1820. Duet for equal voices.
J. PARRY. 1824. Tenor Recitative and Air. Sung by Braham **in the** operatized *Merry Wives of Windsor.*

Hamlet, Act III. Scene ii. lines 282-5.

"WHY, LET THE STROOKEN DEERE GOE WEEPE."

[After the Play-scene, when the guilty Claudius has **rusht from** the Hall, Hamlet says (Quarto 2, sign. H 3) :]

" *Why, let the strooken Deere goe weepe,*   282
  The Hart vngauled play ;
  For some must watch, while some must sleepe :
  Thus runnes the World away."   285

M. P. KING, 1803. Glee for **three** voices, unaccompanied.

SNATCHES OF OPHELIA'S SONGS. (IV. ii. Qo. 2, sign. K. 4.)

Hamlet, Act IV. **Scene v.** lines 23-30, 35, 37-39. (Qo. 2, sign. K. 4.)

"HOW SHOULD I YOUR TRUE LOVE KNOW?"

Shee sings.

Ophelia [mad]. *How should I your true* **Loue know,**   23
        from another one ?
      By *his Cockle hat and staffe,*
        and his Sendall shoone.   26
    *   •   *
      He is dead and gone, Lady !   27
        he is dead and gone !
      At his head, a grasgreene turph ;
        at his heeles, a stone.   30
        •   *   •   *   •

White his ſhrowd as the mountaine ſnow   35
Larded all with ſweet flowers ;   37
Which beweept to the ground did go
With true-loue ſhowers.   39

*Old Melody. In Chappell's ' Music of the Olden Time,' p. 236.
Linley's ' Dramatic Songs,' &c., Vol. ii. p. 50. Caulfield, Vol. ii.
p. 83. Charles Knight's *Shakspere*. *Chappell's 'Thirteen Standard
Songs of Shakspere,' No. 13.
SIR J. STEVENSON. 1789. Glee for two Sopranos and one Bass.
M. V. WHITE, 1882. Solo. 1876 (?) (Known as " Ophelia's Song.")
Boosey.

" THEY BORE HIM BARE-FASTE ON THE BEERE."

Hamlet, IV. ii.   (Qo. 2, sign. K. 4.)   Song.

They bore him bare-faſte on the Beere,   164
(Hey non, nony ; nony, hey nony ! [Fo. 1])
And in his graue rain'd many a teare   166

*   *   *   *   *

Old Melody, in Caulfield. Knight. Chappell's ' Songs.'
*W. Linley, 1816. Song. Linley's ' Dramatic Songs,' &c., Vol. ii. p. 51.

" BONNY SWEET ROBIN."

Hamlet, IV. ii.   (Qo. 2, sign. K. 4.)   Song.

For bonny ſweet Robin is all my ioy.   187

*   *   *   *   *

Old Melody. See Chappell's ' Popular Music,' p. 233, to be found in
*ANTHONY HOLBORNE'S ' Cittharn Schoole,' 1597.
*QUEEN ELIZABETH'S ' Virginal Book.'
*WILLIAM BALLET'S ' Lute Book.'
[Repeated in Caulfield, Linley, C. Knight, *Chappell's 'Thirteen
Songs.']

" AND WILL A NOT COME AGAIN ? "

Hamlet, IV. ii.   (Qo. 2, sign. L. 2.)   Song.

And wil a not come againe ?   190
And wil a not come againe ?
No, no! he is dead!
Goe to thy death bed !
He neuer will come againe !   194

His beard was as white as ſnow,   195
Flaxen was his pole.
He is gone, he is gone !
And we caſt away mone.
God a mercy on his ſoule !   199

*Old Melody. "The tune entitled *Merry Milkmaids* in 'The Dancing
    Master,' 1650." (Chappell, p. 237.)
[Caulfield, Linley, C. Knight. Chappell's 'Thirteen Songs.']
SIR JN. A. STEVENSON, 1800 (?). Glee, S.S.B.

Hamlet, IV. v. 48—55, 58—65. Song.

"TO-MORROW IS S. VALENTINE'S DAY."

> To morrow is S. Valentines day,   48
>   All in the morning betime ;
> And I a mayde, at your window,
>   To be your Valentine.   51
>
> Then vp he rofe, and dond his clofe,   52
>   and dupt the chamber doore ;
> Let in the maide, that out a maide,
>   neuer departed more.   55

    *   *   *   *

> By Gis,[1] and by Saint Charitie,   58
>   alack, and fie, for fhame !
> Young men will don't, if they come too't ;
>   by Cock,[2] they are to blame !   61

Quoth she, ' Before you tumbled me,   62
    you promifd me to wed.'

(He anfwers.) ' So would I a done, by yonder funne,
    And thou hadft not come to my bed.'   65

Old air in Chappell's 'Popular Music,' p. 227.
*Old Melody. 'Quaker's Opera,' 1728.
*Cobbler's Opera, 1729. (See Chappell, p. 237.)
[Repeated in Linley, Caulfield, C. Knight, Chappell's 'Thirteen Songs.']
Traditional. The airs sung by Ophelia. In Chappell's 'Thirteen Stan-
    dard Songs of Shakspere,' No. 13.

Hamlet, Act V. Scene i. lines 69—72, 79—82, 102—5. (Qo. 2, sign. M. 2.)

STANZAS FOR GRAVE-DIGGER.

Song.

Clowne. In Youth, when I did loue, did loue,   69
    Me thought it was very fweet,
To contract, o, the time ; for, A ! my behoue,
    O, me thought, there was nothing a meet.   72

   *   *   *   *   *

But Age, with his ftealing fteppes,   79
    hath clawed me in his clutch,
And hath fhipped me into the land,
    as if I had neuer been fuch.   82

   *   *   *   *   *

------

[1] *Gis* is a contraction for *Jesus*.   [2] God.

A pickax, and a fpade, a fpade,   101
 for and a fhrowding fheet ;
O, a pit of Clay for to be made
 for fuch a gueft is meet.   105

Chappell's 'Music of the Olden Time,' vol. i. p. 201.
Name unknown. Caulfield's Collection, vol. ii. p 90.

King Henry the Fourth.

PART II.

Act IV. Scene iv. lines 81-2, with 2 other bits.

"HEALTH TO MY SOUERAIGNE."

Weftmerland (to HEN. IV.). Health to my Soueraigne, and new
happineffe
Added to that [that I am to deliuer . . .]
. . . an Oliue Branche, and Lawrell Crowne [3 *Henry VI.*, IV. vi. 34]
A Foe to Tyrants, and my Countries Friend [Cato, in *Julius Cæsar*,
 V. iv. 5].

*WILLIAM SHIELD, 1809. A Cento for three voices. In 'A Cento,'
p. 2, calld 'The King. A Cento taken from the Works of
Shakespeare.'

Act V. Scene iii. lines 18—23, 35—9, 48—50, 56, 7, 77—9, 134. (Quarto 1,
 sign. K. 2.)

"DO NOTHING BUT EATE, AND MAKE GOOD
CHEERE."

Scilens. [*fomewhat cupfhotten*] A, firra (quoth-a) we fhall
[*fings*] Do *nothing but eate, and make good cheere,*   18
 And praife God for the merry yeere,
 When flefh is cheape, and Females deare,
 And lusty Laddes roame here and there   21
  So merely ;
  And euer among, fo merily !   23

   *   *   *   *   *
Scilens. *Be merry, be mery ! my Wife has all !*   35
 For women are Shrowes, both fhort and tall.
 'Tis merry in Hall, when Beards wagge¹ all !   37
  And welcome mery Shrouetide !
  Be mery ! be mery !   39
   *   *   *   *   *

  ¹ *Hall . . wagge*] F. hal . . wags Q.

Scilens.	*A Cup of Wine, thats briske and fine,*	48

Scilens. *A Cup of Wine, thats briske and fine,*　　48
And drinke vnto the Leman mine!
And a merry heart liues long-a.　　50

*　　*　　*　　*

Fill the Cuppe, and let it come!
Ile pledge you a mile to the[1] bottome.　　57
Silens. *Do me right,*　　77
and dub me Knight!
Samingo!　　79

●　　●　　●　　●　　●

Falstaffe. Carry Maister *Scilens* to bed!　　134

Anonymous. Solo and Chorus in three parts. In Caulfield's Collection; l. 22-3 omitted.
*W. LINLEY, 1816. Tenor Solo, with l. 22-3 and the two following snatches, l. 35-9, 48-50. Linley's 'Sh.'s Dramatic Songs,' p. 34-6.
*SIR H. R. BISHOP, 1820. Introduced in operatized *Twelfth Night.*

King Henry the Eighth.
Act III. Scene i. lines 3—14.
"ORPHEUS WITH HIS LUTE MADE TREES."

By John Fletcher. (III. i. is part of the Fletcher portion of *Henry VIII.* Shakspere wrote only 1168½ of the 2822 lines of the play. The rest are Fletcher's.)

Enter QUEENE, *and her* Women *as at worke.*

Queene. Take thy Lute, wench! My Soule growes sad with troubles!
Sing, and disperse 'em, if thou canst: leaue working!

Song.

Orpheus *with his Lute made Trees,*　　3
And the Mountaine tops that freese,
Bow themselues when he did sing.　　5
To his Musicke, Plants and Flowers
Euer sprung; as Sunne and Showers
There had made a lasting Spring.　　8

Euery thing that heard him play,　　9
Euen the Billowes of the Sea,
Hung their heads, & then lay by.　　11
In sweet Musicke is such Art, [that]
Killing care, & griefe of heart,
Fall asleepe, or hearing, dye.　　14

[1] *to the* Quarto, *too th'* Folio.

DR. ARNE? (ab. 1740). Song. Caulfield's Collection.
DR. M. GREENE, 1741.* [1742 in B. Mus. Catal.] Song. 'A Cantata
 and four English Songs,' by Dr. Greene.
THOMAS CHILCOT (? ab. 1750). Song.
MATTHEW LOCKE (? ab. 1755).
J. CHRISTOPHER SMITH, 1755. In 'The Fairies.'
R. J. S. STEVENS (? ab. 1790). Glee for five voices.
LORD MORNINGTON. Died 1781. Four-part Madrigal.
THOMAS LINLEY, November, 1788. Song. Sung by Mrs. Crouch.
 Music destroyed at the burning of Drury Lane Theatre.
W. LINLEY, 1816. Song, Soprano.
SIR HENRY BISHOP, 1820. Duet, Soprano and Contralto. Originally
 sung by Misses Greene and M. Tree in *Twelfth Night.* 'Shakspere
 Vocal Album' (1864), p. 197. In Chappell's 'Popular English
 Duets,' ed. Na. Macfarren, No. 5.
JOHN L. HATTON, 1855. Duet, Soprano and Contralto.
VIRGINIA GABRIEL, 1862. Song. 'Shakspere Vocal Album,' p. 150.
*E. B. GILBERT, 1863. Part Song, S.A.T.B. Chappell's 'Vocal
 Library,' No. 25.
SIR G. A. MACFARREN, 1864. Four-part Song, S.A.T.B. 'Choral
 Songs,' No. 1. Novello.
SIR ARTHUR SULLIVAN, 1865. Song, Soprano or Tenor. Metzler.
E. D. HEATHCOTE, 1866. Song.
*E. LASSEN, 1877. Song. German translation.
*ALWYN, W. C., 1875. Song.
*R. PAYNE, 1881 to 1882. Duet or Part Song. [Rogers, a country
 publisher.]
*E. ASPA. Song. Novello.
*G. BENSON. Part Song, A.T.T.B. Novello.

King Lear.

Act I. Sc. iv. lines 181-184, 191-194, 217, 218, 235, 236.

FOUR SNATCHES SUNG BY THE FOOL.

Foole. 1. *Fooles had nere leffe grace in a yeere;*   181
 For wifemen are growne foppifh,
 And know not how their wits to weare,
 Their manners are fo apifh.   184

 2. *Then they for fodaine ioy did weepe,*   191
 And I for furrow fung,
 That fuch a King fhould play bo-peepe,
 And goe the Foole among.   194

 3. *He that keepes nor cruft, nor crum,*
 Weary of all, fhall want fome.   218

C

    4. *The Hedge-Sparrow fed the Cuckoo fo* **long,**
       That it's had it[1] head bit off by it **young.**   **236**

(The two alternates, "The lord that counsell'd thee," ll. 154—161, which are only in the Quarto, have not been set. They are said, not sung, in the play.)

Numbers 1, 2, 3, 4. In Caulfield's Collection. Numbers 1 and 2, by W. LINLEY, 1816, in L's. 'Dramatic Songs of Sh.' ii. 47-9.

Lear, Act II. Scene iv. lines 48 —53, 79—86.

TWO SNATCHES FOR THE FOOL.

    1. **Fathers** *that weare rags,*   48
       do *make their Children blind ;*
      But Fathers that weare bags,
      fhall fee their Children kind.   51
      Fortune, that arrant Whore,
      Nere turns the key to th' Poore.   53

---

    2. *That Sir, which ferues and feekes for gaine,*   79
      And followes but for forme,
    Will packe, when it begins **to raine,**
      And leaue thee in the ftorme.   82
    But I will tarry ; the Foole will ftay ;
      And let the wifeman flie :
    The knaue turnes Foole **that runnes away ;**
      The Foole no knaue, **perdie!**   86

In Caulfield's **Collection.**

Lear, Act III. Scene iv. lines 125-9.

"ST. WITHOLD FOOTED THRICE THE WOLD[2]."

[Sung by Edgar when personating a 'Bedlam'.]

Edgar. *S.* With*old footed thrice the old ;*
    He met the Night-Mare, and her nine-fold : 126
      Bid her alight,
      And her troth-plight ;[3]   128
And, aroynt thee, Witch! aroynt thee!

SIR HENRY BISHOP, 1819. Duet, two Tenors. Sung in the *Comedy of Errors* by Mr. Pyne and Mr. Durusett.

---

[1] 'it' was one of the Elizabethan substitutes for the A.Sax. genitive neuter *his.*
    [2] *Old,* Folio 1.   [3] sweetheart, groom.

Love's Labour's Lost.

Act IV. Scene ii. lines 95—108.

"IF LOVE MAKE ME FORSWORNE, HOW SHALL I SWEARE TO LOVE?"

[NATHANIEL reads BEROWNE'S 6-measure Sonnet to ROSALIN.]

If Loue make me forsworne, how shall I sweare to loue?　　95
Ah! neuer fayth could hold, yf not to beautie vowed.
Though to my selfe forsworne, to thee Ile faythfull proue;
Those thoughts to me were Okes, to thee like Osiers bowed.　98
Studie his byas leaues, and makes his booke thine eyes,　　99
Where all those pleasures liue, that Art would comprehend.
If knowledge be the marke, to know thee shall suffise;
Well learned is that tongue, that well can thee commend;　102
All ignorant that soule, that sees thee without wonder;　　103
Which is to mee some prayse, that I thy partes admire:
Thy eie, Ioues lightning beares; thy voyce, his dreadful thunder,
Which, not to anger bent, is musique, and sweete fier.　　106
Celestiall as thou art, Oh pardon loue this wrong,
That singes heauens prayse, with such an earthly tong.　108

JOHN MAJOR, about 1820. Solo, Tenor. 'Shakspere Vocal Album,'
p. 108.
R. HUGHES, about 1840. Solo, Bass. Sung by Mr. Bland.

Love's Labour's Lost, Act IV. Sc. iii. ll. 25—40, 58—71.

[The two following Sonnets do not seem to have been set:]

The KING reads his Sonnet, to be sent to the PRINCESSE.

" So sweete a kisse, the golden Sunne giues not　　25
To those fresh morning dropps vpon the Rose,
As thy eye-beames, when their fresh rayse haue smot
The night of dew, that on my cheekes downe flowes.　28
Nor shines the siluer Moone one halfe so bright,　　29
Through the transparent bosome of the deepe,
As doth thy face, through teares of mine, giue light:
Thou shinst in euerie teare that I do weepe;　　32
No drop, but, as a Coach, doth carrie thee;　　33
So ridest thou triumphing in my wo.
Do but beholde the teares that swell in me,
And they, thy glorie, through my griefe, will show:　36
But do not loue thy selfe! then thou will keepe
My teares for glasses, and still make me weepe.　38
O Queene of queenes! how farre doost thou excell,
No thought can thinke, nor tongue of mortal tell!"　40

C 2

[LONGAUILL reades his Sonnet, to be fent to MARIA.]

"*Did not the heauenly Rethorique of thine eye,*   58
   Gainſt whom the world cannot holde argument,
Perſwade my hart to this falſe periurie?
Vowes for thee broke, deſerue not puniſhment.   61
A Woman, I forſwore; but I will proue,   62
   Thou being a Goddeſſe, I forſwore not thee.
My Vow was earthly; thou, a heauenly Loue!
   Thy grace being gainde, cures all diſgrace in mee.   65
Vowes are but breath; and breath a vapoure is: 66
   Then thou, faire Sunne, which on my earth doſt ſhine,
Exhalſt this vapour-vow; in thee it is:
   If broken then, it is no fault of mine: 69
If by mee broke, What foole is not ſo wiſe,
To looſe an oth, to winn a Parradiſe?"   71

Love's Labour's Lost, Act IV. Scene iii. lines 99—118. (Also in
The Paſſionate Pilgrim.)

"ON A DAY (ALACKE THE DAY!)"

[DUMAINE reades his Sonnet.]

"*On a day, (alacke the day!)*
Loue, whoſe Month is euer May,   100
Spied a bloſſome paſſing faire,
Playing in the wanton aire: 102
Through the Veluet leaues, the wind,
All vnſeene, can paſſage finde;   104
That the Louer, ſicke to death,
Wiſh himſelfe the heauens breath.   106
'Ayre,' (quoth he), 'Thy cheekes may blow;
Ayre, would I might triumph ſo!   108
But, alacke, my hand is ſworne,
Nere to plucke thee from thy thorne: 110
Vow, alacke, for youth vnmeete,
Youth ſo apt to pluck a ſweete!   112
Do not call it ſinne in me,
That I am forſworne for thee;   114
Thou, for whom Ioue would ſweare,
Iuno but an Æthiop were;   116
And denie himſelfe for Ioue,
Turning mortall for thy loue.'"   118

THOMAS CHILCOT, 1750. Solo.
DR T. A. ARNE (? ab. 1750). Solo. Caulfield's Collection.
IN. CHRISTOPHER SMITH, 1755. Solo. Contralto. In "The Fairies."
WILLIAM JACKSON. Three male voices.
T. LYN about 1790. Four voices. 'Six Canzonets' (1795?).

M. P. KING. Duet, Tenor and Bass, or Soprano and Bass. Commences,
"Do not call it sin in me."
JOHN BRAHAM. (See Roffe, p. 36.)
SIR HENRY BISHOP, 1821. Duet, S.C. Sung by Misses M. Tree and
Hallande, in *Two Gent. of Verona.* 'Shakspere Vocal Album'
(1864), p. 176.
W. P. STEVENS, 1852. Glee for four male voices.
*T. D. SULLIVAN, 1864. Quartette for Treble voices.
*ELLA, 1870. Song.
W. H. CUMMINGS, 1875. Part Song, S.A.T.B.
*C. H. HUBERT PARRY, about 1874. Song. 'A Garland,' No. 1. Boosey.
KELLOW J. PYE, 1879. 'To be sung in C, by a Tenor Voice.' (With
"Good Night! Good Rest!" in 'Two little Songs,' from the
Passionate Pilgrim.)

Love's Labour's Lost, Act IV. Scene iii. lines 318—29.

"A LOVER'S EYES WILL GAZE AN EAGLE BLINDE."

[Part of Berowne's speech, to prove to his Companions the wisdom
of breaking their vow to forswear the company of Women for three
years.]

> *A Louers eyes will gaze an Eagle blinde;*
> *A Louers eare will heare the lowest sound,*
> *When the suspitious head of theft is stopt.* 320
> *Loues feeling, is more soft and sensible*
> *Then are the tender hornes of Cockled Snayles.*
> *Loues tongue, proues daintie* Bachus *graffe in taste.*
> *For Valoure, is not Loue a* Hercules, 324
> *Still clyming trees in the* Hesperides?
> *Subtil as* Sphinx; *as sweete and musicall*
> *As bright* Appolos *Lute, strung with his haire.*
> *And when Loue speakes, the voyce of all the Goddes* 328
> *Make heauen drowsie with the harmonie.*

DR. KEMP, 1814. Solo with Violoncello accompaniment. Dr. Kemp's
'Illustrations of Shakspere.'
JOHN PARRY, 1824. Song. Sung by Mr. Braham in the *Merry Wives
of Windsor.*

Love's Labour's Lost, Act V. Scene ii. lines 877—912.

"WHEN DASIES PIED, AND VIOLETS BLEW."

[Sung after the show of the 'Nine Worthies' had been presented
before the King and the Princess.]

Re-enter all.

Braggart (ARMADO). This side is *Hiems,* Winter; This, *Ver.* the
Spring : The one maynteined by the Owle, th'other by the Cuckow.
¶ *Ver,* begin!

The Song.

Spring.

When Dafies pied, and Violets blew,	877
And Ladi-fmockes all filuer white,	
And Cuckow-budds of yellow hew,	
Do paint the Meadowes with delight,	880
The Cuckow then, on euerie tree,	
Mocks married men; for thus finges hee:	882
Cuckow!	

Cuckow, Cuckow! O word of feare,	
Vnpleafing to a married eare!	885
When Shepheards pipe on Oten Strawes,	886
And merrie Larkes are Ploughmens Clocks,	
When Turtles tread, and Rookes, and Dawes,	
And Maidens bleach their fummer fmockes,	889
The Cuckow then, on euerie tree,	
Mockes married men; for thus finges hee:	891
Cuckow!	

Cuckow, cuckow! O word of feare,	
Vnpleafing to a married care!	894

RICHARD LEVERIDGE, 1725?, 1727. Solo. On a sheet in **a vol.** in
    Brit. Mus. Lib. G ⅍; with the title 'The Cuckoo.'
DR. T. A. ARNE, 1740. Solo, Soprano. Sung by Mrs. Clive in *As You
    Like It.* 'Shakspere Vocal Album' (1864), p. 14.
JOHN STAFFORD SMITH, 1784. Glee for three male voices.
G. A. MACFARREN, 1864. Part Song, S.A.T.B. Novello. **'Choral
    Songs,'** No. 4.
*RICHARD SIMPSON, about 186—; published **1878. Stanley Lucas.**

"WHEN ISACLES HANG BY THE WALL."

Winter.

When Ifacles hang by the wall,	895
And Dicke the Sheepheard blowes his naile,	
And Thom beares Logges into the hall,	
And Milke coms frozen home in paile,	898
When Blood is nipt, and wayes be fowle,	
Then nightly finges the ftaring Owle	900
Tu-whit, to-who!	
A merrie note,	
While greafie Ione doth keele the pot.	903

When all aloude the winde doth blow,	904
And coffing drownes the Parfons faw,	
And Birdes fit brooding in the Snow,	
And Marrians nofe lookes red and raw;	907

When roasted Crabbs hisse in the bowle,
Then nightly singes the staring Owle,   909
          Tu-whit, to-who!
   A merrie note,
   While greasie Ione doth keele the pot.   912

DR. T. A. ARNE (ab. 1740?). Solo, Tenor or Bass. In 'Shakspere
    Vocal Album,' p. 75.
JOHN PERCY, composer of *Wapping Old Stairs*, d. 1797. Glee.
G. A. MACFARREN, 1864. Part Song, S.A.T.B. Novello. In 'Choral
    Songs,' No. 2.

Macbeth.

Act I. Scene i. lines 1—11.

"WHEN SHALL WE THREE MEET AGAINE?"

Thunder and Lightning. Enter three Witches.

1.   hen shall we three meet againe?
        In Thunder, Lightning, or in Raine?   2
       2. When the Hurley-burley's done,
      When the Battaile's lost, and wonne.
      3. That will be ere the set of Sunne.   5
  1. Where the place?
  2.   Vpon the Heath.
  3. There to meet with *Macbeth*.   7
  1. I come, *Gray-Malkin!*
  2.   *Padock* calls.
  3.   Anon!
All. Faire is foule, and foule is faire;
Houer through the fogge and filthie ayre!   [*Exeunt.* 11

M. P. KING, 1780. [1810, 1851, 1857, B. Mus. Cat.] Glee, S.S.B.
SAMUEL WEBBE. Two Baritones and one Bass.
*WILLIAM HORSLEY. Trio. S.S.B. Novello.

Macbeth, Act IV. Scene i. lines 1—47.

"ROUND ABOUT THE CALDRON GO."

Thunder. Enter the three Witches.

  1. Thrice the brinded Cat hath mew'd.
  2. Thrice, and once the Hedge-Pigge whin'd.
  3. *Harpier* [1] cries, "'tis time, 'tis time!"

  1. Round about the Caldron go!
In, the poyfond Entrailes, throw!   5
Toad, (that vnder cold ftone,
Dayes and Nights, ha's, thirty one,   7

      [1] ? *Harpier* (Rom. type in F.) = Harper.

Sweltred Venom, ſleeping got,)
Boyle thou firſt i'th'charmëd pot!   9
   All. Double, double, toile and trouble;
Fire burne, and Cauldron bubble!   11
   2. Fillet of a Fenny Snake,
In the Cauldron, boyle and bake!   13
Eye of Newt, and Toe of Frogge,
Wooll of Bat, and Tongue of Dogge;   15
Adders Forke, and Blinde-wormes Sting,
Lizards legge, and Howlets wing;   17
For a Charme of powrefull trouble,   18
Like a Hell-broth, boyle and bubble!
   All. Double, double, toyle and trouble;
Fire burne, and Cauldron bubble!   21
   3. Scale of Dragon, Tooth of Wolfe,
Witches Mummey, Maw and Gulfe   23
Of the ravin'd ſalt Sea ſharke;
Roote of Hemlocke, digg'd i'th'darke   25
Liuer of Blaſpheming Iew;
Gall of Goate, and Slippes of Yew,   27
Sliuer'd in the Moones Eeclipſe;
Noſe of *Turke*, and *Tartars* lips;   29
Finger of Birth-ſtrangled Babe,
Ditch-deliuer'd by a Drab,
Make the Grewell thicke, and ſlab.   31
Adde thereto a Tigers Chawdron.[2]
For th'Ingredience of our Cawdron.   34
   All. Double, double, toyle and trouble;
Fire burne, and Cauldron bubble!   36
   2. Coole it with a Baboones blood!
Then the Charme is firme and good.   38

Enter Hecat, *to*[3] *the other three* Witches.

   Hecat. O, well done! I commend your paines,
And euery one ſhall ſhare i'th'gaines: 40
And now about the Cauldron ſing,
Like Elues and Fairies in a Ring,
Inchanting all that you put in.   43
        [*Muſicke and* **a Song**. *Blacke Spirits, &c.*
   2. By the pricking of my Thumbes,
Something wicked this way comes: 45
Open, Lockes!
Who euer knockes.   47

Enter Macbeth.

M. P. King, about 1800. Glee in three parts. Beginning, "Round
   about the Caldron go."

[2] entrails.   [3] *and* F.

Macbeth, Act IV. Scene i. lines 127—132.

"COME, SISTERS, CHEERE WE UP HIS SPRIGHTS!"

A fhew of eight Kings, (the Eighth with a glaffe in his hand,) and
BANQUO *laft.*

Macbeth.   Thou art too like the Spirit of *Banquo:* Down!
Thy Crowne do's feare mine Eye-bals!   ¶ And thy haire
Thou other Gold-bound-brow, is like the firft:
A third, is like the former.   ¶ Filthy Hagges!
Why do you fhew me this?———A fourth? Start, eyes!
What, will the Line ftretch out to'th'cracke of Doome?
Another yet?   A feauenth?   Ile fee no more!
And yet the eighth[1] appeares, who beares a glaffe,
Which fhewes me many more: and fome, I fee,   120
That two-fold Balles, and trebble Scepters carry.
Horrible fight!   Now I fee 'tis true;
For the Blood-bolter'd *Banquo* fmiles vpon me,
And points at them for his.   [*They vanifh.*]   ¶ What! is this fo?
     1. I, Sir, all this is fo.   But why
Stands *Macbeth* thus amazedly?

¶ Come, Sifters! cheere we vp his fprights,
And fhew the beft of our delights!   128
Ile Charme the Ayre to giue a found,
While you performe your Antique round;   130
That this great King may kindly fay,
Our duties did his welcome pay.   [*Muficke.* 132
                    [*The Witches Dance, and vanifh.*
     Macbeth.   Where are they?   Gone?   Let this pernitious houre
Stand aye accurfëd in the Kalender!

M. P. KING, about 1800.   Glee for three voices, and Chorus.

Measure for Measure.

Act IV. Scene i. lines 1—8.

"TAKE, OH, TAKE THOSE LIPS AWAY!"

[*The Moated Grange at S. Lukes.*]

Enter MARIANA, *and Boy finging.*

[1] eight, Fo.

2 MEASURE FOR MEASURE.

Song.

Take, oh, take thofe lips away,
that fo fweetly were forfworne!
And thofe eyes, the breake of day;   4
lights that doe miflead the Morne!
But, my kiffes bring againe,
                          bring againe;   6
Seales of loue, but feal'd in vaine,
                      feal'd in vaine!   8

[Mariana has been deserted by her base **lover Angelo, because her**
fortune was loft.]

DR. JOHN WILSON. Song. Published 1653-59. From 'Select Mus.
    Airs and Dialogues.' The printed copy is called 'Love's Ingratitude,'
    and will be found in the Brit. Mus. Lib. in a MS. volume.
JOHN WELDEN, about 1707. Solo. Col. of New Songs by Welden.
J. E. GALLIARD, 1730. In a volume of the 'Musical Miscellany.'
THOMAS CHILCOT, 1750. Solo, Soprano.
Name unknown. See Ruffe, p. 44.
CHRISTOPHER DIXON, 1760. [1760? **B.** Mus. Cat.] Song. Two English
    Cantatas and Four Songs by C. S.
W. N., 1770. In the Library of the Sacred **Harmonic Society.**
G. GIORDANI, 1780. Glee for four voices.
G. GIORDANI, 1780. The same adapted for one voice and harpsichord.
J. S. SMITH, 1780. Glee for A.T.B.
W. JACKSON, soon after 1780. Duet. (Twelve Canzonets, **No. 7.**)
W. TINDAL, 1785. Duet : Soprano and Tenor. Six vocal **pieces, No. 2.**
    (Op. prima.)
T. TREMAIN, 1786. Duet. Thirteen Canzonets for two voices.
SIR JOHN STEVENSON, about 1795. Glee for four voices.
*L. ATTERBURY, died 1796. Round. Bland's 'Glee Collect.,' p. 215.
HON. A. BARRY, 1810. Three-voice Glee.
WM. LINLEY, 1816. Solo, Treble. Linley's 'Dram. Songs of Shaksp.'
    Vol. 1. p. 30.
SIR HENRY BISHOP, 1819. Song, Soprano. Sung by Miss Stephens
    in the operatized 'Comedy of Errors.'
W. GARDINER, 1838. See 'Music and Friends,' by W. G.
F. LANCELOTT, 1838. Round. 'Cyclopedia of Music.' No. 12.
ALFRED MELLON, 1864. Song, Bass. Sung by Mr. Santley.
*C. A. MACIRONE, 1864. Song. Shakspere Vocal Magazine, No. 70.
*G. A. MACFARREN, 1864. Part Song, S.A.T.B. Novello.
*S. REAY, 1869. Part Song. S.A.T.B. Novello's Part Song Book.
    (Bk. 14; No. 164.)
*E. N. GRAZIA, 1872. Song. Weekes.
*JAMES COWARD, 1872. Solo. Cramer.
*C. H. H. PARRY, 1875. 'Three Trios,' &c., No. 3. Song.
*A. H. D. PRENDERGAST, 1878. Part Song, A.T.T.B. Novello.
*J. GREENHILL, 1883. Song, for Tenor or Soprano.

𝔐erchant of 𝔙enice.

Act II. Scene vii. lines 65—73.

"ALL THAT GLISTERS IS NOT GOLD."

Morrocho. [*opens the Golden Casket*] O hell! what haue wee
heare?
A carrion Death, within whofe emptie eye
There is a written fcroule! Ile reade the writing:[1]   64
[Reads] *"All that glifters is not gold!"*
          Often haue you heard that told;   66
          Many a man his life hath fold,
          But my outfide to behold;   68

---

[1] The lines in the 'fhedule' of the Silver Casket opend by Arragon
(II. ix.), and those in the 'fcroule' of the Leaden Casket opend by Bassanio
(III. ii.) do not seem to have been set to music. They follow here:—

Arragon. . . What is here?

     [Reads] *The fier feauen times tried this.*   II. ix. 62
             " Seauen times tried" that iudgement is,
             That did neuer choofe amis.
             Some there be that fhadowes kis;   65
             Such haue but a fhadowes blis.
             There be fooles aliue, Iwis,
             Siluer'd o're; and fo was this.   68
             Take what wife you will to bed,
             I will euer be your head:
             So be gone! you are fped!   II. ix. 71

Arragon. Still more foole I fhall appeare
By the time I linger heere.
With one fooles head I came to woo,
But I goe away with two.
[To PORTIA] Sweet, adiew!

Baffanio.   Heeres the fcroule,
The continent and fummarie of my fortune!

                        (1)
     [Reads] *You that choofe not by the view,*   III. ii. 131
             Chaunce as faire, and chcofe as true!
             Since this fortune falls to you,
             Be content, and feeke no new!   134

                        (2)
             If you be well pleafd with this,   135
             And hold your fortune for your bliffe,
             Turne you where your Lady is,
             And claime her with a louing kis!   138

A gentle fcroule! ¶ Faire Lady! by your leaue!   [*kisses her.*

Guilded timbers wormes infold!
Had you beene as wise as bold,   70
Young in limbs, in iudgement old,
Your aunswere had not beene inscrold,
" Fareyouwell ! your sute is cold !"   73

CHARLES HORN, 1823.   Duet.   Sung in the *Merry Wives of Windsor.*

Merchant of Venice, Act III. Scene ii. lines 63—72.

"TELL ME, WHERE IS FANCIE BRED?"

Here Musicke.

A Song, the whilst BASSANIO comments on the Caskets to himselfe.

(1)

Tell me, where is Fancie bred ?
Or in the hart, or in the head ?
How begot, how nourished ?   65
        Replie ! replie !

(2)

It is engendred in the eyes ;
With gazing fed ; and Fancie dies
In the cradle where it lies !   69

(3)

Let vs all ring Fancies knell !
Ile begin it : Ding, dong, bell !
        All. Ding, dong, bell !   72

DR. T. A. ARNE, 1741.   Solo.   Sung by Mrs. Clive in *Twelfth Night.*
    Caulfeld's Collection.
SIR J. STEVENSON. 1798.   Duet.   Tenor and Bass.   Arranged for two
    Trebles by Sir H. R. Bishop. ('Shakspere Vocal Magazine,' No. 40.)
R. J. S. STEVENS, 1802.   Three Sopranos and One Tenor ; instrumental
    Bass.
*REV. L. RICHMOND, about 1810 or 1820.   **Round.**
WM. LINLEY, 1816.   Duet, with Chorus.   **Linley's 'Dramatic Songs of**
    Shakspere.'
JOHN HATTON, 1855 (and 1859).   Solo and Ladies' Chorus.   **Sung by**
    Miss Poole in the *Merchant of Venice.*
*M. BARTHOLOMEW (MRS. MOUNSEY).   Part-Song.   S.A.T.B.   **Novello.**
*G. A. MACFARREN, 1869.   Part Song, S.A.T.B.   Novello.
*B. LUETZEN, 1877.   Duettino.   Brighton.
*C. PINSUTI, about 1880.   Part Song.   A.T.T.B.   Novello.
*C. PINSUTI.   The same arranged for S.C.T.B.
*J. G. CALLCOTT, 1883.   Part Song.   S.S.C.   Novello.

Merchant of Venice, Act V. Scene i. lines 1—22.

"IN SUCH A NIGHT AS THIS."

[Belmont.   Portias Park.]

Enter LORENZO *and* IESSICA.

Lorenzo.   The moone fhines bright.   In fuch a night as this,
When the fweet winde did gently kiſſe the trees,
And they did make no noyſe; in ſuch a night,
Troylus (me thinks) mounted the *Troian walls,*   4
And figh'd his foule toward the *Grecian* tents
Where *Creſſed* lay that night.
       Ieſſica.   In fuch a night,
Did *Thisbie* fearefully ore-trip the dewe,
And faw the Lyons ſhadow, ere him felfe,   8
And ranne dismayed away.
       Lorenzo.   In fuch a night,
Stoode *Dido,* with a willow in her hand,
Vpon the wilde fea banks, and waft her Loue
To come againe to *Carthage.*
       Ieſſica.   In fuch a night,   12
Medea gathered the inchanted hearbs
That did Renew old *Eſon.*
       Lorenzo.   In fuch a night,
Did *Ieſſica* ſteale from the wealthy *Iewe,*
And, with an vnthrift Loue, did runne from *Venice,*   16
As farre as *Belmont.*
       Ieſſica.   In fuch a night,
Did young *Lorenzo* fweare he lou'd her well,
Stealing her foule with many vowes of faith,
And nere a true one!
       Lorenzo.   In fuch a night,   20
Did pretty *Ieſſica* (like a little ſhrow,)
Slander her Loue; and he forgaue it her.

SIR A. S. SULLIVAN, 1865.   Duet for Soprano and Tenor, introduced
into the Cantata of *Kenilworth.*

Merchant of Venice, Act V. Scene i. lines 54—65.

"HOW SWEET THE MOONE-LIGHT SLEEPES
UPON THIS BANKE!"

[Lorenzo to Jessica, in Portia's park, by moonlight.]

How fweet the moone-light fleepes vpon this banke!
Heere will we fit, and let the founds of muficke
Creepe in our eares. foft ſtilnes, and the night,   56
Become the tutches of fweet harmonie.

Sit, *Ieſſica*! looke how the floore of Heauen
Is thicke inlayed with pattens of bright gold!
There's not the ſmalleſt orbe which thou beholdſt,   60
But, in his motion, like an Angell, ſings,
Still quiring to the young eyde Cherubins:
Such harmonie is in immortall ſoules!
But whilſt this muddy veſture of decay   64
Dooth groſly cloſe it in, we cannot heare it.

JOHN PERCY. Died, 1797. **Solo.**
CHARLES DIGNUM, 1800. **Duet: Soprano, Tenor.** In a volume of
      Mr. Dignum's compositions.
THOMAS HUTCHINSON, 1807. Duet: Soprano, Tenor.
M. P. KING, 1825 (?). Trio for three voices. Chappell, **New Bond**
      Street.
MISS E. NAYLOR, 1845. Duet.
*SIR A. S. SULLIVAN, 1865. Recitative for Tenor before the Duet for
      Soprano and Tenor, introduced into the Cantata of *Kenilworth*.
*HENRY LESLIE, 1866. Part Song. Novello.
*T. BLANCHARD. Song. Blockley, Junr., 3, Argyll Street, Regent Street.
*J. G. CALCOTT, 1883. Part Song, S.C.T.B.B. First sung by Leslie's
      choir, Feb. 2, 1883.
*J. G. CALCOTT, 1883. **The same arranged as** a Trio, S.S.C. Patey
      and Willis.

Merchant of Venice, Act V. Scene i. lines 71—88.

"FOR DOE BUT NOTE A WILDE AND WANTON HEARD."

[Lorenzo, while sitting in Portia's park with Jessica in the moonlight,
   calls on the Musicians to play, and thus greet Portia on her
   home-coming from Venice.]

Come, hoe! and wake *Diana* with a himne!
With ſweeteſt tutches, pearce your Miſtres eare,
And draw her home with muſique.   [*Play Muſique.* **68**
Ieſſica. I am neuer merry, when I heare ſweet muſique.
Lorenzo. The reaſon is, your ſpirits are attentiue:

For doe but note a wilde and wanton heard
Or race of youthfull and vnhandled colts,   72
Fetching mad bounds, bellowing and neighing **loud**,
(Which is the hote condition of their blood;)
If they but heare perchance a Trumpet ſound,
Or any ayre of Muſique touch their ears,   76
You ſhall perceaue them make a mutuall ſtand,
Their ſauage eyes turn'd to a modeſt gaze,
By the ſweet power of Muſique: therefore the Poet
Did faine that *Orpheus* drew trees, ſtones, and floods;   80
Since naught ſo ſtockiſh, hard, and full of rage,

But Mufique, for the time, doth change his nature :
The man that hath no Musique in himselfe,
Nor is not moued with concord of fweet founds,   84
Is fit for treafons, ftratagems, and fpoiles ;
The motions of his fpirit are dull as night,
And his affections darke as *Erebus*.
Let no fuch man be trusted! marke the musique!   88

T. COOKE, 1828. Part of this speech as a Solo, Tenor. Sung by
    Braham in the *Taming of a Shrew*, operatized. (See Geneste's
    English Stage, ix. 418.)

Merry Wives of Windsor.[1]

Act II. Scene ii. lines 186—7.

"LOVE LIKE A SHADOW FLIES, WHEN SUBSTANCE LOVE PURSUES."

[Ford, as Brooke, tells Falstaff, of his imaginary successless pursuit of
his own wife, whom he wishes Falstaff to try and corrupt.]

(181) "briefly, I haue purfu'd her, as Loue hath purfued mee,
which hath beene on the wing of all occafions; but whatfoeuer I
haue merited, (either in my minde, or in my meanes,) meede (I am
fure) I haue receiued none, vnlefle Experience be a Iewell that I haue
purchafed at an infinite rate; and that hath taught mee to fay thus

    " *Loue like a fhadow flies, when fubftance Loue purfues,*
    " *Purfuing that that flies, and flying what purfues.*"   187

JOHN BRAHAM, 1824. Duet: Soprano and Tenor. Sung in *Merry
Wives of Windsor*. (See the amusing account in Geneste's *English
Stage*, ix. 234.)
EDWARD FITZWILLIAM, 1853. Solo. 'A Set of Songs,' No. 2.

Merry Wives, Act III. Scene i. lines 15—19, 21—24. (See *Pass. Pilgr.*)

"TO SHALLOW RIVERS."

[The Welsh Parson, Sir Hugh Evans, is waiting in vain in Windsor
Park, near Frogmore, to fight a duel with the French physician, Dr.
Caius, who has challenged him for being his rival for the hand of
'sweet Anne Page'. To keep up his courage, he attempts to sing a
snatch from Marlowe's song, *Come live with me and be my love*,
(printed as Shakspere's by Iaggard in 1599; but given to Marlowe in
England's Helicon, 1600) which, in the original, runs thus :

[1] See O. Nicolai's *Die lustigen Weiber von Windsor*, komische Oper nach
Shakespeares Lutspiel, &c. 1853, folio.

> " There will we fit vpon the Rocks,
> And fee the Shepheards feed their flocks,
> *By* fhallow Riuers, *by* whofe fals
> Melodious birds fing Madrigals.
>
> There will *I* make thee a *bed* of Rofes
> *With* a thoufand fragrant pofes, &c. &c."

In his nervous condition, Evans misquotes the words of the Song, and at laſt breaks down altogether. The mention of *Riuers*, however, recalls profeſſional aſſociations; **so** that, in his " trembling of minde," and with his " difpofitions to cry," he unconſciouſly mingles the ſacred and the ſecular, by tacking on to Marlowe's verſes the firſt line of the old metrical verſion of the 137th Pſalm (*Super flumina*):—

> " *When we did ſit in Babylon*,
> The *rivers* round about;
> Then, in remembrance of Sion,
> The *tears for grief burſt out*."]

Euan. 'Pleſſe my foule! how full of Chollors I am, and trembling of minde! I ſhall be glad if he haue deceiued me! How melancholies I am! I will knog his Vrinals about his knaues coſtard, when I haue good opportunities for the orke! Pleſſe my foule!   **14**

> [Sings]   *To ſhallow Riuers, to whoſe falls,*
>   *Melodious Birds ſings Madrigalls:*   **16**
>   *There will we make our Peds of Rofes,*
>   *And a thouſand fragrant pofies.*   **18**
>   *To ſhallow—*

Mercie on mee! I haue a great difpofitions to cry—

> [Sings]   *Melodious birds ſing Madrigalls:—*
>   *When as I fat in Pabilon:—*   **21**
>   *And a thouſand vagram Pofies.*
>   *To ſhallow, &c.*

" Melody by an unknown author in a MS. as old as Shakspere's time." (Sir John Hawkins's 'History of Muſic.') Reproduced in Charles Knight's 'Shakspere.'

Dr. JOHN WILSON, about 1600. **This** Melody is harmonized by Sir H. Bishop, as " To by Rivers."

THOS. CHILCOT, about 1750. The whole Poem, *Come live with me*, &c. (see *The Paſſionate Pilgrim*, below), ſet as a Song.

Name unknown, 1770. In the British Museum.

DR. SAMUEL ARNOLD, 1774. Song. Sung by Mr. Reinhold. In 'A Collection of Songs ſung at Vauxhall and Marylebone Gardens.'

DR. ARNE, 1777. Known as " A Favourite Scotch Air.' Sung by Miss Catley, in ' Love in a Village.'

SAMUEL WEBBE, about 1780. Glee for four male voices.

T. TREMAIN, 1760. Duet, two Sopranos, or two Tenors. 'A Book of Cantonets,' by T. T.

F. DALBERG (Baron), 1792. Solo. 'Three English Songs and a Glee.'

THOMAS HUTCHINSON, 1807. Duet : Soprano and Contralto. Commences " Here will we sit." Hutchinson's Collection.
SIR HENRY BISHOP, 1819. Song. Sung by Miss Stephens in the Comedy of Errors. ' Shakspere Vocal Album,' 1864.
W. TURNBULL, 1830. Song.
JOHN HATTON, 1855. Song, Tenor. Sung by Signor Mario.
JOHN HATTON. Part Song, S.A.T.B. Novello.
J. B. TURNER, 1859. Song.
DR. STERNDALE BENNETT, 1816—1875. Part Song. Mr. Hullah's Collection. Hutchins and Romer.
Name Unknown. " To Shallow Rivers." Caulfield's Collection.

Merry Wives, Act V. Scene v. lines 92—8.

"FIE ON SINNEFULL PHANTASIE."

[Falstaffe, with a buck's head and horns on him, has come into Windsor Park to meet Mrs. Ford and Mrs. Page at Herne's Oak. Their friends, disguised as Fairies, &c, have surprised him, and he has thrown himself to the ground, face downwards. The Fairies have lighted their Tapers :]

[*They put the Tapers to his fingers, and he starts.*
Falstaff. Oh, oh, oh !
Queene [Anne Page]. Corrupt, corrupt, and tainted in defire ! 89
About him, (Fairies,) fing a fcornfull rime ;
And as you trip, ftill pinch him to your time ! 91

[*Here they pinch him, and fing about him, & the* Doctor *comes one way & fteales away a* Fairy *in White. And* SLENDER *another way : he takes a* Fairy *in Greene. And* FENTON *fteales* Mifteris ANNE, *being in White.*

The Song.

Fie on finnefull phantafie ! Fie on Luft, and Luxurie ! 92
Luft is but a bloudy fire, kindled with vnchafte defire,
  Fed in heart whofe flames afpire,
  As thoughts do blow them higher and higher. 95
Pinch him, (Fairies,) mutually ! Pinch him for his villanie !
  Pinch him, and burne him, and turne him about,
  Till Candles, & Star-light, & Moone-fhine be out ! 98

[*A noife of hunting is made within : and all the* Fairies *runne away.* FALSTAFFE *pulls off his bucks head, and rifes vp. And enter* Mafter PAGE, *Mafter* FORD, *and their Wiues, Mafter* SHALLOW, *& Sir Hugh* EUANS.]

C. ADDISON, ? 1811. Solo up to the word "villanie," l. 96. Sung by Sir Hugh Evans, with Chorus for S.S.B., on the words, "Pinch him," &c. Caulfield's Collection.

D

Midsummer Night's Dream.

Act I. Scene i. lines 171—8, 182—5, 204—7, 234—9.

"BY THE SIMPLICITIE OF VENUS DOVES."

[Hermia loves Lysander, and he loves her. Demetrius also loves
her; and her father wishes to give her to him, as by the Athenian
law he can. To prevent this, Lysander proposes to take Hermia to
his widow-aunts', 7 leagues from Athens, and there marry her.]

Lysander. . . . If thou louest **mee**, then,
Steale forth thy fathers house to-morrow night;   164
And in the wood, a league without the towne,
(Where I did meete thee once with *Helena*,
To do obseruance to a morne of May,)
There will I stay for thee.
Hermia.   My good *Lysander!*   168
I sweare to thee, by *Cupids* strongest bowe,
By his best arrowe, with the golden heade,
By the simplicitie of *Venus* doues,
By that which knitteth soules, and prospers loues,   172
And by that fire which burnd the *Carthage* queene,   [Dido.]
When the false *Troian* vnder faile was seene,   [Æneas] 174
By all the vowes that euer men haue broke,
(In number more then euer women spoke,)   176
In that same place thou hast appointed mee,
To-morrow truely will I meete with thee.   178
Lysander. Keepe promise, loue! Looke, here comes *Helena!*

SIR HENRY BISHOP, 1816. Solo for Soprano. Sung by Miss Stevens,
     as Hermia, in *Midsummer Night's Dream.*

M. N. Dream, I. i. 182—5.

"O HAPPY FAIRE!
YOUR EYES ARE LOADSTARRES; AND YOUR
TONGUE'S SWEETE AIRE."

Enter HELENA [*in love with* DEMETRIUS, *who loves* HERMIA.]

Hermia. God speede, faire *Helena!* whither away?
Helena. Call you mee 'faire'? That 'faire' againe vnsay! 181
Demetrius loues your faire:
                    o happy faire!
Your eyes are loadstarres; and your tongue's sweete aire   183
More tunable then larke, to sheepeheards eare,
When wheat is greene, when hauthorne buddes appeare.   185
Sicknesse is catching: O, were fauour so,
Your words Ide catch, faire *Hermia*, ere I goe;   187

My eare fhould catch your voice, my eye, your eye,
My tongue fhould catch your tongues fweete melody ! 189
Were the world mine, (*Demetrius* being bated,)
The reft ile giue to be to you tranflated. 191
O, teach mee how you looke ; and with what Art,
You fway the motion of *Demetrius* heart ! 193

CHRISTOPHER SMITH, 1754. Solo, Soprano. In the operatized *M. N. Dream*, called ' Fairies.'

W. SHIELD, 1796 (?). No. 2 in ' Shakespears Duel[1] and Loadstars.' Glee for three voices. Also in ' Shakspere Vocal Magazine,' 1864, No. 43.

E. J. LODER, 1844. Solo, Soprano or Tenor, from lower D to upper G. No. 5 of a set of six ' Songs of the Poets,' by Loder.

EDWARD HINE. Solo, Soprano or Tenor, from lower D to upper G ; key of E♭.

M. N. Dream, I. i. 204—7.

"BEFORE THE TIME I DID LISANDER SEE."

[Hermia promises Helena that she'll leave Athens (with Lysander), so that Demetrius—who loves her inftead of Helena—fhall be no longer tempted, by the fight of her, to refufe Helena his love.]

Hermia. Take comfort ! he no more fhall fee my face :
Lufander and my felfe will fly this place. 203

Before the time I did *Lifander* fee,
Seem'd *Athens* as a Paradife to mee. 205
O then, what graces in my loue dooe dwell,
That hee hath turnd a heauen vnto a hell ! 207

CHRISTOPHER SMITH, 1754. Song. In the ' Fairies.'

M. N. Dream, I. i. 234—9.

"LOVE LOOKES NOT WITH THE EYES, BUT WITH THE MINDE."

[Hermia and Lyfander having gone, Helena foliloquifes on Love's power and blindnefs, and laments her lover Demetrius's faithlessness in giving her up for Hermia.]

Helena. How happie fome, ore otherfome can be !
Through *Athens*, I am thought as faire as fhee. 227
But what of that ? *Demetrius* thinkes not fo ;
He will not knowe, what all but hee doe know. 229
And as hee erres, doting on *Hermias* eyes,
So I, admiring of his qualities. 231

1 The Duel is, ' It was a lordlings Daughter.'—*Pass. Pilgrim.*

D 2

Things bafe and vile, holding no quantitie,
Loue can tranfpofe to forme and dignitie.   233

Loue lookes not with the eyes, but with the minde;
And therefore is wingd *Cupid* painted blinde.   235
Nor hath loues minde, of any iudgement tafte;
Wings, and no eyes, figure vnheedy hafte.   237
And therefore is loue faid **to** bee **a** childe,
Becaufe, in choyce, he is **fo** oft beguil'd.   239
As waggifh boyes, in game themfelues **forfweare,**
So the boy, Loue, is periur'd euery where.   241
For, ere *Demetrius* lookt on *Hermias* eyen,
Hee hayld downe othes, that he was onely **mine.**   243
And when this haile, fome heate from *Hermia* felt,
So he diffolued, and fhowrs of oathes did melt.   245

CHRISTOPHER SMITH, 1754. **Solo.** In the 'Fairies.'

M. N. Dream, II. i. 2—15.

"OVER HILL, OVER DALE."

[*A Wood neere Athens.* April 30.]

Enter, a Fairie *at* one *doore, and* ROBIN GOODFELLOW (PUCKE) *at another.*

Robin. How now, fpirit? **whither** wander you?

    Fairie. Ouer hill, ouer dale,   2
    Thorough buth, thorough brier,
  Ouer parke, ouer pale,
    Thorough flood, thorough fire,   5
  I do wander euery where,
  Swifter **than** the Moons fphere;   7
  And I ferue the Fairy Queene,
  To dew her orbs vpon the greene.   9
  The cowflippes tall, her Penfioners bee;
  In their gold coats, fpottes you fee: 11
  Thofe be Rubies, Fairie fauours;
  In thofe freckles, liue their fauours.   13
  I muft goe feeke fome dew-droppes here,
  And hang a pearle in euery cowflippes eare.   15

Farewell, thou Lobbe of fpirits! Ile be gon.
Our Queene, **and** all her Elues, come here anon.   17

WM. JACKSON, 1770-5 (?). Glee for two Sopranos, one Tenor, and one Bass. This is the middle movement in his arrangement of Arne's Air " Where the bee sucks."
*T. COOKE, 1840. Florid Song. Ashdown.
EDWARD FITZWILLIAM, 1855. Solo, with Clarionet Obbligato. In 'Songs for a Winter Night,' No. 3.

G. A. MACFARREN, 1856. Solo. Composed for and sung by Madame
　Viardot.
*W. WILSON, 1858. Duet. Sung by the Misses Brougham.
J. F. DUGGAN, 1862. Solo.
*J. HATTON. Part Song, S.A.T.B. Novello.

M. N. Dream, II. ii. 155—68, 249—58.

"THAT VERY TIME I SAW," &c.

Oberon. . . . My gentle *Pucke,* come hither!　Thou remembreft, 148
Since once I fat vpon a promontory,
And heard a Mearemaide, on a Dolphins backe,
Vttering fuch dulcet and harmonious breath,
That the rude fea grewe ciuill at her fong,　　　　　　　　　152
And certaine ftarres fhot madly from their Spheares,
To heare the Sea-maids muficke.
　　Puck.　　　　　　　　　I remember.
　　Oberon. That very time, I faw, (but thou could'ft not,)
Flying betweene the colde Moone and the earth,　　　　　156
Cupid, all arm'd : a certaine aime he tooke
At a faire Veftall, throned by the weft,
And loof'd his loue-fhaft fmartly from his bowe,
As it fhould pearce a hundred thoufand hearts ;　　　　　160
But, I might fee young *Cupids* fiery fhaft
Quencht in the chaft beames of the watry Moone ;
And the imperiall Votreffe paff'd on,
In maiden meditation, fancy-free.　　　　　　　　　　164
Yet markt I, where the bolt of *Cupid* fell.
It fell vpon a little wefterne flower ;
Before, milke white ; now purple, with Loues wound,
And maidens call it, ' Loue-in-idleneffe.'　　　　　　　168
Fetch mee that flowre ! the herbe I fhewed thee once.
The iewce of it, on fleeping eyeliddes laide,
Will make, or man or woman, madly dote
Vpon the next liue creature that it fees.　　　　　　　172
Fetch mee this herbe, and be thou here againe
Ere the *Leuiathan* can fwimme a league !
　　Puck. Ile put a girdle, round about the earth,
In forty minutes.　　　　　　　　　　　　　　[*Exit.*

T. COOKE, 1840. Soprano. Sung by Madame Vestris. Called " Love
　in Idleness."

M. N. Dream, II. i. 249—58.

"I KNOW A BANKE, WHERE THE WILDE TIME
BLOWES."

Oberon [*to* PUCKE.]　¶ Haft thou the flower there ? Welcome,
wanderer !

Puck.   I, there it is!
Oberon.   I pray thee, glue it mee.   248

I know a bauke, where the wilde time blowes,
Where Oxlips, and the nodding Violet growes,   250
Quite ouercanopi'd, with lufhious woodbine,
With fweete mufke rofes, and with Eglantine   252
There fleepes *Tytania,* fumetime of the night,
Luld in thefe flowers, with daunces and delight;   254
And there the fnake, throwes her enammeld fkinne,
Weed, wide enough, to wrappe a Fairy in.   256
And, with the iuyce of this, Ile ftreake her eyes,
And make her full of hatefull phantafies.   258

JOHN PERCY, died 1797.   Soprano : Flute Obbligato.
CHARLES E. HORN, about 1827 (ed. 1856, 1858).   Duet for Soprano
    and Mezzo-Soprano.
*J. BARNETT, 1830.   Duet.

M. N. Dream, II. ii. 9—24, 66—83.

"YOU SPOTTED SNAKES, WITH DOUBLE TONGUE."

Enter TYTANIA, Queene of Fairies, *with her traine.*

Queen.   Come, now a Roundell, and a Fairy fong!   1
Then, for the third part of a minute, hence!
Some to kill cankers in the mufk rofe buds;
Some warre with Reremife, for their lethren wings,   4
To make my fmall Elues coattes; and fome keepe backe
The clamorous Owle, that nightly hootes and wonders
At our quaint fpirits. Sing me now a-fleepe!
Then to your offices, and let mee reft.   8

Fairies *fing.*

You fpotted Snakes, with double tongue,   9
Thorny Hedgehogges, be not feene!
Newts and blindewormes, do no wrong!
Come not neere our Fairy Queene!   12
Philomele, with melody,
Sing in our fweete Lullaby,
Lulla, lulla, lullaby! lulla, lulla, **lullaby**!

Neuer harme,   16
Nor fpell, nor charme,
Come our louely lady nigh!
So, good night, with lullaby!   19
1. *Fairy.*   Weauing Spiders, come not heere!   20
Hence, **you** long legd Spinners! hence!

Beetles blacke, approach not neere!
Worme nor snaile, doe no offence!   23
   Philomele, *with melody, &c.*   [TITANIA *sleepes.*
  2. *Fairy.* Hence, away! now all is well:
    One aloofe, ftand Centinell!   [*Exeunt* Fairies.

CHRISTOPHER SMITH, 1794. Solo, Soprano. Sung by Titania. In
  the 'Fairies.'
W. B. EARLE, 1794. Glee for four voices.
R. J. S. STEVENS, 1800(?). Four-voice Glee, S.A.T.B. Novello.
Name unknown. Solo.
MENDELSSOHN, 1843. Soprano Solo, with a Chorus of Sopranos and
  Altos. Novello.
*W. HILLS, 1865, &c. 'Vocal Trios,' &c., No. 4. Robert Cocks.
*J. MOUNT, 1879. 'The Fairies' Song.'
*G. A. MACFARREN, 1879. For four Ladies' voices, S.S.A.A. Novello.

M. N. Dream, II. ii. 66–83.

"THROUGH THE FORREST HAVE I GONE."

[Oberon sends Puck into the Forest to find a youth in Athenian
dress ('weedes'), Demetrius, that despises Helena who loves him.
Puck is to squeeze pansy-juice on Demetrius's eyes, so that he may
fall in love with Helena the moment he wakes. But Puck finds
Lysander near Hermia, both asleep; and, mistaking them for
Demetrius and Helena, squeezes the pansy-juice on Lysander's eyes.
(Lysander on waking sees Helena, and falls furiously in love with her,
to Hermia's great angerment.)]

            Enter PUCKE.

Puck. Through the forreft haue I gone;
But *Athenian* found I none,   67
On whofe eyes I might approue
This flowers force in ftirring loue.   [*Sees* LYSANDER. 69
Night aud filence! Who is heere?
Weedes of *Athens* he doth weare: 71
This is hee (my matter faide)
Defpifed the *Athenian* maide: [*Sees* HERMIA. 73
And here the maiden, fleeping found,
On the danke and dirty ground!   75
Pretty fowle! fhe durft not lye
Neere this lack-loue, this kil-curtefie.   [*Points to* LYSANDER. 77
¶ Churle! vpon thy eyes I throwe
All the power this charme doth owe: 79
When thou wak'ft, let loue forbidde
Sleepe, his feat on thy eye lidde!   81
So awake, when I am gon;
For I muft now to *Oberon.*   [*Exit.* 83

MRS. J. B. GATTIE, 1825(?). Solo, Canzonet.

M. N. Dream, III. i. 109—112, 114—117.

"THE WOOSELL COCK, SO BLACKE OF HEWE."

[Puck frightens Bottom's companions, and they run away.]

Bottom. Why doe they runne away? This is a knauery of
them, to make mee afeard.   100

Re-enter SNOWTE.

Snowte. O *Bottom*, thou art chaung'd! What do I fee on thee?
Bottom. What doe you fee? You fee an Affe-head of your
owne, Do you?   [*Exit* SNOWTE.

Re-enter QUINCE.

Quince. Bleffe thee, *Bottom!* bleffe thee! Thou art tranflated.
                                                [*Exit.* 104
Bottom. I fee their knauery! This is to make an affe of mee;
to fright me, if they could. But I wil not ftirre from this place, do
what they can! I will walke vp and downe heere, and I will fing,
that they fhall heare I am not afraide: 108

[*Sings*] *The Woofell cock, fo blacke of hewe,*   109
          With Orange tawny bill,
          The Throftle, with his note fo true,
          The Wren, with little quill,   112

(*Tytania.* [*Waking*] What Angell wakes me from my flowry
bed?)

Bottom [*Sings*]. *The Fynch, the Sparrowe, and the Larke,* 114
          The plainfong Cuckow gray,
          (*Whofe note, full many a man doth marke,*
          And dares not anfwere, 'nay!')   117

For indeede, who would fet his wit to fo foolifh a birde? Who
would giue a bird the ly, though hee cry 'Cuckow,' neuer fo?

(PURCELL probably set this; but his setting has been loft. Roffe,
    p. 60.)
Name unknown. Caulfield's Collection.
BURNEY, 1762. Song. Roffe, p. 60.

M. N. Dream, III. ii. 102—9.

"FLOWER OF THIS PURPLE DY."

[To remedy Puck's mistake of taking Lysander for Demetrius,
and to restore the latter's love to Helena (from Hermia), Oberon,
finding Demetrius asleep in the wood, says to Puck :]

Oberon. About the wood, goe fwifter then the winde,
And *Helena* of *Athens*, looke thou finde!   95
All fancy-ficke fhe is, and pale of cheere,
With fighes of loue, that cofts the frefh blood deare.   97

By fome illufion, fee thou bring her here!
Ile charme his eyes, againft fhe doe appeare.   99
   Robin. I goe, I goe! looke how I goe!
Swifter then arrow, from the *Tartars* bowe!   [*Exit.* 101

  Oberon. Flower of this purple dy,   102
Hit with *Cupids* archery,
Sinke in apple of his eye!   [*Drops iuice into* DEMETRIUS *eyes.*
When his loue he doth efpy,   105
Let her fhine as glorioufly
As the *Venus* of the fky!   107
When thou wak'ft, if fhe be by,
Begge of her, for remedy.   109

CHRISTOPHER SMITH, 1754. Solo. Sung by Oberon. 'The Fairies.'

M. N. Dream, III. ii. 379—87, 396—99.
"LO,¹ NIGHT'S SWIFT DRAGONS CUT THE CLOUDS FULL FAST."

[Demetrius, on waking, falls violently in love with his old sweetheart Helena, with whom Lysander—under the influence of the pansy-
juice—is also in love. Lysander challenges Demetrius to fight for
Helena. Oberon bids Puck 'overcast the night,' and lead the rivals
apart and astray, and tire them out till they fall asleep. He'll then
cure Lysander, and give him back to Hermia. Puck answers:]

  Puck. My Faiery Lord, this muft be done with hafte,

For Nights fwift Dragons cut the clouds full faft,   379
And yonder fhines *Auroras* harbinger;
At whofe approach, Ghofts, wandring here and there,   381
Troope home to Churchyards: damnëd fpirits all,
That in croffe-waies and floods haue buriall,   383
Already to their wormy beds are gone;
For feare leaft day fhould looke their fhames vpon,   385
They wilfully themfelues exile from light,
And muft for aye confort with black-browed night.   387

T. COOKE, 1840. Solo, Soprano. Sung by Miss Rainforth as 1st Fairy
  in the *Midsummer Night's Dream.*

M. N. Dream, III. ii. 396—9.
"UP AND DOWN, UP AND DOWN."

[Puck assures Oberon that he'll mislead, and tire out, the angry
rivals for Helena's Love, Lysander (when under the charm) and
Demetrius:]

¹ *For,* Shakspere.

42 MIDSUMMER NIGHT'S DREAM.

> *Puck.* Vp & down, vp & down, 396
>   I will lead them vp & down!
>   I am feard in field & town!
>   *Goblin*, lead them vp & downe! 399

DR. C. BURNEY, 1762. Solo.
CHRISTOPHER SMITH, 1754. **Solo.** In the ' Fairies.'
T. COOKE, 1840. Solo, Soprano. **Sung by Madame Vestris as ' Oberon,'** compass from F to lower C.

M. N. Dream, V. i.

"A TEDIOUS BRIEFE SCENE OF YOUNG PYRAMUS AND HIS LOVE THISBE;" VERY TRAGICAL MIRTH.

Re-enter BOTTOM as PYRAMUS.

> *Theseus.* Pyramus drawes neare the wall: filence! 167
> *Pyramus.* O grim-lookt night! a night, with hue fo blacke!
> O night, which euer art, when day is not!
> O night, O night! alacke, alacke, alacke!
> I feare my Thisbyes promife is forgot! 171
> [To SNOUT as Wall.] And thou, ô wall, ô fweete, ô louely wall,
> That flandft betweene her fathers ground and mine!
> Thou wall, ô wall, O fweete and louely wall!
> **Showe mee thy** chinke, to blink through with mine eyne! 175
>   {SNOUT holds up his hand, with his fingers thus <
> Thankes, curteous wall! Ioue fhield thee well, for this!
> But what fee I? No Thifby doe I fee.
> O wicked wall, through whome I fee no bliffe!
> Curft be thy ftones, for thus deceiuing mee! 179

Re-enter FLUTE as THISBY.

> *   *   *   *   *   *
> *Thifby.* My loue! thou art my loue, I thinke.
> *Pyramus.* Thinke what thou wilt, I am thy louers Grace; 193
> And, like Limander, am I trufty ftill.
> *Thifby.* And I, like Helen, till the Fates me kill. 195
> *Pyramus.* Not Shafalus, to Procrus was fo true.
> *Thifby.* As Shafalus to Procrus, I to you. 197
> *Pyramus.* O, kiffe mee through the hole of this vilde wall!
> *Thifby.* I kiffe the walles hole; not your lips at all! 199
> *Pyramus.* Wilt thou, at Ninnies tombe, meete me ftraight way?
> *Thufby.* Tide life, tyde death, I come without delay! 201

Enter PYRAMUS.

> *Pyramus.* Sweete Moone, I thanke thee for thy funny beames!
> I thanke thee, Moone, for fhining now fo bright;
> For by thy gratious, golden, glittering beames,
> I truft to take, of trueft Thifby, fight. 206
>   [Sees her bloody Mantle.

But flay : ô fpight!
But marke, poore knight,
What dreadfull dole is here!   269
Eyes, do you fee?
How can it bee?
O dainty duck! o deare!   272
Thy mantle good,—
What! flaind with blood?
Approach, ye Furies fell,   275
O Fates come, come!
Cut thread and thrumme!
Quaile, crufh, conclude, and quell!   278

Duke. This paffion, & the death of a deare friend, would goe
neere to make a man looke fad.
Hyppolita. Befhrewe my heart, but I pitty the man.
Pyramus. *O, wherefore, Nature, didft thou Lyons frame?*   282
Since Lyon vilde hath here deflour'd my deare,
Which is—no, no!—which was, the faireft dame
That liu'd, that lou'd, that lik't, that look't with cheere.   285
Come teares, confound!
Out, fword! and wound
The pappe of Pyramus :   288
I, that left pappe,
Where heart doth hoppe.
Thus dy I, thus, thus, thus! [Stabs himselfe. 291
Now am I dead!
Now am I fled!
My foule is in the fky!   294
Tongue, loofe thy light!
Moone, take thy flight?
Now dy, dy, dy, dy, dy!   [Dies. 297

———

In " Pyramus and Thifbe," a Burlesque Opera.
*   *   *   *   *   *   *
Re-enter THISBY.   *Sees* Pyramus's *Corpse.*
*   *   *   *   *

Thifby. *A-fleepe, my loue?*
What? dead! my doue?
O Pyramus, arife!   315
Speake, fpeake! Quite dumbe?
Dead! dead? A tumbe
Muft couer thy fweete eyes.   318
Thefe lilly lippes,
This cherry nofe,
Thefe yellow cowflippe cheekes,   321
Are gon! are gon!
Louers make mone!

His eyes were greene as leekes.   324
  O Sisters three,
  Come, come to mee,
With hands as pale as milke!   327
  Lay them in gore,
  Since you haue shore
With sheeres, his threede of silke.   330
  Tongue, not a word!
  Come, trusty sword!
  Come, blade, my breast imbrew!   [*Stabs herselfe.*
  And farewell, friends!
  Thus Thisby ends:
  Adieu, adieu, adieu!   [*Dies.* 336

1. 'And thou, O wall.' (l. 172—75, above).   Song, Tenor, S.
2. 'O wicked wall!' (l. 178—9, above).   Song.   „
3. 'Not Cephalus to Procris.' (l. 196—97, above).   Duet, S.T.
4. 'Approach, ye Furies.' (l. 275- 8, above).   Song, Tenor, S.
5. 'Now am I dead.' (l. 292—7, above'.   Song.   „
5. 'These lily lips.' (l. 319- 330, above).   Song.   „

JOHN FREDK. LAMPE, 1745.   *Pyramus and Thisbe.*   A Mock Opera.

M. N. Dream, V. i. 358—369.

"NOW THE HUNGRY LYON ROARES."

[After Duke Theseus and his Bride, and all their guests have gone.]

Enter PUCKE.

Pucke. Now the hungry Lyon roares,   358
        And the wolfe behowls the Moone;
    Whilst the heauie ploughman snores,
        All with weary talke foredoone.   361
    Now the wasted brands doe glowe,
        Whilst the scriech-owle, scrieching lowd,
    Puts the wretch that lyes in woe,
        In remembrance of a shrowde.   365
    Now[1] it is the time of night,
        That the graues, all gaping wide,
    Euery one lets forth his spright,
        In the Churchway paths to glide.   369
    And wee Fairies—that doe runne
        By the triple *Hecates* teame,
    From the presence of the Sunne,
        Following darkenesse like a dreame—   373
    Now are frollick: not a mouse
    Shall disturbe this hallowed house.   375

---

[1] 'Now,' alter'd to 'When,' by C. Horn.

I am fent with broome, before,
To fweepe the duft behinde the dore.   377
Enter King and Queene of Fairies, with all their traine.

Oberon. Through the houfe giue glimmering light,   378
By the dead and drowfie fier:
Euery Elfe and Fairy fpright,
Hop as light as birde from brier;   381
And this dittie, after mee,
Sing, and daunce it trippingly.
Titania. Firft, rehearfe your fong by rote,
To each word a warbling note.   385
Hand in hand, with Fairy grace,
Will we fing and bleffe this place.   387

OBERONS *Song*[1] : *the* Fairies *repeat it & daunce.*

Oberon. Now, vntill the [2] breake of day,
Through this houfe each Fairy ftray.   389
To the beft bride-bed will wee,
Which by vs fhall bleffed be;   391
And the iffue there create,
Euer fhall be fortunate: 393
So fhall all the couples **three,**
Euer true in louing **be :**   395
And the blots of Natures hand,
Shall not in their iffue ftand.   397
Neuer mole, hare-lippe, nor fcarre,
Nor marke prodigious, fuch as **are**   399
Defpifed in natiuitie,
Shall vpon their children be.   401
With this field-deaw confecrate,
Euery Fairy take his gate,   403
And each feuerall chamber bleffe,
Through this palace with fweete peace;   405
And the owner of it bleft,
Euer fhall in fafety reft.   407
Trippe away! make no ftay!
Meete me all, by breake of day!   409

R. LEVERIDGE, 1727. Solos for 1st, 2nd, 3rd, &c., up to 8th Fairy,
and a Chorus to finish. May be found in his two volumes. Collection published, 1727.
DR. COOKE, about 1775. **Five-part Glee.** Begins, 'Hand in hand,'
l. 386 above. Novello.
R. J. S. STEVENS, about 1790? **Glee for four voices, S.A.T.B.,** begins,
"Now the hungry lion."

[1] The Song is not given in Shakspere's text; only Oberon's speech to his
Fairies.
[2] 'Now, vntill the,' alterd to '**Meet me all by**' (see l. 409, below), by
Bishop.

CHRISTOPHER SMITH, 1794. Begins, 'Now, until the break of day.'
In the 'Fairies.'
W. LINLEY, 1816. Solo, Bass.
SIR HENRY BISHOP, 1816. Four male voices. A.T.T.B. Sung in *Two Gentlemen of Verona.*
SIR HENRY BISHOP, 1816. Chorus. Oberon's words, l. 388-409 above.—
l. 388 being alterd to 'Meet me all by break of day,'—are introduced in Bishop's Chorus, 'Spirits advance.'
CHARLES HORN, 1840. Song and Chorus. Sung in *Merry Wives.*
Commences, 'When it is the time of night,' l. 366 above.
MENDELSSOHN. Chorus. Female voices. Novello.

𝔐uch 𝔄do about 𝔑othing.[1]

Act III. Scene i. lines 57—68.

"SIGH NO MORE, LADIES, SIGH NO MORE."

The Song.[2]

Balthaser. *Sigh no more, Ladies, figh no more!*	57
Men were deceiuers euer :	
One foote in fea, and one on fhore,	
To one thing conftant neuer.	60
Then figh not fo, but let them go!	61
And be you blith and bonnie,	
Conuerting all your foundes of woe,	
Into ' hey nony, nony.'	64
Sing no more ditties, fing no moe,	65
Of dumps fo dull and heauy!	
The fraud of men was euer fo,	
Since fummer firft was leauy ;	68
Then figh not fo, &c.	

DR. ARNE, about 1740. Song, Bass. For Mr. Beard, in *Much Ado About Nothing.* 'Shakspere Vocal Album,' 1864.
CHRISTOPHER SMITH, 1794. Solo, S. For 'Oberon' in the 'Fairies.' Caulfield's Collection.
R. J. S. STEVENS, 1790 (1800, 1846, &c.). Five-part Glee.
WM. LINLEY, 1816. Solo. Melody of Stevens's Glee as Solo.
SIR ARTHUR SULLIVAN, 1865. Solo, Tenor. Metzler.
*F. STANISLAUS, 1868. Solo : Tenor or Soprano. Ashdown.
G. A. MACFARREN, 1869. Part Song, S.A.T.B. Novello.
W. BALFE. Duet : Soprano and Contralto.

[1] See Hector Berlioz's *Beatrice et Bénédict.* Opéra . . . imité de Shakspere. 1862. 8vo.
[2] Sung by 'Iacke Wilson,' a singer of the Burbages' Company, to which Shakspere belongd. See Dr. Rimbault's pamflet 'Who was Jack Wilson?' identifying the singer with the composer, Dr. John Wilson.

G. *BARKER. Solo. Robert Cocks.
*G. E. FOX, 1876. Solo, Baritone. D to (upper) G. 'Very pretty
   Song, if well sung.'—G. B. Shaw.
*ETHEL HARRADEN, 1877. Solo, Mezzo-Soprano. Duff and Stewart.
*F. G. COLE, 1879. Tenor Solo : 'Composed expressly for his friend
   Walter Allen.'
*MALCOLM LAWSON, 1880. Glee for Ladies' Voices, S.S.A.A, unac-
   companied. With piano-forte accompaniment. Stanley Lucas,
   Weber, & Co.
*H. C. HILLER, 1880.

_____

Much Adoe, V. ii. 24—7.

"THE GOD OF LOVE."

Margaret [*to* BENEDICKE]. Well, I will call *Beatrice* to you,
who I thinke hath legges.   [*Exit* MARGARITE.
Benedicke. And therefore wil come.   [*Sings.*

            The God of loue
            That sits aboue,   25
            And knowes mee, and knowes me,
            How pittiful I deserue . . .   27

I meane in singing; but in louing, *Leander* the good swimmer,
Troilus, the first imploier of pandars, and a whole booke full of these
quondam carpet-mongers, whose names yet runne smoothly in the
euen rode of a blancke verse, why, they were neuer so truly turnd
ouer and ouer as my poore selfe in loue.

Anonymous. Caulfield's Collection.

_____

Much Adoe, V. iii. 3—10.

"DONE TO DEATH BY SLANDEROUS TONGUES."

[A Church in Messina.]

Enter CLAUDIO,[1] PRINCE, *and three or four with tapers.*

Claudio. Is this the monument of *Leonato?*
A Lord. It is, my Lord.

CLAUDIO *reads his Epitaph on* HERO *from a Paper.*

            Done to death by slanderous tongues,   3
            Was the Hero *that heere lies :*
            Death, in guerdon of her wronges,
            Giues her fame which neuer dies :   6
            So the life that dyed with shame,
            Liues in death with glorious fame.   8

[1] Claudio has slanderd his love Hero, and believes that his slanders have
kild her.

Hang thou there vpon the toomb,
Praifing hir when I am dead![1] 10

THEODORE AYLWARD, 1770. Glee for four voices. 'Elegies and Glees,
by T. A.

Much Adoe, Act V. Scene ii. lines 12—21.

"PARDON, GODDESSE OF THE NIGHT!"

Claudio. Now, Mufick, found, & fing your folemne hymne! 11

  Song. *Pardon! Goddeffe of the Night!*
    Thofe that flew thy virgin knight;
    For the which, with fongs of woe,
    Round about her tombe they goe: 15
    Midnight! affift our mone!
    Help vs to figh & grone,
     Heauily, heauily! 18
    *Graues! yawne and yeeld your **dead**,*
    Till death be vttered,
     Heauily, heauily![2]

DR. ARNE, about 1740. Solo for Soprano. In Caulfield's Collection.
T. CHILCOT, about 1745. Solo. In 'Shakspere Vocal Album,' 1864
 (transposed into D minor).
W. LINLEY, 1816. Duet and Chorus. In Linley's 'Dramatic Songs of
 Shakspere.'

Othello.

Act II. Scene iii. lines 71—5.

"AND LET ME THE CANNAKIN CLINKE,
CLINKE!"

Iago. Some Wine, hoa!   [*Sings.* 70

  And let me the Cannakin clinke, clinke!
  And let me the Cannakin clinke! 72
  A Souldiers a man;
  Oh, man's life's but a fpan! 74
  Why, then let a Souldier drinke!

Some Wine, Boyes!
Caffio. 'Fore Heauen, **an excellent Song!** 77

  [1] Some Editors emend 'dead' to 'dumb.' But the emendation is only
a 'fancy' one, for ryme's sake.
  [2] The Folio reads 'Heauenly, heauenly.'

Iago. I learn'd it in *England;* where indeed they are moſt potent in Potting. Your *Dane,* your *Germaine,* and your ſwag-belly'd *Hollander,* (drinke, hoa!) are nothing to your *Engliſh.*[1]   80

*PELHAM HUMFREY, 1673. Song. Solo, Soprano. In *Musica Antiqua,* ii. 171, ed. J. Stafford Smith. 1812.
Name Unknown. Caulfield's Collection.
W. LINLEY, 1816. Round for three male voices. In Linley's ' Dramatic Songs of Shakspere.'

Othello, IV. iii. 34, &c.

"SONG OF 'WILLOUGH.'"

[Desdemona talks to her woman Æmilia, who is undressing her to go to the bed in which Othello strangles her.]

Deſdemona. My Mother had a Maid call'd *Barbarie:*   26
She was in loue; and he the lou'd prou'd mad,
And did forſake her. She had a Song of ' Willough '
An old thing 'twas; but it expreſſ'd her Fortune,
And ſhe dy'd ſinging it. That Song, to night,   30
Will not go *from* my mind: I haue much to do,
But to go hang *my* head all at one ſide,
And ſing it like *poore Barbarie.* Prythee, diſpatch!

*   *   •   •   *   *   *

Deſdemona [ſings]. *The poore Soule ſat ſinging, by a Sicamour tree.*
Sing all a greene Willough!   35
Her hand on her boſome, her head on her knee;
Sing Willough, Willough, Willough!   37
The freſh Streames ran by her, and murmur'd her moanes;
Sing Willough, &c.
Her ſalt teares fell from her, and ſoftned the ſtones;
Sing Willough, &c.

(Lay by these.) *Willough, Willough!*   42
(Prythee, high thee! he'le come anon.)
Sing, all a greene Willough muſt be my Garland.

---

[1] Iago's next song is an old English ballad, which has its own tune. The music is in Caulfield's Collection (II. 68).
Iago. Oh, sweet England!
King Stephen was and a worthy Peere,   92
His Breeches coſt him but a Crowne;
He held them Six pence all to deere,
With that he cal'd the Tailor ' Lowne!'   95
He was a wight of high Renowne,   96
And thou art but of low degree:
'Tis Pride that pulls the Country downe,
And take thy awld Cloake about thee.   99
Some Wine, hoa!

E

Let no body blame him! his scorne I approue.   45

(Nay, that's not next.   Harke! who is't that knocks?
Æmil. It's the wind.)

Desdemona. I call'd my Loue 'falfe Loue' : but what faid he then?
Sing Willough, &c.   49
If I court mo women, you'le couch with mo men.

Ancient, 1600.[1] **Solo,** Contralto.   Chappell's 'Music of the Olden Time,'
vol. i. p. 207.
SIGNOR GIORDANI, 1783. **Solo.**
*Anonymous. 'Willow! a **Glee** for four **voices.'**   London, 1800 ?',
folio.[2]   S1, S2, S3, or Contra Alto, B.
J. MOREHEAD. Glee for three voices. Giordani, arranged by J. M.
JAMES HOOK, 1800. Solo, Mezzo-Soprano. Sung by Mrs. Jordan.
'Shakspere Vocal Album,' 1864.
DR. I. KEMP, 1807. Song, Soprano. 'Vocal Magazine of Canzonets,'
&c. &c., p. 100.
W. LINLEY, 1816. Solo. Linley's 'Dramatic Songs of Shakspere.'
SIR HENRY BISHOP, 1819. Solo. Sung in *Comedy of Errors*, by Miss
Stevens.
SIR ARTHUR SULLIVAN, 1865. Solo, Contralto. Metzler.
*W. SHIELD set the introduction to this Song, beginning '*My Mother
had a maid called Barbara*,' but he did not go on with it, so as to
include *Willow*, *Willow*. (See Linley, vol. ii. p. 24.)
*W. MICHAEL WATSON. Part Song. (Cross-reference in Brit. Mus.
Catalogue, but no principal entry.)

Romeo and Juliet.

Act I. Scene v. lines 95—112.   Quarto 2, ed. Daniel.

"IF I PROPHANE WITH MY VNWORTHIEST HAND."

Romeo [to IULIET].   If I prophane with my vnworthieft hand,
This holy fhrine, the gentle fin is this ;   96
My lips, two blufhing Pilgrims, readie ftand,
To fmoothe that rough touch, with a tender kis.   98

---

[1] The music of 'Willow, willow' is older than 1600. It is found in
Thomas Dallis's MS. 'Lute-book,' with the title 'All a greane willow.'
Dallis taught music at Cambridge; and his book, dated 1583, is now in the
Library of Trin. Coll., Dublin. (D. iii, 30.)
[2] The finger is made a man. The words are much altered : After 37
above, **are**

    He figh'd in his singing, and after each groan,
       O Willow, &c.
    I'm dead to all pleasure, my true love is gone.
          &c.   &c.

Iuliet. Good Pilgrime, you do wrong your hand too much,
Which mannerly deuocion fhowes in this;
For Saints haue hands, that Pilgrims hands do **tuch**;
And palme **to palme, is** holy Palmers kis.   102
  Romeo. Haue not Saints lips, and holy Palmers too?
  Iuliet. I, Pilgrim! lips that they mufl vfe in praire.
  Romeo. O then, deare Saint, let lips do what hands do!
They pray (grant thou) leaft faith turne **to** difpaire.   106
  Iuliet. Saints do not moue, thogh grant for praiers fake.
  Romeo. Then moue **not** while my praiers effect I take :   108
Thus from my lips, by thine, my fin is purg'd.
  Iuliet. Then haue **my** lips the fin that **they haue tooke.**
  Romeo. Sin **from my** lips? ò trefpas fweetly **vrgd!**
Giue me my fin againe!
  Iuliet.   Youe kiffe bith booke.   1:3

FRANCIS HUTCHINSON, 1807.   Duet, Soprano and Tenor.

———

Romeo and Juliet, II. ii. 107—24. Quarto 2, ed. Daniel.

"LADY! BY YONDER BLESSED MOONE I VOW."

  Romeo. Lady! by yonder bleffed Moone I **vow**,[1]   107
That tips with filuer all thefe Fruite tree tops. . .
  Iuliet. O fweare not by the Moone,—th'inconfiant Moone,
That monethly changes in her circled Orbe,—
Leaft that thy Loue proue likewife variable.   111
  Romeo. What fhall I fweare by?
  Iuliet.   Do not fweare at all!
Or, if thou wilt, fweare by thy gracious felfe,
Which is the **God of my Idolatrie,**
And Ile beleeue thee.
  Romeo.   If my hearts deare loue. . . .   115
  Iuliet. Well, do not fweare! although I ioy in thee,
I haue no ioy of this contráct to night;
It is too rath, too vnaduifd, too fudden,
Too like the lightning, which doth ceafe to bee   119
Ere one can fay, 'It lightens.' Sweete! goodnight!
This bud of Loue, by Sommers ripening breath,
May proue a bewtious Floure when next we meete.
Goodnight! goodnight! As fweete repofe and reft,
Come to thy heart, as that within my breft!   .   124

DR. J. KEMP, about 1799. Duet, Soprano and Tenor. Violoncello
  Obbligato. In 'Illustrations of Shakspere,' by Dr. J. Kemp.

[1] sweare. Folio 1.

E 2

DR. J. KEMP. Solo. Violoncello Ob. Begins, 'Love heralds should
be thoughts.' 'Illustrations of Shakspere,' by Dr. J. Kemp.
HOWARD GLOVER, 1861. Song, Soprano. Called 'Sweet good night!'
or Juliet's Song.
COUNTESS MARIE CORELLI, 1882. Recitative and Air. Called 'Romeo's
good night!' Stanley Lucas.
(See W. S. STEVENS'S 'Lyric Recitation of the Garden Scene in *Romeo
and Juliet*, paraphrased from Shakspere,' 1881.)

Romeo and Juliet, III. v. 1—11.   Quarto 2, ed Daniel.

"WILT THOU BE GONE? IT IS NOT YET NEARE DAY."

[After their one night together, as husband and wife.]

Enter ROMEO *and* JULIET *aloft*.

Juliet. Wilt thou be gone? It is not yet neare day: 1
It was the Nightingale, and not the Larke,
That pierst the fearefull hollow of thine eare;
Nightly she sings on yond Pomgranet tree: 4
Beleeue me, Loue, it was the Nightingale!
Romeo. It was the Larke, the Herauld of the Morne;
No Nightingale! Looke, Loue, what enuious streakes
Do lace the seuering Cloudes in yonder East!   8
Nights Candles are burnt out, and Iocand Day
Stands tipto on the mystie Mountaine tops.
I must be gone, and liue; or stay, and die.   11

PERCY, 1785. Duet. Called 'The Garden Scene' in *Romeo and Juliet*.
J. REEKES, about 1850. Solo. J. Reekes, 'Six Songs from Shakspere.'

Taming of the Shrew.

Induction.   Scene ii. lines 33—54.

"WILT THOU HAVE MUSICKE? HARKE! APOLLO PLAIES."

[The humourous Lord who has taken the drunkard Sly to his
house, and told his men to treat Sly as a Lord, says to him:]

Lord. Wilt thou haue Musicke? Harke! *Apollo* plaies, [*Musick*.
And twentie cag'd Nightingales do sing: 34
Or wilt thou sleepe? Wee'l haue thee to a Couch,
Softer and sweeter then the lustfull bed   36
On purpose trim'd vp for *Semiramis*.
Say thou wilt walke; we wil bestrow the ground:
Or wilt thou ride? Thy horses shall be trap'd,

Their harneſſe ſtudded all with Gold and Pearle. 40
Doſt thou loue hawking? Thou haſt hawkes will ſoare
Aboue the morning Larke : Or wilt thou hunt?
Thy hounds ſhall make the Welkin anſwer them,
And fetch ſhrill ecchoes from the hollow earth. 44
  1. *Man.* Say thou wilt courſe ; thy gray-hounds are as ſwift
As breathëd Stags, I, fleeter than the Roe.
  2. *Man.* Doſt thou loue pictures? we wil fetch thee ſtrait
Adonis, painted by a running brooke, 48
And *Citherea* all in ſedges hid,
Which ſeeme to moue and wanton with her breath,
Euen as the wauing ſedges play with winde.
  Lord. Wee'l ſhew thee *Io*, as ſhe was a Maid ; 52
And how ſhe was beguilëd and ſurpriz'd,
As liuelie painted as the deede was done.

T. COOKE, 1828. Song. Sung by Miss Fanny Ayton in *Taming of the Shrew*.

Taming of the Shrew, Act II. Scene i. lines 167—77.

"SHOULD HE UPBRAID, I'LL OWN THAT HE PREVAIL."[1]

ALTERED FROM THE SPEECH BEGINNING,
"SAY, THAT SHE RAILE."

[Baptista, the father of Kate the Shrew, speaks to Petruchio, who
wants to marry her :]

Signior *Petruchio*, will you go with vs,
Or ſhall I ſend my daughter *Kate* to you? 164
  Petruchio. I pray you do! [*Exit.* Manet PETRUCHIO.
          I will attend her heere,
And woo her with ſome ſpirit when ſhe comes.

Say, that ſhe raile ; why, then Ile tell her plaine,
She ſings as ſweetly as a Nightinghale : 168
Say, that ſhe frowne ; Ile ſay ſhe lookes as cleere
As morning Roſes newly waſht with dew :
Say, ſhe be mute, and will not ſpeake a word ;
Then Ile commend her volubility, 172

[1] The words in Bishop's song are as follows, the alterd ones being in
italics :
          Should he upbraid, I'll *own that he prevail*,
          And sing as sweetly as *the* Nightingale.
          Say that *he* frown, I'll say ' *his* looks *I view*
          As morning roses newly *tipt* with dew,'
          Say *he* be mute, I'll *answer with a smile*,
          And dance and play, and wrinkled Care beguile.

And say she vttereth piercing eloquence :
If she do bid me packe, Ile giue her thankes,
As though she bid me stay by her a weeke
If she denie to wed, Ile craue the day   176
When I shall aske the banes, and when be married.
But heere she comes; and now, *Petruchio,* speake !

Enter KATERINA.

Good morrow, *Kate!* for thats your name, I heare.

SIR H. R. BISHOP, 1821. Solo. Composed for and sung by Miss M.
Tree in *The Two Gentlemen of Verona.*

Tempest.

Act I. Scene ii. lines 198—206.

"NOW I FLAM'D AMAZEMENT."

Prospero [to ARIEL].   Hast thou, Spirit,   193
Perform'd to point, THE TEMPEST that I bad thee ?
Ariel. To euery Article !
I boorded the Kings ship. Now on the Beake,   196
Now in the Waste, the Decke, in euery Cabyn,
I flam'd amazement. Sometime I'ld diuide,
And burne in many places ; on the Top-mast,
The Yards, and Bore-spritt, would I flame distinctly ;   200
Then meete, and ioyne. *Ioues* Lightning, the precursers
O'th dreadfull Thunder-claps, more momentarie
And sight out-running, were not ; the fire, and cracks
Of sulphurous roaring, the most mighty *Neptune,*   204
Seeme to besiege, and make **his** bold waues tremble,
Yea, **his** dread Trident shake.

IN. CHRISTOPHER SMITH, 1756. Recitative in Smith's 'Tempest,'
p. 12.

Tempest, Act I. Scene ii. lines 375—85.

"COME UNTO THESE YELLOW SANDS."

Enter FERDINAND ; *&* ARIEL, *inuisible, playing* **and** *singing.*

Ariel. [Song.] *Come ento these yellow sands,*
              and then take hands;   376
         Curtsied when you haue, and kist
              the wilde waues whist !   378
         Foote it featly heere and there,
              and, sweete Sprights, beare the burthen !   380

[Burthen, difperfedly.] *Harke, harke! lough waugh!*
       The watch-Dogges barke, lough waugh! 382
   Ariel.   *Hark, hark, I heare,*
       the ftraine of ftrutting Chanticlere
       cry, ' Cockadidle-dowe!' 385

JOHN BANISTER. In the time of Charles II. Solo.
HENRY PURCELL, 1675. Soprano Solo and Chorus.
JN. CHRISTOPHER SMITH, 1756. Solo. Smith's 'Tempest.'
SIR JOHN STEVENSON, 1798 (?). Glee for S.S.B. 4-hand Piano
   accompaniment.
*SIR ARTHUR S. SULLIVAN, 1866. Solo and Chorus.

Tempest, Act I. Scene ii. lines 395—402.

"FULL FADOM FIVE THY FATHER LIES."

[Ariel's song tells Prince Ferdinand that his Father is drownd.
(He is, in fact, alive and well.)]

   Ariell. [Song.] *Full fadom fiue thy Father lies :* 395
       Of his bones are Corrall made :
       Thofe are pearles that were his eies,
       Nothing of him that doth fade, 398
       But doth fuffer a Sea-change
       Into fomething rich & ftrange : 400
   Sea-Nimphs hourly ring his knell :
          [Burthen :] *ding dong!*
   Harke! now I heare them : ding-dong, bell! 402

ROBERT JOHNSON. Shakspere's time. Harmonized for three voices by
   Dr. Wilson. 'Cheerful Ayres or Ballads,' by Dr. Wilson.
JOHN BANISTER. In the time of Charles II. Song, Soprano. Arranged
   (C. or B.) with Chorus, S.A.T.B., by Edw. J. Loder. Lonsdale.
HENRY PURCELL, 1675. Soprano Solo and Chorus.
JN. CHRISTOPHER SMITH, 1756. Solo : Contralto or Bass.
*SIR ARTHUR SULLIVAN, 1865. Solo. Novello.
*C. H. HUBERT PARRY, 1874. Song, Contralto, C to E♭. 'A Garland,'
   &c., No. 5. Sung by Miss Antoinette Sterling. Boosey. Called
   "A Sea Dirge."
*A. M. WARREN, 1874. Solo, Bass. Weekes and Co.
*G. R. VICARS, June 1, 1883. Part Song. Novello.

Tempest, Act II. Scene i. lines 298—303.

"WHILE YOU HERE DO SNOARING LIE."

[Sebastian has arranged with Antonio, that when he (S.) raises his
hand, Antonio shall kill the sleeping Gonzalo, while he, Sebastian,
kills king Alonso, who lies asleep, too. Ariel, sent by Prospero,
wakes Gonzalo, and frustrates the plot.]

Re-enter ARIELL, *invisible, with* **Muficke and Song.**

Ariel [*to* GONZALO *fleeping*].   My Mafter (through his Art)
   forefees the danger
That you (his friend) are in ; and fends me forth   296
(For elfe his proiect dies) to keepe them liuing.
                                       [*Sings in* GONZALOES *eare*.

         While you here do fnoaring lie,
         Open-ey'd Confpiracie
              His time doth take.   300
         If of Life you keepe a care,
         Shake off flumber and beware!
              Awake, awake!   303

DR. ARNE (?), 1746.   Song.   In Caulfield's Collection.
THOMAS LINLEY, 1789.   Linley's 'Dramatic Songs of Shakspere.'

Tempest, Act II. Scene ii. lines 41, 42, 45~53.

"SNATCHES OF SONG FOR STEPHANO."

Sung by Mr. Bannister.

Enter STEPHANO *finging,* & *holding a large Bottle of Sacke.*

Stephano.   *I fhall no more to fea, to fea,*
                 Here fhall I dye afhore. . .

This is a very fcuruy tune to fing at a mans Funerall : well, here's
my comfort !   [*Drinkes.* 44

[*Sings.*] *The Mafter, the Swabber,* **the Boate-fwaine &** *I,*   45
       The Gunner, and his Mate,
       Lou'd Mall, Meg, and Marrian, and Margerie,
       But none of vs car'd for Kate.   48
          For fhe had a tongue with a tang,
          Would cry to a Sailor 'goe hang!'   50
       She lou'd not the fauour of Tar nor of Pitch;
       Yet a Tailor might fcratch her where ere fhe did itch.
          Then, to Sea, Boyes! and let her goe hang!   53
This is a fcuruy tune too : But here's my comfort !   [*Drinkes.*

Anonymous.   Caulfield's Collection.

Tempest, Act II. Scene ii. lines 173-79.

"NO MORE DAMS I'LL MAKE FOR FISH."

[Caliban, Prospero's slave, made drunk by Stephano's sack,—made
" a howling Monster, a drunken Monster," as Trinculo says,—swears
to be Stephano's subject, and no longer serve Prospero.]

Caliban. *No more dams I'le make for fijh,*
    Nor fetch in firing,
    At requiring,   175
    Nor fcrape trenchering,
    Nor wajh dijh !   177
    Ban', ban', Ca . . calyban,
    Has a new Majter. 'Get a new Man !   179

Freedome, high-day! high-day, freedome! freedome! high-day, freedome!

JN. CHRISTOPHER SMITH, 1756. Solo, Bass. Smith's 'Tempest.'
    Caulfield's Collection.
J. W. HOBBS, 1861. Song, Bass. Called 'Caliban.'
J. F. DUGGAN, 1870. Tenor or Bass Song. Called 'Caliban.'

Tempest, Act III. Scene ii. lines 118, 19.

"FLOUT 'EM, AND COUT 'EM."

Caliban [to STEPHANO]. Thou mak'ft me merry! I am full ot
    pleafure!
Let vs be iocond! Will you troule the Catch   114
You taught me but whileare?
    Stephano. At thy requeft, Monfter, I will do reafon; any reafon.
¶ Come on, *Trinculo !* let vs fing!   117

Sings.

Flout'em, and cout'em ! and skowt'em, and flout'em !
Thought is free.

HENRY PURCELL, 1675. Round for three. Caulfield's Collection.

Tempest, Act IV. Scene i. lines 44-8.

"BEFORE YOU CAN SAY, 'COME, AND GOE'."

[Ferdinand and Miranda are to witness a Masque of Prospero's
Spirits.]

    Profpero [to ARIEL]. . . . Goe bring the rabble
(Ore whom I giue thee powre) here, to this place!
Incite them to quicke motion, for I muft
Beftow vpon the eyes of this yong couple[1]   40
Some vanity of mine Art : it is my promife,
And they expeft it from me.

        [1] Ferdinand and Miranda.

Ariel.   Prefently ?
Profpero.   I ! with a twincke !
Ariel.   Before you can fay ' come, **and goe,'**   44
And breathe twice, and cry ' fo, fo ' :
Each one, tripping on his Toe,
Will be here with mop and mowe.
Doe you lone me, Mafter ?   no ?   48

JN. CHRISTOPHER SMITH, 1756.   Solo.   Smith's ' Tempest.'
THOS. LINLEY, 1789.   Solo.   Linley's ' Dramatic Songs of Shakfpere.'

Tempest, Act IV. Scene i. lines 106—17.

"HONOR, RICHES, MARRIAGE-BLESSING."

IVNO *defcends, & enters.*

Iuno [to CERES].   How do's my bounteous fifter ?   **Goe with me**
To blefſe this twaine,[1] that they may profperous be,   104
And honourd in their Iſſue !

Iuno.   *Honor, riches, marriage-bleſſing,*
          Long continuance, and encreaſing,   107
          Hourely ioyes, be ſtill vpon you !
          Iuno *ſings her bleſſings on you.*   109

Ceres.   *Earths increaſe, foyzon plentie,*
           Barnes and Garners, neuer empty,   111
           Vines, with cluſtring bunches growing,
           Plants, with goodly burthen bowing :   113
           Spring come to you at the fartheſt,
           In the very end of Harueſt !   115
           Scarcity and want ſhall ſhun you,
           Ceres bleſſing ſo is on you.   117

SIGNORINA **DE** GAMBERINI, 1785 (?).   Solo.   Entitled, " The friendly
    wiſh from Shakſpere."   'Twelve English and Italian Songs,' by
    Gamberini.   No. 2.   Brit. Mus. Lib.
WILLIAM LINLEY, 1816.   Duet for two Sopranos.
T. S. COOKE, 1840 (?).   Duet for two Sopranos.   Novello.
H. VAN DEN ABEELEN, 1859.   Duet.   Known as "Homage to Shakſpere."
    Ashdown and Parry.
SIR ARTHUR S. SULLIVAN, 1862.   Duet for Soprano and Contralto,
    with Chorus.   'Duet for two Sopranos,' 1863.   Novello.

---

[1] Ferdinand and Miranda.

Tempest, Act IV. Scene i. lines 134—8.

"YOU SUN-BURN'D SICKLEMEN, OF AUGUST WEARY."

Re-enter IRIS.

Iris. You Nimphs, cald *Nayades*, of ye windring brooks,
With your fedg'd crownes, and euer-harmleffe lookes,   129
Leaue your crifpe channels, and on this greene-Land
Anfwere your fummons! *Iuno* do's command!   131
Come, temperate Nimphes, and helpe to celebrate
A Contract of true Loue! be not too late!   133

Enter Certaine Nimphes.

¶ You Sun-burn'd Sicklemen, of Auguft weary,
Come hether from the furrow, and be merry!   135
Make holly-day! your Rye-ftraw hats put on,
And thefe frefh Nimphs encounter, euery one,   137
In Country footing!

Enter certaine Reapers (*properly habited*): *they ioyne with the* Nimphes, *in a gracefull dance; towards the end whereof,* PROS-PERO *ftarts fodainly, and fpeakes; after which, to a strange hollow and confufed noyfe, they heauily* [1] *vanifh.*

FRANCIS HUTCHINSON, 1807.   Glee for two Tenors and one Bass. Collection of Vocal Music by Hutchinson.

———

Act V. Scene ii. lines 152—6.

"THE CLOWD-CAPT TOWRES, THE GORGEOUS PALLACES."

Profpero [*to* FERDINAND].   Our Reuels now are ended.   Thefe our actors
(As I foretold you) were all Spirits, and   149
Are melted into Ayre, into thin Ayre,
And, like the bafeleffe fabricke of this vifion,

The Clowd-capt Towres, the gorgeous Pallaces,
The folemne Temples, the great Globe it felfe,   153
Yea, all which it inherit, fhall diffolue,
And (like this infubftantiall Pageant faded)
Leaue not a racke behinde.
                    We are fuch ftuffe
As dreames are made on; and our little life   157
Is rounded with a fleepe.

R. J. STEVENS, about 1795.   Glee for six voices, S.A.T.T.B.B.   Novello.

———

[1] *heauily* = mournfully.

Tempest, Act V. Scene i. lines 1—8.

"NOW DO'S MY PROIECT GATHER TO A HEAD."

Before PROSPEROES *Cell.*

Enter PROSPERO *(in his Magicke robes), and* ARIEL.

Prospero. Now do's my Proiect gather to a head :   1
My charmes cracke not ; my Spirits obey ; and Time
Goes vpright with his carriage. How's the day ?
Ariel. On the fixt hower ; at which time, my Lord,   4
You faid our worke fhould ceafe.
Prospero.   I did fay fo,
When firft I raif'd *THE TEMPEST.* Say, my Spirit,
How fares the King, and's followers ?
Ariel.   Contin'd together,
In the fame fafhion, as you gaue in charge, ...   8

JN. CHRISTOPHER SMITH, 1756.   Recitative.   Smith's 'Tempest.'

Act V. Scene i. lines 88—94.

"WHERE THE BEE SUCKS, THERE SUCK I."

[Prospero is about to present himself before King Alonso,
Antonio, and the rest.]

Prospero. . . . . . .   *Ariell.*
Fetch me the Hat, and Rapier in my Cell !   84
I will difcafe me, and my felfe prefent
As I was fometime *Millaine.*   Quickly, Spirit !
Thou fhalt ere long be free.   87

[ARIELL *fings, and helps to attire him.*

Where the Bee fucks, there fuck I;
In a Cowflips bell, I lie ;
There I cowch when Owles doe crie ;
On the Batts backe I doe flie
after Sommer merrily.   92
Merrily, merrily, fhall I liue now,
Vnder the bloffom that **hangs on** *the* ***Bow!***   94

Prospero.   Why ! that's my dainty *Ariell !*   I fhall miffe thee ;
But yet thou fhalt haue freedome : fo, fo, fo !

ROBERT JOHNSON, Shakspere's time.   Harmonized for three voices,
   by Dr. Wilson.   'Cheerful Ayres,' by Dr. Wilson, Oxford, 1660.
   Printed in Hullah's 'Singers' Library,' No. 21, 1859.
PELHAM HUMFREY, 1665.   Called "A Song in the machines, by Ariel's
   Spirits."   Printed on a sheet in Brit. Mus.
PURCELL, 1675.   Dr. Rimbault had it in MS.

DR. ARNE, 1746. Solo, Soprano. The same, harmonized for S.S.T.B.,
  by W. Jackson. Caulfield's Collection.
NICOLO PASQUALI, 1750. Solo. It alters "On the Batts backe I doe
  flie," l. 91, to "On the swallow's wings I fly." Twelve English Songs
  in Score, collected from several Masques, &c. No. II. 'A Song
  in the Tempest.'
JN. CHRISTOPHER SMITH, 1756. Solo. Smith's 'Tempest.'
SIR ARTHUR SULLIVAN, 1862. Solo. Novello.

Troylus and Cressida.

Act IV. Scene iv. lines 15—18.

"O, HEART, HEAUIE HEART!"

[Troylus comes to Pandaruses house, to fetch his love Cressid, in
order to deliver her up to Diomed and the Geeeks, who are to take
her to her father, Calchas, in the Grecian camp.]

Enter TROYLUS.

Cref. O Troylus, Troylus!   [*Embracing him.*
Pan. What a paire of spectacles is here! let me embrace too!
' Oh heart,' as the goodly faying is ;   14

  ' Oh heart, heauie heart,
  Why fighest thou without breaking ?'

where he answers againe ;

  ' Becaufe thou canft not eafe thy fmart
  By friendfhip, nor by fpeaking' :   18

There was neuer a truer rime! Let vs caft away nothing, for we
may liue to haue neede of fuch a Verfe! We fee it, we fee it!
How now, Lambs?   21

M. P. KING, 1810 (?).

Twelfth Night.

Act I. Scene i. lines 1—15.

"IF MUSICKE BE THE FOOD OF LOVE, PLAY ON!"

The Dukes Palace.

Enter ORSINO, Duke *of* Illyria, CURIO, *and other Lords* ; Musicians
attending.

Duke.

F Muficke be the food of Loue, play on!   1
Giue me exceffe of it, that, furfetting,
The appetite may ficken, and fo dye.
That ftraine agen! it had a dying fall :   4

O, it came ore my eare, like the sweet sound
That breathes vpon a banke of Violets,
Stealing, and giuing, Odour!—Enough; no more!
'Tis not so sweet now, as it was before.   8
O spirit of Loue, how quicke and fresh art thou,
That, notwithstanding thy capacitie
Receiueth as the Sea: nought enters there,
Of what validity, and pitch so ere,   12
But falles into abatement, and low price,
Euen in a minute! so full of shapes is Fancie,
That it alone is high fantasticall.

JAMES CLIFTON, 1781. Solo. Reproduced in 'Shakspere Vocal Album,' 1864.
SIR JOHN STEVENSON. Air, Contralto or Bass. Commences, 'That straun again.' L 4. In a set of eight Songs and four Duets.
SIR J. STEVENSON and T. COOKE, 1828. Quartet. Opera, *Taming of the Shrew.*
A. MATTHEY, 1847. Canzonet.
CHARLES HORSLEY. Solo. Chappell, New Bond Street.
GEORGE BENSON, 1861. Glee.
*W. C. SALLE, 1863. Canzonet.

Twelfth Night, Act I. Scene v. lines 254—262.

"MAKE ME A WILLOW CABINE AT YOUR GATE."

[Viola, drest as Duke Orsino's page, Cesario, takes her Master's message of love to Olivia, who, not caring for him, falls in love with his page Cesario-Viola. The latter says to Olivia:]

Viola. If I did loue you in my masters flame,
With such a suffring, such a deadly life,
In your deniall I would finde no sence;
I would not vnderstand it.
   Oliuia.   Why, what would you?   253
   Viola. Make me a willow Cabine at your gate,
And call vpon my soule within the house;
Write loyall Cantons of contemnèd loue,
And sing them lowd, euen in the dead of night;   357
Hallow your name to the reuerberate hilles,
And make the babling Gossip of the aire
Cry out, 'Oliuia!' O, you should not rest
Betweene the elements of ayre, and earth,   261
But you should pittie me!

JOHN BRAHAM, 1828. Solo, Tenor. Sung by himself in *Taming of the Shrew.*

Twelfth Night, Act II. Scene iii. lines 36—41, 44-9.

"O MISTRIS MINE, WHERE ARE YOU ROMING?"

Sir Andrew. Excellent! Why, this is the beft fooling, when
all is done. Now, a fong!
Sir Toby. Come on; there is fixe pence for you! Let's haue a
fong!   31
Sir Andrew. There's a teftrill of me too! if one knight giue a ...
Clowne. Would you haue a loue-fong, or a fong of good life?
Sir Toby. A loue fong, a loue fong!
Sir Andrew. I, I! I care not for 'good life.' [*Clowne fings.* 35

     O Miftris mine, where are you roming?
     O, ftay and heare! your true loue's coming,
     That can fing both high and low: 38
     Trip no further, prettie fweeting!
     Iourneys end in louers meeting.
     Every wife mans fonne doth know.   41

Sir Andrew. Excellent good, ifaith!
Sir Toby. Good, good!   43

     Clowne. *What is Loue? tis not heereafter;*
     Prefent mirth hath prefent laughter;
     What's to come is ftill vnfure   46
     In delay there lies no plentie;
     Then come kiffe me, Sweet and twentie!
     Youth's a ftuffe will not endure!   49

Sir Andrew. A mellifluous voyce, as I am true knight!

Anonymous, 1599 and 1611. Morley's 'Consort Lessons.' Also in
    Queen Elizabeth's Virginal Book, arranged by Byrd. Solo, Tenor
    or Bass. (Chappell, 'Music of the Olden Time,' vol. i. p. 209.)
R. J. S. STEVENS, 1755. Glee. Novello.
WILLIAM LINLEY, 1815. Solo. Linley's 'Dramatic Songs of Shakspere.'
J. ADDISON, 1820. Solo, Tenor. In Caulfield, vol. i. p. 137.
ELIZABETH CRAVEN, MARGRAVINE OF ANSPACH. Madrigal for two
    voices.
J. MAJOR, 1856. ('Cyclopædia of Music,' No. 356.) An adaptation of
    Elizabeth Craven's Madrigal. Duct.
J. REEKES, 1850 to 1860. Song. 'Six Songs from Shakspere.'
SIR ARTHUR S. SULLIVAN, 1866. Solo, Bass. Sung by Mr. Santley.
    Metzler.
*F. STANISLAUS, 1870. Song. Ashdown.
*G. A. MACFARREN, 1872. Part Song, S.A.T.B. (Fofter's 'Choral
    Harmonist,' No. 4.)
*REV. C. E. HEY, 1877. Part Song: Soprano, Contralto, Tenor, Bass,
    in *Twelfth Night*. Patey and Willis.
*A. H. D. PRENDERGAST, 1878. Part Song, A.T.B. Stanley Lucas,
    Weber, and Co.
*H. W. WAREING, 1878. Part Song. Novello.

*J. MOUNT, 1879. Song.
*T. E. GLADSTONE, 1880. Song. Novello.
*L. CARROTT, 1881. Song. Stanley Lucas, Weber, and Co.
E. T. DRIFFIELD. Part Song, A.T.T.B. Novello.

Twelfth Night, Act II. Scene iii.

"SNATCHES OF SONG FOR SIR TOBY."

Enter MARIA.

Maria. What a catterwalling doe you keepe heere! If my
Ladie haue not call'd vp her Steward *Maluolio*, and bid him turne
you out of doores, neuer trust me!   68
Toby. My Lady's a *Catayan*, we are politicians: *Maluolio's* a
Peg-a-ramsie, and [*sings*] '*Three merry men be wee.*' Am not I con-
sanguinious? Am I not of her blood? Tilly vally! '*Ladie'*:
[*sings*] '*There dwelt a man in Babylon, Lady, Lady!*'   73
Clowne. Beshrew me, the knight's in admirable fooling!
Sir Andrew. I, he do's well enough if he be dispos'd, and so
do I too: he does it with a better grace, but I do it more naturall.
Toby. [*sings*] '*O, the twelfe day of December,*' . . .   77
Maria. For the loue o' God, peace!

Enter MALUOLIO.

*   *   *   *   ●   *   ●   *   *

Maluolio. Sir Toby, I must be round with you! My Lady [86
bad **me** tell you, that, though shee harbors you as her kinsman, shee's
nothing ally'd to your disorders. If you can separate your selfe and
your misdemeanors, you are welcome to the house; if not, and it
would please you to take leaue of her, shee is very willing to bid you
farewell.   91
Toby. [*sings*] '*Farewell, deere heart! since I must needs be gone.*'
(*Maria.* Nay, good Sir Toby!)
Clowne. [*sings*] '*His eyes do shew his dayes are almost done.*' 94
(*Maluolio.* Is't euen so?)
Toby. '*But I will **neuer** dye.*'
Clowne. Sir Toby, there you lye.   97
(*Maluolio.* This is much credit to you.)
Toby. '*Shall I bid him go?*'
Clowne. '*What and if you do?*'   100
Toby. '*Shall I bid him go, and spare not?*'
Clowne. '*Oh, no, no, no, no, you dare not!*'   102

In Caulfield's Collection, vol. i. p. 147. Composer unknown.
*ROBERT JONES, 1601 (12th from the 1st Book). Song, in four Parts.
    In *Musica Antiqua*, vol. ii. 204, ed. J. Stafford Smith. 1812. Cald
    'Farewell, dear Heart!'

Twelfth Night, Act II. Scene iv. lines 51—66.

"COME AWAY! COME AWAY, DEATH!"

Re-enter CURIO *&* Clowne (FESTE).

The Duke. [to FESTE]   O, fellow, come! the fong we had laft
   night!

¶ Marke it, *Cefario!* it is old and plaine;
The Spinfters and the Knitters in the Sun,
And the free maides that weaue their thred with bones,   45
Do vfe to chaunt it : it is filly footh,
And dallies with the innocence of loue,
Like the old age.

Clowne. Are you ready, Sir?   49
Duke. I; prethee, fing!   [*Muficke.*

The Song.

Clowne. Come away! come away, Death!   51
   And in fad cypreffe let me be laide;
   Fye, away! fie, away,[1] breath!
   I am flaine by a faire cruell maide: 54
   My fhroud of white, ftuck all with Ew,   55
   O, prepare it!
   My part of death, no one fo true
   did fhare it.   58

Not a flower, not a flower fweete,   59
   On my blacke coffin, let there be ftrewne;
Not a friend, not a friend greet
   My poore corpfe, where my bones fhall be throwne! 62
   A thoufand thoufand fighes to faue,   63
   lay me, ô, where
   Sad true louer neuer find my graue,
   to weepe there!   66

DR. ARNE, 1741.   Solo.   Sung by Mr. Lowe.   'Shakspere Vocal Album.'
R. J. S. STEVENS, 1790.   Glee.   Novello.
MARIA HESTER PARK, 1790.   Solo.   Inscribed to Dr. Parsons.
By a Lady (anonymous).   Solo.
WILLIAM LINLEY, 1816.   Solo, Bass.   Linley's 'Dramatic Songs of
   Shakspere.'
*SAMUEL WEBBE, JUN., 1830.   Glee.
*J. BRAHMS.   Published with English words, November, 1833.   (It is
   older in Germany.)   Trio, Ladies' voices.   Novello.
G. A. MACFARREN, 1864.   Glee, S.A.T.T.B.   Novello.

   [1] Editors generally read '*Fly away . . . fly away.*'

F

Twelfth Night, **Act II.** Scene iv. lines 110—115.

"SHE NEVER TOLD HER LOVE."

[Viola, as the page Cesario, says to her master, Orsino, Duke **of** Illyria :]

My Father had a daughter lou'd a man,
As it might be, perhaps, were I a woman,
I should your Lordship.
  Duke.   And what's her history?   109
  Viola. **A blanke,** my Lord.
                She neuer told her **loue,**
But let concealment, like **a** worme i'th budde,
Feede on her damaske cheeke : the pin'd in thought ;
And, with a greene and yellow melancholly,   113
She sate like Patience on a Monument,
Smiling at greefe.

HAYDN, 1790. **Solo. Dedicated to Lady** C. Bertie. (Canzonets, 2nd set, No. 4.)
DR. HARRINGTON of Bath, about 1790. Terzetto. Called 'Viola's account of her own concealed love,' in *Twelfth Night.* Book of Dr. Harrington's Compositions.
GEORGE NICKS, 1842. Duet for two Sopranos. **Robert Cocks.**
EDWARD L. HIME, 1856. Glee for four male **voices.**
*A. C. ROWLAND, 1874. Part Song, S.S.T.B. **Lamborn Cock.**

Twelfth Night, Act III. Scene i. lines 147—162.

"CESARIO! BY THE ROSES OF THE SPRING."

[Olivia, scorned by the page Cesario-Viola, with whom she is **in** love, first speaks to herself, and then to Viola, as Cesario :—]

  Olivia. ([*aside*] O, what a deale of scorne lookes beautifull
In the contempt and anger of his lip!   **144**
A murdrous guilt shewes not it selfe more soone
Then loue that would seeme hid : Loues night **is noone !**)   **146**

Cesario ! **by the Roses of** the Spring,
By maid-hood, honor, truth, and euery thing,   **148**
I loue **thee** so, that, maugre all thy pride,
Nor wit, nor reason, can my passion hide !   **150**
Do not extort thy reasons from this clause,
For that I woo, thou therefore hast no cause ;   **152**
But, rather, reason thus with reason fetter :
Loue sought, is good : but, giuen vnsought, is better !   **154**

Viola. By innocence I fweare, and by my youth,
I haue one heart, one bofome, and one truth,   156
And that no woman has! nor neuer none
Shall miftris be of it, faue I alone!   158
And fo adieu, good Madam! neuer more
Will I my Mafters teares to you deplore!   160
Olivia. Yet come againe! for thou perhaps mayft moue
That heart, which now abhorres, to like, his loue.   [*Exeunt.* 162

SIR HENRY BISHOP, 1820. Duet. Altered from Winter. Sung by
Misses Greene and Tree, in the operatised *Twelfth Night.*

Music for the Clowne's Snatches, in lines 72-9 and 118-121, is
given in Caulfield, I. 153; but his Song, which ends IV. ii., does not
seem to have been set [yet of course it has been].

Clowne. [*aduances & sings*] *Hey,* Robin! *iolly* Robin!
Tell me how thy Lady does!
Maluolio. Foole!   74
Clowne. *My Lady is vnkind, perdie.*
Maluolio. Foole!
Clowne. *Alas, why is fhe so?*
Maluolio. Foole, I fay!   78
Clowne. *She loues another* . . . Who calles, ha?

[Malvolio, having been made to believe that Olivia loves him, is
bound in a dark room as a madman. He calls to the Clown, Feste,
whom he hears singing. Malvolio wishes to write to Olivia, in
proof of his sanity, and Feste promises to be the bearer of the
letter.]

Clowne. [*sings*] *I am gone, fir;*   118
              And anon, fir,
              Ile be with you again,   120
              In a trice,
              Like to the old Vice,
              Your neede to fuftaine;   123

              Who, with dagger of lath,   124
              In his rage and his wrath,
              Cries, ' ah, ha!' to the Diuell: 126
              Like a mad lad,
              ' Paire thy nayles, dad;
              Adieu, good man Diuell!'   129

                                                      F 2

Twelfth Night, Act V. Scene i. lines 378—396.

"WHEN THAT I WAS AND A LITTLE TINE BOY."

[When all the other Players have left the Stage, the Clowne, Feste, winds up the Play with this Song:]

Clowne sings.

When that I was and a little tine[1] boy,	378
with hey, ho, the winde and the raine,	
A foolish thing was but a toy,	380
for the raine, it raineth every day.	
But when I came to mans estate,	382
with hey, ho, &c.	
Gainst Knaues and Theeues men shut their gate,	384
for the raine, &c.	
But when I came, alas! to wiue,	386
with hey, ho, &c.	
By swaggering could I neuer thriue,	388
for the raine, &c.	
But when I came vnto my beds,	390
with hey, ho, &c.	
With tosspottes still had drunken heades,	392
for the raine, &c.	
A great while ago the world begun,	394
hey, ho, &c.	
But that's all one; our Play is done:	396
and weel striue to please you euery day.	[Exit.

J. VERNON, 1770 (?). Solo. In 'The new Songs,' &c, No. 2. (Attributed by Linley to Fielding; but Dr. Rimbault says 'Vernon.') Linley's 'Dramatic Songs of Shakspere.' 'Handbook of Standard English Songs.' R. Cocks.
SIR J. STEVENSON, 1854. Glee, S.A.T.B.
*RICHARD SIMPSON, 1878. Solo. Lucas and Weber.
*J. L. HATTON. Part Song, S.A.T.B. Williams, Berners Street.
*SCHUMANN. Solo. Augener, Newgate St.

Two Gentlemen of Verona.
Act I. Scene iii. lines 84—7.
"OH, HOW THIS SPRING OF LOVE RESEMBLETH."

[Protheus is found by his father Antonio, reading a letter from his love Julia, whom he wants his father's consent to marry. Askt

[1] *tine* = tiny.

whose letter it is, Protheus shams that it is one from his friend
Valentine, describing how happily he gets on at the Emperor's court.
On this, Antonio resolves to send Protheus at once to the Court, to
join Valentine, and thus separate him from Julia. Protheus, caught
in his own trap, thus soliloquises:]

Protheus. Thus haue I shund the fire, for feare of burning,
And drench'd me in the fea, where I am drown'd.
I fear'd to shew my Father *Iulias* Letter, 80
Leaft he should take exceptions to my loue;
And, with the vantage of mine own excufe,
Hath he excepted moft againft my loue.

Oh, how this fpring of loue refembleth 84
The vncertaine glory of an Aprill day,
Which now shewes all the beauty of the Sun,
And by and by a clowd takes all away! 87

SIR HENRY BISHOP, 1819. Solo. Sung by Miss M. Tree, in the
Operatised *Comedy of Errors.*

Two Gentlemen of Verona, Act II. Scene vii. lines 33—38.

"HINDER NOT MY COURSE."

[Julia resolves to go to the Emperor's court, after her lover
Protheus. Her maid Lucetta tries to prevent her, and counsels her
to wait at home till Protheus returns. Julia answers:]

Iulia. Oh, know'ft thou not, his looks are my foules food?
Pitty the dearth that I haue pinëd in, 16
By longing for that food fo long a time!
Didft thou but know the inly touch of Loue,
Thou wouldft as foone goe kindle fire with fnow,
As feeke to quench the fire of Loue with words! 20
Lucetta. I doe not feeke to quench your Loues hot fire,
But qualifie the fires éxtreame rage,
Left it should burne aboue the bounds of reafon,
Iulia. The more thou dam'ft it up, the more it burnes: 24
The Current, that with gentle murmure glides,
(Thou know'ft,) being ftop'd, impatiently doth rage;
But, when his faire courfe is not hinderëd,
He makes fweet muficke with th'enameld ftoues, 28
Giuing a gentle kifle to euery fedge
He ouer-taketh in his pilgrimage;
And fo, by many winding nookes, he ftraies,
With willing fport, to the wide Ocëan. 32

Then let me goe, and hinder not my courfe!
Ile be as patient as a gentle ftreame,
And make a paftime of each weary ftep,

Till the laſt ſtep haue brought me to my Loue ;   36
And there He reſt, as, after much turmoile,
A bleſſed ſoule doth, in *Elizium !*

M. M. ALLNAT, 1860. Song.

_____

Two Gentlemen of Verona, Act IV. Scene ii. lines 38—52.

"WHO IS SILVIA? WHAT IS SHE?"

[Julia, having reacht the Emperor's city, in man's attire, is taken
by her Host to hear her faithless lover Protheus serenade Silvia, the
love of his friend Valentine, to whom he has turnd traitor, in order
that he may win Silvia for himſelf.]

Song.

Who is Siluia? what is ſhe,   38
That all our Swaines commend her ?
Holy, faire, and wiſe is ſhe ;   40
The heauen ſuch grace did lend her,
That ſhe might admired be.   42

Is ſhe kinde as ſhe is faire ?   43
For beauty liues with kindneſſe.
Loue doth to her eyes repaire,   45
To helpe him of his blindneſſe,
And, being help'd, inhabits there.   47

Then to Siluia let vs ſing,   48
That Siluia is excelling :
She excels each mortall thing,   50
Vpon the dull earth dwelling !
To her let vs Garlands bring !   52

RICHARD LEVERIDGE, 1727. Solo. Reproduced in 'Shakspere Vocal
    Album,' 1864, and Caulfield's Collection, 1864, with Chorus for T.T.B.
    'The New Songs, &c.', No. 7.
J. VERNON, 1770 (?). Solo, Tenor (' Key of F, ranging up to B♭'.—Roſſe).
R. J. S. STEVENS, 1810 (?). Glee.
WILLIAM LINLEY, 1816. Solo. Linley's 'Dramatic Songs of Shakspere.'
SIR H. BISHOP, 1820. Pasticcio. Morley, 1595: Raven-croft, 1614.
    Novello. In the operatised *Twelfth Night.* Glee for five voices.
SIR HENRY BISHOP, 1821. Concerted Piece. Pasticcio. 'By the sim-
    plicity,' an air in ' Midas '. In the Operatised *Two Gentlemen of
    Verona.* Glee for S.A.T.T.B.
SAMUEL WEBBE, JUNR., 1830. Glee for five voices.
FRANZ SCHUBERT, 1852. Solo, Mezzo-Soprano. **'Shakspere Vocal
    Album,' 1864.**
J. F. DUGGAN, 1854. Duet, Soprano and Bass.
*GEORGE A. MACFARREN, 1864. Part Song, S.A.T.B. 'Choral Songs,'
    No. 5.
*MISS M. A. MACIRONE. **Part Song, S.A.T.B.** Ashdown.

*LIONEL S. BENSON, 1873. Duet : Soprano, Contralto, or Tenor and
  Bass. Stanley Lucas and Weber.
*W. H. HOWELLS. Part Song, S.A.T.B. Lamborn Cock.
*C. S. HEAP. Part Song, S.A.T.B. Stanley Lucas and Weber.
*R. H. WAITHMAN, 1882. Part Song. Weekes.
*ISIDORE DE SOLLA, June, 1883. Solo. Stanley Lucas & Co.
*WALTER MACFARREN. Sept. 15, 1883. Part Song, S.C.T.B. 'The
  Lute.' Patey and Willis.
*W. J. YOUNG. Nov. 1883. Part Song, S.A.T.B. Novello.

Winter's Tale.[1]

Act IV. Scene iii. lines 1—12.

"WHEN DAFFADILS BEGIN TO PEERE."

[A Road near the Shepheards Cottage.]

Enter AUTOLICUS, *singing.*

When Daffudils begin to peere,
  With (heigh!) the Doxy ouer the dale,
Why, then comes in the sweet o'the yeere,
  For the red blood raigns in y' winters pale.   4

The white sheete bleaching on the hedge,
  With (hey!) the sweet birds, O, how they sing!
Doth set my pugging[2] tooth an edge;
  For a quart of Ale is a dish for a King!   8

The Larke, that tirra-Lyra chaunts,
  With (heigh!) the Thrush and (hey!) the Iay!
Are Summer songs for me and my Aunts,
  While we lye tumbling in the hay.   12

DR. WM. BOYCE, about 1759. Song. In Linley's 'Dramatic Songs
  of Shakspere,' and Caulfield, II. 46.
*H. W. WAREING, Mus. Bac. S.A.T.B. Novello.
*MISS C. A. MACIRONE. S.A.T.B. Novello.

Winter's Tale, Act IV. Scene ii. lines 15—22.

"BUT SHALL I GO MOURNE FOR THAT, MY DEERE."

Autolycus. . . . I haue seru'd Prince *Florizell,* and in my time
wore three pile ; but now I am out of seruice :   14

[1] See M. Bruch's '*Hermione,* grosse Oper . . . nach Sh.'s *Wintermärchen,*'
&c. 1872, folio.   [2] thieving.

> But shall I go mourne for that, (my deere?)   15
> The pale Moone shines by night:
> And when I wander here and there,
> I then do most go right.   18
>
> If Tinkers may haue leaue to liue,   19
> and beare the Sow-skin Bowget,
> Then my account I well may giue,
> **and in** the Stockes auouch it.   22

My Trafficke is 'fleeces': when the Kite builds, looke to leffer Linnen! My Father nam'd me *Autolicus*; who, being (as I am) lytter'd vnder *Mercurie*, was likewife a fnapper-vp of vnconfidered trifles. With Dye and drab, I purchas'd this Caparison; and my Reuennew is the filly Cheate. Gallowes, and Knocke, are too powerfull on the Highway. Beating and hanging are terrors to mee! For the life to come, I fleepe out the thought of it.   29

Anonymous. Caulfield's Collection, vol. ii. p. 52.
J. F. LAMPE, 1745. Solo, S. or M.S. British **Museum**. **G.** 306, piece 251.

Winter's Tale, Act IV. Scene iii. line 119—122.

"JOG-ON, JOG-ON, THE FOOT-PATH WAY."

(SNATCH OF SONG.)

[Autolycus has shammed illness, and **robd the Clowne**, the old Shepherd's son, who takes leave of him :]

Clowne. Then fartheewell! I muft go buy Spices for our fheepe-fhearing.   113

Autolycus. Profper you, fweet fir! [*Exit* CLO.] Your purfe is not hot enough to purchafe your Spice. He be with you at your fheepe-fhearing too! If I make not this Cheat bring out another, and the fheerers proue fheepe, let me be vnrold, and my name put in the booke of Vertue!   118

> **Song.** *Jog-on, Jog-on, the foot-path **way**,*   119
> *And merrily hent the Stile-a!*
> *A merry heart goes all the day!*
> *Your fad, **tyres** in a Mile-a.*   [*Exit.* **122.**

Anonymous. This tune is in the 'Dancing Master' (1650 to 1698), called *Jog on.* Also in Q. Elizabeth's 'Virginal Book,' with the name of *Hanskin.* Solo. (Chappell's 'Music of Olden Time,' p. 211.)
Anonymous. Snatch. Caulfield's Collection.
DR. BOYCE, about 1759. The centre of his 'When Daffodils.'
MISS C. A. MACIRONE, 1860. Part Song, S.A.T.B. Novello.

Winter's Tale, Act IV. Scene iv. lines 217—229.

"LAWNE, AS WHITE AS DRIVEN SNOW."

[The Old Shepherd's Servant describes to him and his Clowne-
son, to his supposed daughter Perdita, and their guests at their Sheep-
shearing, the goods and the singing of Autolycus, disguised as a
Pedler :]

Servant. Hee hath Ribbons of all the colours i'th Rainebow; [205
Points, more then all the Lawyers in *Bohemia* can learnedly
handle, though they come to him by th'groffe ; Inckles,[1] Caddyffes,[2]
Cambrickes, Lawnes : why, he fings em ouer, as they were Gods,
or Goddeffes ! you would thinke a Smocke were a fhee-Angell, he
fo chauntes to the fleeue-hand, and the worke about the fquare
on't.　　　　　　　　　　　　　　　　　　　　　　　　　210
Cloune.　Pre'thee bring him in ! and let him approach finging.
Perdita.　Forewarne him, that he vfe no fcurrilous words in's
tunes !　　　　　　　　　　　　　　　　　　　　[*Exit* Seruant. 213
Cloune.　You haue of thefe Pedlers, that haue more in them then
youl'd thinke (Sifter !)
Perdita.　I, good brother, or go aboute to thinke.　　　216

Enter AUTOLICUS *finging.*

Lawne, as white as driuen Snow;
Cypreffe, blacke as ere was Crow ;　　　　　　　　218
Gloues, as fweete as Damafke Rofes ;
Mafkes for faces, and for nofes ;　　　　　　　　220
Bugle-bracelet, Necke-lace Amber,
Perfume for a Ladies Chamber :　　　　　　　　222
Golden Quoifes and Stomachers,
For my Lads to giue their deers ;　　　　　　　224
Pins, and poaking-flickes of fleele ;[3]
What Maids lacke, from head to heele :　　　　226
　Come buy of me, come ! come buy ! come buy !
　Buy, Lads ! or elfe your Laffes cry :
　　　　　　　　　　　　　　　　Come, buy !

DR. WILSON, 1660. Solo.
Anonymous. Solo. Caulfield's Collection.
DR. BENJAMIN COOKE, 1780 (?). Glee.
*E. S. BIGGS, 1800 (?). Solo, Tenor. 'Here's lawn as white.'
THOS. HUTCHINSON, 1807. Song. 'Vocal Collection' of Mr. Hutchinson.
WILLIAM LINLEY, 1816. Song, Tenor. Linley's 'Dramatic Songs of
　Shakspere.'
*CARL NESTOR. Song. Baritone.

---

　　　[1] *Incles,* tapes.　　　　　[2] *Caddyffes,* worsted lace.
　　　　　　[3] To ftiffen the curls of their Ruffs on.

Winter's Tale, Act IV. Scene iv. lines 291—302.

"GET YOU HENCE, FOR I MUST GOE!"

[Autolycus, Mopsa (with whom the Clowne is in love), and her
friend Dorcas, fing a Ballad together :]

Autolycus. This is a merry ballad, but a very pretty one!   281
Mopfa. Let's haue fome merry ones!
Autolycus. Why, this a patling merry one, and goes to the tune
of ' *Two maids wooing a man :*' there's fearfe a Maide weftward, but
the fings it : 'tis in requeft. I can tell you!   285
Mopfa. [*looking at it*] We can both fing it : if thou'lt beare a
part, thou fhalt heare ; 'tis in three parts.
Dorcas. We had the tune on't, a month agoe!
Autolycus. I can beare my part, you muft know 'tis my occupa-
tion : Haue at it with you!   290

Song.

Aut.	*Get you hence, for I mufi goe!*	
	Where, it fits not you to know.	292
Dor.	*Whether?*	
Mop.	*O, whether ?*	
Dor.	*Whether ?*	
Mop.	*It becomes thy oath full well,*	
	Thou to me thy fecrets tell.	295
Dor.	*Me too! Let me go thether!*	296
Mop.	*Or thou goeft to th' Grange, or Mill ;*	
Dor.	*If to either, thou doft ill.*	298
Aut.	*Neither !*	
Dor.	*What, neither ?*	
Aut.	*Neither !*	
Dor.	*Thou haft fworne, my Loue to be,*	
Mop.	*Thou haft fworne it more to mee!*	301
Both.	*Then whether goeft ? Say whether ?*	302

DR. WM. BOYCE, about 1759.   Trio.   Linley's ' Dramatic Songs of
Shakspere.   Also in Caulfield, II. 60.

Winter's Tale, Act IV. Scene iv. lines 309—314.

"WILL YOU BUY ANY TAPE?"

[AUTOLYCUSES Song.]

Will you buy any Tape, or Lace for your Cape?   309
    My dainty Ducke, my deere-a ?
Any filke, any Thred, any Toyes for your head,
    Of the new'ft, and fin'ft, fin'ft weare-a!   312
Come to the Pedler!   Money's a medler,
That doth vtter all men's ware-a.   [*Exit.* 314

Anonymous. Solo. Caulfield's Collection.
DR. BOYCE, about 1769. Solo. Linley's 'Dramatic Songs of Shakspere.'
DR. COOKE, about 1780. Catch.
*MISS C. A. MACIRONE, 1864. **Part Song, S.A.T.B.** Novello.

Sonnets.

[Sonnets 5, 6, and 7 are of those in which Shakspere appeals to his handsome young friend, William Herbert, afterwards (A.D. 1601) Earl of Pembroke, to marry, and beget children.]

5. "THOSE HOWERS THAT WITH GENTLE WORKE."

Thofe howers, that with gentle worke did frame
  The louely gaze where euery eye doth dwell,
Will play the tirants to the very fame,
  And that vnfaire which fairely doth excell;   4

For neuer refting time leads Summer on
  To hidious winter, and confounds him there;
Sap-checkt with froft, and luftie leau's quite gon,
  Beauty ore-fnow'd, and bareues euery where.   8

Then—were not fummers diftillation left,
  A liquid prifoner pent in walls of glaffe,—
Beauties effect with beauty were bereft,
  Nor it, nor noe remembrance what it was: 12

  But flowers diftil'd, though they with winter meete,
  Leefe but their fhow; their fubftance ftill liues fweet. 14

*RICHARD SIMPSON, publisht (after his death) April 1878. Solo. Lucas and Weber, New Bond St. (All Richard Simpson's are of the same date. He had set all the Sonnets to music, and many other pieces. Out of them, Mrs. G. A. Macfarren chose a thin folio volume for publication.)

6. "THEN, LET NOT WINTERS WRAGGED HAND."

Then let not winters wragged hand deface
  In thee, thy fummer, ere thou be diftil'd!
Make fweet fome viall! treafure thou fome place
  With beauties treafure, ere it be felfe kil'd!   4

That vfe is not forbidden vfery,
  Which happies thofe that pay the willing lone;
That's for thy felfe to breed an other thee,
  Or ten times happier, be it ten for one!   8

Ten times thy selfe, were happier then thou art!
If ten of thine, ten times refigur'd thee :
Then what could Death doe, if thou should'st depart,
  Leauing thee liuing in posterity ?   12

    Be not selfe-wild! for thou art much too faire
    To be deaths conquest, and make wormes thine heire. 14

*RICHARD SIMPSON, 1878. Solo. Lucas and Weber, New Bond St.

------

7. "LOE! IN THE ORIENT, WHEN THE
          GRACIOUS LIGHT."

Loe! in the Orient, when the gracious light
Lifts vp his burning head, each vnder eye
Doth homage to his new appearing sight,
  Seruing with lookes his sacred maiesty ;   4

And hauing climb'd the steepe vp heauenly hill,
  Resembling strong youth in his middle age,
Yet mortall lookes adore his beauty still,
  Attending on his goulden pilgrimage ;   8

But when from high-most pich, with wery car,
  Like feeble age, he reeleth from the day,
The eyes (fore dutious) now conuerted are
  From his low tract, and looke an other way :   12

So thou, thy selfe out-going in thy noon,
  Vnlok'd-on diest, vnlesse thou get a sonne.   14

SIR HENRY BISHOP, 1820. Glee and Chorus, l. 1-8 in As You Like It.
*RICHARD SIMPSON, 1878. Solo. Lucas and Weber, New Bond St.

------

18. "SHALL I COMPARE THEE TO A
          SUMMERS DAY?"

[Shakspere assures his friend William Herbert of eternal life
through his (Sh.'s) Sonnets to him. See nos. 54, 63, and 81 below.]

Shall I compare thee to a Summers day ?
  Thou art more louely and more temperate :
Rough windes do shake the darling buds of Maie,
  And Summers leafe hath all too short a date :   4

Sometime, too hot the eye of heauen shines,
  And often is his gold complexion dimm'd :
And euery faire, from faire some-time declines,
  By chance, or natures changing course, vntrim'd ;   8

But thy eternall Sommer fhall not fade,
Nor loofe poffeffion of that faire thou ow'ft;
Nor fhall Death brag thou wandr'ft in his fhade,
When, in eternall lines, to time thou grow'ft : 12

So long as men can breath, or eyes can fee,
So long liues this, and this giues life to thee. 14

CHARLES HORN, 1821. Duet. It was sung in the *Tempest*.
E. LODER, 1838. Solo. One of a set of 'Six Songs.'
J. REEKES, about 1850. The three first and ninth lines have been used.
'Six Shakspere Songs.'
*ROBERT HOAR, 1876. Song. Hutchins and Romer, 9, Conduit St.
*LADY RAMSEY OF BANFF. Czerny, 211, Oxford St.

Sonnet 25. Lines 1—4.

[Shakspere contrasts his lowly state with that of Fortune's favourites. Yet they may feel her fickle change, while he is sure of his Friend's constant Love.]

Let those who are in fauour with their ftars,
Of publike honour and proud titles boft,
Whilft I, whome Fortune of fuch tryumph bars,
Vnlookt for, ioy in that I honour moft. 4

Great Princes fauorites, their faire leaues fpread
But as the Marygold at the funs eye,
And in them-felues their pride lies buried,
For, at a frowne, they in their glory die. 8

The painefull warrier, famosëd for worth,
After a thoufand victories once foild,
Is from the Booke of Honour rafëd quite,
And all the reft forgot, for which he toild. 12

Then happy I, that loue, and am beloued
Where I may not remoue, nor be remoued! 14

*SIR HENRY R. BISHOP, 1821. In his operatised *Two Gentlemen of Verona*, he has introduced the first 4 lines as a sequel to the Chorus from *As you like it* 'Good Duke, receive thy Daughter', which is preceded by the first 4 lines of *Sonnet* 97. He makes Julia and Sylvia sing a duet, Julia singing Sonnet 25, and Sylvia, Sonnet 97, the first 4 lines of each—both at the same time.

27. "WEARY WITH TOYLE."

[Shakspere, away from his young friend, cannot sleep on his weary bed, for thinking of him.]

Weary with toyle, I haft me to my bed,
(The deare repofe for lims with trauaill **tired.**)
But then begins a iourny in my head,
To worke my mind, when boddies work's expired :   4

For then my thoughts (from far where I abide)
Intend a zelous pilgrimage to thee,
And keepe my drooping eye-lids open wide,
Looking on darknes which the blind doe fee :   8

Saue that my foules imaginary fight
Prefents their fhaddoe to my fightles view,
Which, (like a iewell hunge in gaftly night),
Makes blacke night beautious, and her old face new.   12

Loe ! thus, by day my lims, by night my mind,
For thee, and for my felfe, noe quiet finde.   14

*RICHARD SIMPSON, 1878. Solo. Lucas and Weber, New Bond St.

---

29. "WHEN IN DISGRACE WITH FORTUNE AND MENS EYES."

[Shakspere, when forlorn and **sad, has but to think of** his Friend and then is lifed into bliss.]

When, in difgrace with Fortune and mens eyes,
I all alone beweepe my out-caft ftate,
And trouble deafe heauen with my bootleffe cries,
And looke vpon my felfe, and curfe my fate,   4

Wifhing me like to one more rich in **hope,**
Featur'd like him, like him with **friends** poffeft,
Defiring this mans art, and that mans fkope,—
With what I moft inioy, contented leaft,—   8

Yet, in thefe thoughts my felfe almoft defpifing,
Haplye I thinke on thee ; and then my ftate,
(Like to the Larke, at breake of daye arifing,
From fullen earth) fings himns at Heauens gate !   12

For, thy fweet loue remembred, fuch welth brings,
That then I fkorne to change my ftate with Kings.   14

SIR HENRY BISHOP, 1821. Solo **brillante.** Sung by Miss M. Tree **in**
Two Gentlemen of Verona : **2 movements,** 1. andante, 2. allegro

---

33. "FULL MANY A GLORIOUS MORNING HAVE I SEENE."

[Shakspere excuses his young Friend's neglect of him, and complains not of it.]

F\ll many a glorious morning haue I feene,
  Flatter the mountaine tops with foueraine eie,
Kiffing with golden face the meddowes greene,
  Guilding pale ftreames with heauenly alcumy ;   4
Anon permit the bafeft cloudes to ride,
  With ougly rack, on his celeftiall face,
And from the fór-lorne world his vifage hide,
  Stealing vnfeene to weft with this difgrace :   8
Euen fo my Sunne one early morne did fhine,
  With all triumphant fplendor on my brow ;
But, out, alack! he was but one houre mine ;
  The region cloude hath mafk'd him from me now !   12
    Yet, him for this, my loue no whit difdaineth :
    Suns of the world may ftaine, when heauens fun ftaineth.

J. REEKES, about 1850. Solo. 'Six Shakspere Songs.' Eight lines:
  1-4, 9-12. Two octaves, lower to upper C.
SIR H. BISHOP. 1820. Soprano Song. Sung by Miss M. Tree. Opera,
  Twelfth Night.

40. "TAKE ALL MY LOVES, MY LOVE! YEA,
       TAKE THEM ALL!"

[Shakspere says he is willing to give up his dark Lady-love (? Mrs.
Fytton[1]) to his young Friend, William Herbert, later, Earl of Pembroke. Whatever she does, the Poet and Earl must not quarrel.]

Take all my loues, my Loue! yea, take them all!
  What haft thou then more then thou hadft before?
No loue, my Loue, that thou maift 'true loue' call :
  All mine was thine, before thou hadft this more :   4
Then, if for my loue, thou my Loue receiueft,
  I cannot blame thee, for my loue thou vfeft;
But yet be blam'd, if thou this felfe deceaueft
  By wilfull tafte of what thy felfe refufeft.   8
I doe forgiue thy robb'rie, gentle Theefe,
  Although thou fteale thee all my pouerty ;
And yet, loue knowes, it is a greater griefe
  To beare loues wrong, then hates knowne iniury.   12
    Lafciuious Grace, in whom all il, wel fhowes,
    Kill me with fpights! yet we muft not be foes.   14

SIR HENRY BISHOP, 1820. Solo, Soprano. Sung by Miss Greene in
  Twelfth Night.
CHARLES HORN, 1821. Solo, Tenor or Bass. Sung by him in the
  Tempest.

---

[1] See Mr. T. Tyler's letters in the Academy of March 8, March 22,
and April 19, 1884. Mrs. Fytton was Lord Pembroke's 'caufe', and
had a child by him.

54. "OH, HOW MUCH MORE DOTH BEAUTIE, BEAUTIOUS SEEME!"

[Shakspere assures his young Friend that when his youth fades, his Truth shall live for ever in Shakspere's verse. Compare Sonnet 18 above, and 63 and 81 below.]

Oh, how much more doth Beautie, beautious feeme,
  By that fweet ornament which Truth doth giue!
The Rofe lookes faire; but fairer we it deeme,
  For that fweet odor, which doth in it liue: 4
The Canker bloomes haue full as deepe a die,
  As the perfumèd tincture of the Rofes;
Hang on fuch thornes, and play as wantonly,
  When fommers breath their malk'd buds difclofes: 8
But, for their virtue only is their fhow,
  They liue vnwoo'd, and vnrefpected fade,
Die to themfelues. Sweet Rofes doe not fo:
  Of their fweet deathes, are fweeteft odors made: 12
    And fo of you, beautious and louely youth,
    When that fhall vade, by[1] verfe diftils your truth.   14

SIR HENRY BISHOP, 1820. Firft 4 lines. **Solo, Soprano. Sung by** Miss Greene in *Twelfth Night.*
GEORGE BARKER, 1870. Solo. Composed for, and **printed in, the** 'Ballad Album.'

58. "THAT GOD FORBID."

[Shakspere will **not presume** to blame his young Friend for ill spending of his time **or neglecting** Shakspere.]

That God forbid, that made me firft your flaue,
  I fhould in thought controule your times of pleafure,
Or at your hand th' account of houres to craue,
  Being your vaffaii, bound to ftaie your leifure!   4
Oh, let me fuffer (being at your beck)
  Th' imprifon'd abfence of your libertie;
And patience, tame to fufferance, bide each check,
  Without accufing you of iniury!   8
Be where you lift! your charter is fo ftrong,
  That you your felfe may priuiledge your time
To what you will; to you it doth belong,
    Your felfe to pardon of felfe-doing crime.   12
    I am to waite, (though **waiting** fo be hell;)
    Not blame your pleafure; be it ill or well.   14

*RICHARD SIMPSON, 1875. Solo. Lucas and Weber, New Bond St.

[1] by, generally emended **to my.**

59. "IF THERE BEE NOTHING NEW."

[Shakspere wishes he could see old records, to find whether any
one has ever been so handsome as his young Friend, Pembroke.]

If their bee nothing new ; but that which is,
　Hath beene before ; how are our braines beguild,
Which, laboring for inuention, beare amiſſe
　The ſecond burthen of a former child !　　　　　　4

Oh that record could (with a back-ward looke,
　Euen of fiue hundreth courſes of the Sunne,)
Show me your image in ſome antique booke,
　Since minde at firſt in carrecter was done,　　　　8

That I might ſee what the old world could ſay,
　To this compoſëd wonder of your frame ;
Whether we are mended, or where [1] better they,
　Or whether reuolution be the ſame.　　　　　　12

Oh, ſure I am, the wits of former daies,
　To ſubiects worſe, haue giuen admiring praiſe !　　14

*RICHARD SIMPSON, 1878.　Song.　Lucas and Weber, New Bond St.

---

63. "AGAINST MY LOVE."

[Shakspere declares his Friend's beauty shall, when it fades, live in
his (Sh.'s) lines.　Compare Sonnets 18 and 54, above, and 81, below.]

Againſt my Loue ſhall be, as I am now,
　(With Times iniurious hand chruſht and ore-worne,)
When houres haue dreind his blood, and fild his brow
　With lines and wrincles ; when his youthfull morne　　4

Hath trauaild on to Ages ſteepie night ;
　And all thoſe beauties, whereof now he's King,
Are vaniſhing, or vaniſht out of ſight,
　Stealing away the treaſure of his Spring ;—　　　8

For ſuch a time do I now fortifie
　Againſt confounding Ages cruell knife,
That he ſhall neuer cut from memory
　My ſweet Loues beauty, though my louers life.　　12

His beautie ſhall in theſe blacke lines be ſeene :
And they ſhall liue ; and he in them ſtill greene.　　14

*RICHARD SIMPSON, 1878.　Solo.　Lucas and Weber, New Bond St.

[1] where, whether.

G

64. "WHEN I HAVE SEENE THE HUNGRY OCEAN."

[Looking at the destruction wrought by Time, Shakspere sees
that it will some day take his **young** Friend from him.]

When I haue feene, by Times fell hand defaced
  The rich proud coft of outworne buried age ;
When fometime loftie towers, I fee downe rafed,
  And brafle, eternall flaue to mortall rage ;   4

When I haue feene the hungry Ocean gaine
  Aduantage on the Kingdome of the fhoare,
And the firme foile win of the watry maine,
  Increafing ftore with lofle, and lofle with ftore ;   8

When I haue feene fuch interchange of ftate,
  Or ftate it felfe confounded, to decay,
Ruine hath taught me thus to ruminate :
  That Time will come, and take my loue away.   12

    This thought is as a death which cannot choofe,
    But weepe to haue, that which it feares to loofe. 14

SIR HENRY BISHOP, 1821. Solo. Sung by Master Longhurst in *Two
Gentlemen of Verona.* Commences, " When I have seen the hungry
ocean," line 5.

---

71. "NOE LONGER MOURNE."

[Shakspere begs his Friend **not to** mourn for him when he dies,
and **not** even to love his memory, **lest** the World should mock his
friend **for** so doing.]

Noe Longer mourne for me when I am dead !
  Then you fhall heare the furly fullen bell
Giue warning to the world, that I am fled
  From this vile world, with vildeft wormes to dwell :   4

Nay, **if** you read this line, remember not,
  The hand that writ it ! for I loue you fo,
That I in your fweet thoughts would be forgot,
  If thinking on me then fhould make you woe.   8

O ! if (I fay) you looke vpon this verfe,
  When I (perhaps) compounded am with clay,
Do not fo much as my poore name reherfe ;
  But let your loue, euen with my life decay,   12

    Leaft the wife world fhould looke into your mone,
    And mocke you with me, after I am gon. 14

*RICHARD SIMPSON, 1878. **Solo.** **Lucas and** Weber, New Bond St.

73. "THAT TIME OF YEEARE THOU MAIST IN ME BEHOLD."

[Shakspere is growing old (? 34),[1] and this, his young Friend sees; and therefore values him the more, as he may lose him soon.]

That time of yeeare thou maift in me behold,
When yellow leaues, or none or few, doe hange
Vpon thofe boughes which fhake againft the could,
Bare ruin'd quiers, where late the fweet birds fang.   4

In me thou feeft the twi-light of fuch day,
As after Sun-fet fadeth in the Weft,
Which by and by blacke night doth take away,
Deaths fecond felfe that feals vp all in reft.   8

In me thou fceft the glowing of fuch fire,
That on the afhes of his youth doth lye,
As the death-bed, whereon it muft expire,
Confum'd with that which it was nurrifht by.   12

This thou perceu'ft, which makes thy loue more ftrong,
To loue that well, which thou muft leaue ere long.   14

Sir Henry Bishop, 1821. Lines 1—8 only. Cavatina, sung by Miss
M. Tree in *Two Gentlemen of Verona.*
*Richard Simpson, 1878. Solo. Lucas and Weber.

81. "OR SHALL I LIVE."

[Shakspere assures his young Friend of future life in his (S.'s) verse. Compare Sonnets 18, 54, and 63, above.]

Or I fhall liue, your Epitaph to make,
Or you furuiue when I in earth am rotten :
From hence, your memory Death cannot take,
Although in me each part will be forgotten.   4

Your name from hence, immortall life fhall haue,
Though I (once gone) to all the world muft dye :
The earth can yeeld me but a common graue,
When you intombëd in mens eyes fhall lye :   8

Your monument fhall be my gentle verfe,
Which eyes not yet created, fhall ore-read,
And toungs to be, your beeing fhall rehearfe,
When all the breathers of this world are dead,   12

You ftill fhall liue (fuch vertue hath my Pen)
Where breath moft breaths, euen in the mouths of men. 14

*Richard Simpson, 1878. Solo. Lucas and Weber.

87. "FAREWELL! THOU ART TOO DEARE
FOR MY POSSESSING."

[Shakspere, thinking his Friend (Lord W. Herbert) has withdrawn
his friendship from him, acquiesces in the fact.]

Farewell! thou art too deare for my poſſeſſing!
  And, like enough, thou knowſt thy eſtimate :
The Charter of thy worth giues thee releaſing ;
  My bonds in thee are all determinate.   **4**

For how do I hold thee, but by thy granting ?
  And for that ritches, where is that deſeruing ?
The cauſe of this faire guift in me is wanting,
  And ſo my pattent back againe is ſweruing.   **8**

Thy ſelfe thou gau'ſt, thy owne worth then not knowing,
  Or mee to whom thou gau'ſt it, elſe miſtaking ;
So thy great guift, vpon miſpriſion growing,
  Comes home againe, on better iudgement making.   **12**

    Thus haue I had thee, as a dreame doth flatter :
    In ſleepe a King ; but waking, no ſuch matter.   **14**

J. REEKFS, about 1850. Solo. 'Six Shakspere Songs.' Lines 1-4.
*CARACCIOLO. Solo. Ricordi.

---

92. "SAY THO' YOU STRIVE TO STEAL
YOURSELF AWAY."

[Shakspere so loves his Friend, that if that Friend withdraws his
love from him, he will die, and be happy in his death. But even if
his Friend is falſe to him, he may not know it.]

Bvt doe thy worſt to ſteale thy ſelfe away,
  For tearme of life thou art aſſurëd mine ;
And life no longer then thy loue will ſtay,
  For it depends vpon that loue of thine.   **4**

Then need I not to feare the worſt of wrongs,
  When in the leaſt of them my life hath end ;
I ſee, a better ſtate to me belongs,
  Then that which on thy humor doth depend :   **8**

Thou canſt not vex me with inconſtant minde,
  Since that my life on thy reuolt doth lie :
Oh ! what a happy title do I finde !
  Happy to haue thy loue ; happy to die !   **12**

    But whats ſo bleſſed faire, that feares no blot ?
    Thou maiſt be falſe, and yet I know it not.   **14**

*SIR HENRY R. BISHOP, 1821. Duet, S.A., in the Operatised *Two Gentlemen of Verona.* No. 3, p. 11. Line 1 is alterd to 'Say tho' you strive to steal yourself away.'

96. "SOME SAY THY FAULT IS YOUTH."

[Shakspere's Friend has committed faults. Though these, in him, look graces, Shakspere prays him to abstain from them, for his good name is Shakspere's too.]

> Some fay thy fault is youth ; fome, wantoneffe ;
> Some fay thy grace is youth and gentle fport :
> Both grace and faults are lou'd of more and leffe :
> Thou makft faults graces, that to thee refort :   4
>
> As on the finger of a thronëd Queene,
> The bafeft Iewell will be well efteem'd,
> So are thofe errors that in thee are feene,
> To truths tranflated, and for true things deem'd.   8
>
> How many Lambs might the fterne Wolfe betray,
> If, like a Lambe, he could his lookes tranflate ?
> How many gazers mighft thou lead away,
> If thou wouldft vfe the ftrength of all thy ftate ?   12
>
> But doe not fo! I loue thee in fuch fort,
> As thou, being mine, mine is thy good report.   14

*RICHARD SIMPSON, 1878. Solo. Lucas and Weber.

97. "HOW LIKE A WINTER HATH MY ABSENCE BEEN."

[Shakspere has been away from his Friend; and tho' he has been prosperous, yet his gain has seemd loss, for all his joy is in his Friend.]

> How like a Winter, hath my abfence beene
> From thee, the pleafure of the fleeting yeare !
> What freezings haue I felt ! what darke daies feene !
> What old Decembers barenefle euery where !   4
>
> And yet this time remou'd, was Sommers time,
> The teeming Autumne big with ritch increafe,
> Bearing the wanton burthen of the prime,
> Like widdowed wombes, after their Lords deceafe.   8
>
> Yet this aboundant iffue feem'd to me,
> But hope of Orphans, and vn-fathered fruite ;
> For Sommer, and his pleafures, waite on thee ;
> And thou away, the very birds are mute ;   12

No! Time! thou shalt not bost that I doe change!
Thy Piramyds, buylt vp with newer might,
To me are nothing nouell, nothing strange :
They are but dreslings of a former sight.   4

Our dates are breefe; and therefor we admire
What thou dost foy st vpon vs that is ould,
And rather make them borne to our desire,
Then **thinke** that we before haue heard them tould.   8

Thy Regisers and Thee, I both defie,
Not wondring at the Present, nor the Past ;
For thy Records, and what we fee, doth lye,
Made more or les by thy continuall hast.   12

   This I doe vow, and this shall euer be :
   I will be true, dispight thy Syeth and Thee.   14

SIR HENRY R. BISHOP, 1824.   Solo, S.   In the operatised *As you like it.*   Opens with a *largo*, and closes with an *allegro.*   Rolfe, p. 107.
Only lines 1—4, and 13—4, are set.

---

148. "O ME! WHAT EYES HATH LOVE PUT IN MY HEAD."

[Shakspere asks himself how he can think his plain dark Mistress (? Mrs. Fytton) fair, when she is foul. It is, because she keeps him tearful, anxious for her love, and thus blind.]

O me! what eyes hath loue put in my head,
   Which haue **no** correspondence with true sight ?
Or, if they haue, where is my iudgment fled,
   That censures falsely what they fee aright?   4

If that be faire whereon my false eyes dote,
   What meanes the world to say it is not so?
If it be not, then loue doth well denote,
   Loues eye is not so true as **all** mens : No!   8

How can it?   O, how can loues eye be true,
   That is so vext with watching and with teares ?
No maruaile then though I mistake my view :
   The sunne it felfe fees not, till heauen cleeres.   12

   O cunning loue, with teares thou keepst me blinde,
   Least eyes well feeing, thy foule faults should finde.   14

SIR HENRY BISHOP, 1824.   Song, Soprano.   Sung by Miss M. Tree as Rosalind, in *As You Like It.*   Rolfe, p. 107.

Venus and Adonis.

STANZA I. "EVEN AS THE SUN, WITH PURPLE-COLOURED FACE."

[Venus comes to woo Adonis, bent on hunting.]

(1)

EVen as the funne, with purple-colourd face,   1
   Had taue his laft leaue of the weeping morne,
Rofe-cheekt *Adonis* hied him to the chace :
   Hunting he lou'd ; but loue, he laught to fcorne :   4
   Sick-thoughted *Venus* makes amaine vnto him,
   And like a bold-fac'd futer ginnes to woo him.   6

CHARLES EDWARD HORN, 1823. Hunting Song, Soprano. Sung by
Anne Page in the operatised *Merry Wives.* In 'Shakspere Vocal
Mag.,' No. 15, 1864, &c.
SIR HENRY BISHOP, 1824. Glee, A.T.T.B. Operatised *As You Like It.*

Venus and Adonis, Stanza 24, lines 145—150.

"BID ME DISCOURSE, I WILL ENCHANT THINE EAR."

[Venus is rehearsing her charms, in order to tempt Adonis.]

(25)

Bid me difcourfe : I will inchaunt thine eare ;   145
   Or like a Fairie, trip vpon the greene ;
Or, like a Nimph, with long difheueled heare,
   Daunce on the fands, and yet no footing feene.   148
   Loue is a fpirit all compact of fire,
   Not groffe to finke, but light, and will afpire.   150

SIR HENRY BISHOP, 1820. Solo, Soprano. Sung by Miss M. Tree as
Viola in the operatised *Twelfth Night.* Roffe, p. 110.

Venus and Adonis, Stanza 34, lines 169—174.

"ART THOU OBDURATE, FLINTIE, HARD AS STEELE."

[Adonis has refuzed Venus's advances. She remonstrates with
him, and asks for one kiss.]

(34)

Art thou obdurate, flintie, hard as fteele ?   169
Nay more then flint, for ftone at raine relenteth,
Art thou a womans fonne, and canft not feele
What tis to loue, how want of loue tormenteth ?   172

O, had thy mother borne fo bad a mind,
She had not brought foorth thee, but dyed vnkind. 174

(35)

What am I, that thou fhouldft contemne me this[1]? 175
Or what great danger dwels vpon my fute?
What were thy lips the worfe, for one poore kiffe?
Speake, Faire : but fpeake faire words or elfe bee mute. 178
Giue me one kiffe, Ile giue it thee again ;
And one for int'reft, if thou wilt haue twaine. 180

SIR HENRY BISHOP, 1824. Song : Soprano or Tenor. **Sung in** *As You Like It.*

Venus and Adonis, Stanza 130, lines 775—780.

"IF LOVE HATH LENT YOU TWENTIE THOUSAND TONGUES."

[Adonis refuzes Venus's pressing offers of love,]

(130)

If Loue haue lent you twentie thoufand tongues, 775
And euerie tongue more mouing then your owne,
(Bewitching like the wanton Marmaides Songs,)
Yet from mine eare the tempting tune is blowne. 778
 For know, my heart ftands armed in my eare,
 And will not let a falfe found enter there : 780

(131)

Left the deceiuing harmony fhould **runne** 781
Into the quiet clofure of my breft,
And then my little heart were quite vndone,
In his bed-chamber to be bard of reft : 784
 No Lady, no : my heart longs not to grone,
 But foundly fleeps, while now it fleeps alone. 785

SIR HENRY BISHOP, 1824. Song, **Soprano.** **Sung by** Miss Tree in the operatized *As You Like It.*
G. REEKES, ab. 1850. Solo, Alto **or Bass.** J. Reekes, 'Six Songs of Shakspere.'

Venus and Adonis, Stanza 143, lines 753-8.

"LO, HERE THE GENTLE LARKE, WEARIE OF REST."

[Adonis has run from Venus. She laments all night ; and in the dawning, greets the Lark, and Sun.]

[1] *this* = thus.

(143)

Loe here the gentle Larke, wearie of reſt,   753
From his moiſt cabinet mounts vp on high,
And wakes the morning, from whoſe ſiluer breſt,
The Sunne ariſeth in his Maieſtie;   756
  Who doth the World ſo gloriouſly behold,
  That Cedar tops and hils ſeeme burniſht Gold.   758

(144)

Venus ſalutes him with this faire good morrow;   759
O thou cleere God, and Patron of all light,
From whom each lamp & ſhining ſtar doth borrow
The beautious influence that makes him bright,   762
  There liues a Son, that ſuckt an earthly mother,
  May lend thee light as thou doſt lend to other.   764

SIR HENRY BISHOP, 1819. Song, Soprano. Flute Obbligato. Sung
by Miss Stephens in *Comedy of Errors* (p. 88, ed. 1819). Only
stanza 143 is set.

Venus and Adonis, Stanza 183, lines 1093—8.

183. "TO SEE HIS FACE, THE LION WALKT
ALONG."

(st. 183 only, set)

[Adonis being kild by the Boar he was hunting, Venus laments
him, and describes his gentleness, and the love of all other animals
for him. Even the Boar who kild him, did so because it wanted to
kiss him.]

(183)

To ſee his[1] face, the Lion walkt along,   1093
Behind ſome hedge, becauſe hee would not fear[2] him;
To recreate himſelfe when he hath ſong,
The Tygre would be tame, and gently heare him: 1096
  If he had ſpoke, the Wolfe would leaue his prey,
  And neuer fright the ſilly Lambe that day.   1098

(184)

When he beheld his ſhadow in a Brooke,   1099
The fiſhes ſpred on it their golden gils:
When he was by, the birds ſuch pleaſure tooke,
That ſome would ſing ſome other in their bils,   1102
  Would bring him Mulberies, and ripe red Cherries:
  He fed them with his ſight, they him with berries.   1104

    [1] Adonis's.   [2] frighten.

(185)

But this foule, grim and vrchinsnouted Boare,   1105
Whose downward eye still looketh for a graue,
Ne're saw the beauteous liuery that he wore ;
Witnesse the entertainment that he gaue :   1108
  If he did see his face, why then, I know,
He thought to kisse him, and hath kild him so.   1110

(186)

Tis true, true, true, thus was Adonis slaine,   1111
He ran vpon the Boare with his sharpe speare,
Who would not whet his teeth at him againe,
But by a kisse thought to persuade him there :   1114
  And nouzling in his flanke, the louing Swine,
Sheath'd vnaware the tuske in his soft groine.   1116

(187)

Had I been tooth'd like him, I must confesse,   1117
With killing him I should haue kild him first :
But he is dead and neuer did he blesse
My youth with his ; the more am I accurst :   1120
  With this she falleth in the place she stood,
And staines her face with his congealed blood.   1122

SIR HENRY BISHOP, 1821.   Round for four male voices.   In the
operatised *Two Gentlemen of Verona*, p. 41 ; also publisht
separately by Novello.   Only the first 4 lines of stanza 183 are set.

The Passionate Pilgrim.
7. "FAIR IS MY LOVE, BUT NOT SO FAIR
AS FICKLE."

[None of the following pieces from this miscellaneous Collection
is certainly Shakspere's.   Most are certainly not his.   "Crabbed age
and youth " may perhaps be his.]

VII.

[A jilted lover describes his false Love's beauty and untruth.]

Faire is my loue, but not so faire as fickle,   1
Milde as a Doue, but neither true nor trustie ;
Brighter then glasse, and yet, as glasse is, brittle ;
Softer then waxe, and yet, as Iron, rustie :   4
  A lilly pale, with damaske die to grace her ;
None fairer, nor none falser to deface her.   6

¹ each. Qo. 1.

Her lips to mine, how often hath fhe ioyned,   7
Betweene each kiffe, her othes of true loue fwearing :
How many tales to pleafe me hath fhe coyned,
Dreading my loue, the loffe whereof ftill fearing.   10
   Yet in the mids of all her pure proteftings,
   Her faith, her othes, her teares, and all were ieaftings.   12

She burnt with loue, as ftraw with fire flameth ;   13
She burnt out loue, as foone as ftraw out burneth :
She fram'd the loue, and yet fhe foyld the framing ;
She bad loue laft, and yet fhe fell a turning.   16
   Was this a louer, or a Letcher whether ?
   Bad in the beft, though excellent in neither.   18

*Name unknown. Madrigal.
SIR HENRY BISHOP, 1824. Song. Sung by Mr. Fawcett in *As You
Like It.*
*RICHARD SIMPSON, 1878. Solo. Lucas and Weber.

Passionate Pilgrim. No. 8. RICHARD BARNFIELD'S Sonnet to a
   Lover of Music.

8. "IF MUSICKE AND SWEET POETRIE AGREE."

VIII.

[A lover of Poetry and Spenser, shows how natural is his love for
a friend who is devoted to Music, and Dowland.]

If Muficke and fweet Poetrie agree,
As they muft needs (the Sifter and the brother,)
Then muft the loue be great twixt thee and me,
Becaufe thou lou'ft the one, and I the other.)   4
Dowland[1] to thee is deere, whofe heauenly tuch
Vpon the Lute, dooth rauifh humane fenfe :
Spenfer to me, whofe deepe Conceit is fuch,
As paffing all conceit, needs no defence.   8
Thou lou'ft to heare the fweet melodious found,
That *Phœbus* Lute (the Queene of Muficke) makes :
And I in deepe Delight am chiefly drownd,
When-as himfelfe to finging he betakes.   12
   One God is God of both (as Poets faine) ;
   One Knight loues Both, and both in thee remaine.   14

JOHN BRAHAM, 1828. Song. Sung by himself in the *Taming of the
Shrew,* and printed in the operatised version of that play.

[1] John Dowland, musician, 15-16.

Passionate Pilgrim, No. 10. To a fair one dead.

10. "SWEET ROSE, FAIRE FLOWER, VN-TIMELY PLUCKT, SOON VADED."

X.

Sweet Rofe, faire flower, vntimely pluckt, foon vaded,   1
Pluckt in the bud, and vaded in the fpring!
Bright orient pearle, alacke, too timely fhaded!
Faire creature kilde too foon by Deaths fharpe fting!   4
  Like a greene plumbe that hangs vpon a tree,
  And fals (through winde) before the fall fhould be.   6

I weepe for thee; and yet no caufe I haue;   7
For why[1] thou letts me nothing in thy will;
And yet thou letts me more then I did craue;
For why I craued nothing of thee ftill;   10
  O yes, (deare friend,) I pardon craue of thee;
  Thy difcontent thou didft bequeath to me.   12

WM. SHIELD, 1790. Elegy, in four vocal Parts. Accompaniments for Muffled Drums, Trumpet, Bells with Sordini and Flute. In 'A Collection of Canzonets, and an Elegy,' by Wm. Shield. p. 27; called "Shakspears Love's Loft, an Elegy sung at the Tomb of a young Virgin."
SIR HENRY BISHOP, 1819. Cavatina. Sung by Miss M. Tree in the operatised *Comedy of Errors*.

Passionate Pilgrim. No. 12.

13. "CRABBED AGE AND YOUTH."

[A Girl sings how she hates her old lover, and loves her young one, whom she bids hie to her soon.]

XII.

Crabbed age and youth cannot liue together,
Youth is full of pleafance, Age is full of care;
Youth like fummer morne, Age like winter weather,
Youth like fummer braue, Age like winter bare.   4

Youth is full of fport; Ages breath is fhort;
Youth is nimble; Age is lame;
Youth is hot and bold; Age is weake and cold;
Youth is wild, and Age is tame.   8

Age, I doe abhor thee! Youth, I doe adore thee!
O my loue my loue is young!
Age, I doe defie thee. Oh fweet Shepheard, hie thee!
For me thinks thou ftaies too long.   12

[1] *For why* = because.

SIGNOR GIORDANI, 1782. Duet : S.S. or T.T.
R. J. S. STEVENS, 1790. Glee for four male voices, A.T.T.B.
SIR HENRY R. BISHOP, 1820. Song. Sung by Miss Greene in Opera
of *Twelfth Night.*
SIR HENRY R. BISHOP, 1824. Dramatic Trio, S.C.B. In *As You
Like It.*
EARL OF WESTMORELAND, 1833. Solo.
*MRS. MOUNSEY BARTHOLOMEW, February 6, 1882. Song, Soprano or
Tenor. 'Six Songs.' No. 1. Lucas and Weber.

Passionate Pilgrim. No. 13.

13. "BEAUTY IS BUT A VAINE AND DOUBTFULL GOOD."

XIII.

(1)

Beauty is but a vaine and doubtfull good ;
A shining glotte, that vadeth foduinly ;
A flower that dies, when first it gins to bud,
A brittle glatte, that's broken presently.   4
   A doubtfull good, a glotte, a glatte, a flower,
   Loft, vaded, broken, dead within an houre.   6

(2)

And, as goods loft, are feld or neuer found ;   7
As vaded glotte, no rubbing will refresh ;
As flowers dead, lie withered on the ground ;
As broken glatte, no fymant can redretle ;   10
   So, beauty blemisht once, for euer's[1] loft,
   In fpite of phificke, painting, paine and coft.   12

*SIR HENRY R. BISHOP, 1819. Solo, Bass. 'Beauty's Valuation.'
Sung by Mr. Durusett in Shakspeare's *Comedy of Errors,* at the
Theatre Royal, Covent Garden.

Passionate Pilgrim. No. 14.

14. "GOOD NIGHT, GOOD REST."

XIV.

(1)

'Good night, good rest '! Ah! neither be my share :
She bad good night : that kept my reft away,
And daft me to a cabben hangde with care,
To defcant on the doubts of my decay.   4
   'Farewell (quoth fhe) and come againe to morrow '!
   Fare well I could not, for I fupt with forrow.   6

[1] euer. Qo. 1.

(2)

Yet at my parting, fweetly did fhe fmile,   7
In fcorne or friendfhip, nill I conster whether :
'T may be, fhe joyd to ieaft at my exile ;
'T may be, againe to make me wander thither,   10
'Wander,' a word for fhadowes like my felfe,
As take the paine, but cannot plucke the pelfe.   12

*SIR HENRY BISHOP, 1821. Glee. S.A.T.B. In the Operatifed *Two Gentlemen of Verona*, p. 25.
WALTER MACFARREN, 1863. Part Song for S.A.T.B.
K. J. PYE, 1879. Solo. In "Two little Songs."

- - - -

Sonnets to Sundry Notes of Musicke.

Paffionate Pilgrim. No. 15.

15. "IT WAS A LORDINGS DAUGHTER."

[How a Girl hesitates between a Learned man and a Knight, and then chooses the Learned man. (Right and wise of her !)]

XV.[1]

It was a Lordings daughter, the faireft one of three,
That liked of her maifter, as well as well might be,
Till looking on an Englifhman, the faireft that eie could fee,
   Her fancie fell a turning.   4

Long was the combat doubtfull, that loue with loue did fight
To leaue the maifter loueleffe, or kill the gallant knight ;
To put in practife either, alas it was a fpite
   Vnto the filly damfell.   8

But one muft be refufed : more mickle was the paine,
That nothing could be vfed, to turne them both to gaine,
For of the two the trufty knight was wounded with difdaine :
   Alas, fhe could not helpe it.   12

Thus Art with Armes contending, was victor of the day,
Which, by a gift of learning, did beare the maid away.
Then lullaby, the learned man hath got the Lady gay ;
   For now my fong is ended.   16

WM. SHIELD, 1796. Song. Sung by Madame Vestris. 'Shakspere
  Vocal Album.' 1864. No. 22.
CHARLES EDWARD HORN, 1823. Song. 'Shakspere Vocal Album,'
  1864.
STEPHEN GLOVER, 1846. Song.

---

[1] The poem usually numbered XV. is but a Continuation of XIV.
'The Lover's Night of Waiting.' See Prof. Dowden's Introduction to the forthcoming Facsimile of the little Quarto of the *P. P.*

[For No. 16, "On a day, alacke the day!" See *Love's La'our's Lost*, IV. iii. 99-118, p. 20-21 above.]

Passionate Pilgrim. No. 17, in 3 Parts.

PART 17. "MY FLOCKES FEEDE NOT."

[The Shepherd Coridon laments his woes (in three outbursts), now that his Love has jilted him, and he must live alone.]

XVII. PART I.

My flocks feede not, my Ewes breed not,
  My Rams fpeed not, all is amis!
Loue is[1] dying, Faithes defying,
  Harts [2]denying, caufer of this.   4
All my merry ligges are quite forgot;
All my Ladies loue is loft (God wot!)   6
Where her faith was firmely fixt in loue,
There a nay is plact without remoue.   8
  One filly crotfe, wrought all my lotfe!
  O frowning fortune! curfed fickle dame!
  For now I fee, inconftancy,
  More in women[3] then in men remaine.[4]   12

2nd PART. "IN BLACKE MORNE I."

In blacke morne I, all feares fcorne I;   13
  Loue hath forlorne me, liuing in thrall:
Hart is bleeding, all helpe needing;
  O cruell fpeeding, fraughted with gall!   16
My fhepheards pipe can found no deale,
My weathers bell rings dolefull knell;   18
My curtaile dogge that wont to haue plaid,
Plaies not at all, but feemes afraid;   20
  My[5] fighes fo deepe, procures to weepe,
  In howling wife, to fee my dolefull plight.
  How fighes refound through hartles ground,
  Like a thoufand vanquifht men in blodie fight.   24

3rd PART. "CLEARE WELS SPRING NOT."

Cleare wels fpring not, sweete birds fing not,   25
  Greene plants bring not forth their die;
Heards ftands weeping, flocks all fleeping,
  Nimphs backe[6] peeping fearefully: 28

---

[1] Loue is — Loues, Love's. [2] nenying, Qo. 1. [3] wowen, Qo. 1.
[4] Signed *Ignoto*, in *England's Helicon*, 1600. It is also in Weelkeses *Madrigals*, 1597.
[5] With, Qo. 1. 'My'—Weelkeses *Madrigals*.
[6] backe (creeping).—Weelkeses *Madrigals*, 'blacke.' *P. P.*, 1599.

All our pleafure knowne to vs poore fwaines,
All our merrie meetings on the plaines,   30
All our euening fport from vs is fled,
All our loue is loft, for loue is dead,   32
  Farewell fweet loue[1] thy like nere was,
  For a fweet content, the caufe of all my woe.[2]
Poore Coridon muft liue alone,
  Other helpe for him I fee that there is none.   36

THOMAS WEELKES, 1597.   Three Madrigals, all for S.S.T.   'Book of
    Madrigals,' by Thomas Weelkes.   (Mus. Antiquarian Soc. 1843.)
*CHARLES EDWARD HORN, 1830(?).   'In black mourn I,' Cald ' Poor
    Corydon.'   Lines 19—28, 52-3 : 27-8, 53-6, slightly alterd.

Passionate Pilgrim.   No. 19, by KIT MARLOWE.

"COME LIVE WITH ME, AND BE MY LOVE."

[The lover recites the pleasures of the country, and asks his Love
to fhare them with him.   She doubts.]

XIX.

Liue with me, and be my Loue ;
And we will all the pleafures proue,   2
That hilles and vallies, dales and fields,
And all the craggy mountaines yeeld.   4

There will we fit vpon the Rocks,
And fee the Shepheards feed their flocks,   6
By fhallow Riuers, by whofe fals[3]
Melodious birds fing Madrigals.   8

There will I make thee a bed of Rofes,
With a thoufand fragrant pofes,   10
A cap of flowers, and a Kirtle
Imbrodered all with leaues of Mirtle.   12

A belt of ftraw and Yuye buds,
With Corall Clafps and Amber ftuds :   14
And if thefe pleafures may thee moue,
Then liue with me, and be my Loue !   16

LOUES ANSWERE.

If that the World and Loue were young,
And truth in euery fhepheards toung,   18
Thefe pretty pleafures might me moue
To liue with thee, and be thy Loue.   20

---

¹ laff : Weelkeses *Madrigals.*   ² moane : *England's Helicon.*
   ³ For the settings of the lines ' By fhallow riuers,' see *Merry Wiues of
Windfor* above, p. 32.

*S. ARNOLD, 1774. 'The words by Marlow.' Solo, with accompaniment for two Violins, Viola, and Basso. In 'A Third Collection of Songs sung at Vauxhall and Marybone Gardens,' p. 21-3.

Passionate Pilgrim. No. 20, by RICHARD BARNFIELD.

"AS IT FELL UPON A DAY."

[A forlorn man sympathises with a Nightingale who is lamenting the loss of her mate. When troubles come, false friends fly. But the true Friend helps in need, and shares all one's sorrows.]

XX.

As it fell vpon a Day,
In the merry Month of May,   2
Sitting in a pleafant fhade
Which a groue of Myrtles made,   4
Beaftes did leape, and Birds did fing,
Trees did grow, and Plants did fpring;   6
Euery thing did banifh mone,
Saue the Nightingale alone.   8
Shee (poore Bird) as all forlorne,
Leand her breaft vp-till a thorne,   10
And there fung the dolefulft Ditty,
That, to heare it was great Pitty: 12
Fie, fie, fie, now would fhe cry;
Teru, Teru, by and by: 14
That, to heare her fo complaine,
Scarce I could from teares refraine: 16
For her griefes, fo liuely fhowne,
Made me thinke vpon mine owne.   18
Ah (thought I) thou mournft in vaine!
None takes pitty on thy paine: 20
Senfleffe Trees, they cannot heare thee;
Ruthleffe Beares,[1] they will not cheere thee.   22
King Pandion,[2] he is dead:
All thy friends are lapt in **Lead**:   24
All thy fellow Birds doe fing,
Careleffe of thy forrowing.[3]   26
Whilft as fickle Fortune fmilde,
Thou **and** I, were both beguild.   28
Euery one that flatters thee,
Is **no friend** in miferie: 30

[1] beasts: *England's Helicon.*
[2] Father of Philomela, the nightingale.
[3] *England's Helicon* adds the lines—
    Euen so, poore Bird, like ther,
    None alue will pitty me.

H 2

Words are easie, like the wind;
Faithfull friends are hard to find: 32
Euery man will be thy friend,
Whilst thou hast wherewith to spend: 34
But if store of Crownes be scant,
No man will supply thy want.   36
If that one be prodigall,
Bountifull they will him call: 38
And with such-like flattering,
Pitty but he were a King!   40
If he be addict to vice,
Quickly him, they will intice.   42
If to Women hee be bent,
They haue at Commaundement: 44
But if Fortune once doe frowne,
Then farewell his great renowne: 46
They that fawnd on him before,
Vse his company no more.   48
Hee that is thy friend indeede,
Hee will helpe thee in thy neede: 50
If thou sorrow, he will weepe;
If thou wake, hee cannot sleepe: 52
Thus of euery griefe, in hart
Hee, with thee, doeth beare a part.   54
These are certaine signes, to know
Faithfull friend, from flatt'ring foe.   56

EARL OF MORNINGTON, ab. 1770.   Four-Part Madrigal.   S.A.T.B.
WILLIAM KNYVETT, about 1812.   Three-Part Madrigal for A.T.B.
SIR HENRY BISHOP, 1819.   Duet.   Sung by Miss Stephens and Miss
    Tree in the operatised *Comedy of Errors*.
*T. COOKE, 1832.   Glee.
*JAMES COWARD, July 28, 1856.   Prize Glee.
*S. REAY, 1862.   Part Song. S.A.T.B.   Novello.
*CHARLES GARDNER, 1872.   Song.

The Rape of Lucrece.

(Qo. 1, 1594, sign. D 2.)

"WITHOUT THE BED HER OTHER FAIRE HAND WAS."

[Shakspere describes Lucrece asleep in bed, as Tarquin sees her.]

[St. 56]

Her lillie hand, her rofie cheeke lies vnder,   386
Coofning the pillow of a lawfull kiffe,
VVho therefore angrie feemes, to part in funder,
Swelling on either fide to want his bliffe;
Betweene whofe hils her head intombed is,   390
VVhere, like a vertuous Monument, thee lies,
To be admir'd of lewd vnhallowed eyes.   392

[St. 57]

VVithout the bed her other faire hand was,   393
On the greene couerlet, whofe perfect white
Showed like an Aprill dazie on the graffe,
VVith pearlie fwet refembling dew of night.
Her eyes like Marigolds had fheath'd their light,   397
And canopied in darkeneffe fweetly lay,
Till they might open to adorne the day.   399

*SIR HENRY R. BISHOP.

Rape of Lucrece, Stanza 160, lines 1114-1120. (Qo. 1, 1594, sign. H 3.)

"TIS DOUBLE DEATH, TO DROWNE IN KEN OF SHORE."

[After Tarquin's rape of her, Lucrece laments.]

[St. 158]

So fhee, deepe drenchëd in a Sea of care,   1100
Holds difputation with ech thing fhee vewes,
And to her felfe, all forrow doth compare.
No obiect, but her paffions ftrength renewes,
And as one fhiftes, another ftraight infewes: 1104
Somtime her griefe is dumbe, and hath no words;
Sometime tis mad, and too much talke affords.   1106

[St. 159]

The little birds that tune their mornings ioy,   1107
  Make her mones mad, with their sweet melodie,
" For mirth doth search the bottome of annoy ;
  " Sad foules are slaine in merrie companie ;
  " Griefe best is pleas'd with griefes societie ;   1111
    " True sorrow then is feelinglie suffiz'd,
  " When with like semblance it is simpathiz'd.   1113

[St. 160]

" Tis double death to drowne in ken of shore :   1114
    " He ten times pines, that pines beholding food :
" To see the salue, doth make the wound ake more :
    " Great griefe greeues most at that wold do it good :
  " Deepe woes roll forward like a gentle flood,   1118
    VVho being stopt, the bounding banks oreflowes :
  Griefe dallied with, nor law nor limit knowes.   1120

RICHARD SIMPSON (the late), published 1878. Song. (The above are
  in the original print ; they are often put before maxims.)

ADDENDA.

Page 11.   " Feare no more the heate," &c.

Add : *DR. NARES, 1780. Glee for A.T.B. (Warren's 'Collection of
  Catches, Glees,' &c., vol. ii.)

Page 56.   " While you here do snoaring lie."

Add : *A. S. SULLIVAN, 1865. Song. (Music to *The Tempest.* p. 22.)

Clay and Taylor. Printers, Bungay, Suffolk.

A LIST OF

ALL THE SONGS AND PASSAGES
IN SHAKSPERE

WHICH HAVE BEEN SET TO MUSIC.

A LIST OF

ALL THE SONGS & PASSAGES
IN SHAKSPERE

WHICH HAVE BEEN SET TO MUSIC.

COMPILED BY

J. GREENHILL, THE REV. W. A. HARRISON,
AND F. J. FURNIVALL.

THE WORDS IN OLD SPELLING, FROM THE QUARTOS
AND FIRST FOLIO,

EDITED BY

F. J. FURNIVALL AND W. G. STONE.

REVISED EDITION.

PUBLISHT FOR

𝔗𝔥𝔢 𝔑𝔢𝔴 𝔖𝔥𝔞𝔨𝔰𝔭𝔢𝔯𝔢 𝔖𝔬𝔠𝔦𝔢𝔱𝔶

BY N. TRÜBNER & CO., 57, 59, LUDGATE HILL,
LONDON, 1884.

Series VIII. 3. Miscellanies.

CLAY AND TAYLOR, THE CHAUCER PRESS, BUNGAY, SUFFOLK.

CONTENTS.

---
[1] Compare Byron's Poem on attaining his 36th year.—T. Tyler.

FOREWORDS.

AFTER the first 'Musical Evening' of the New Shak-spere Society, in May, 1883, several Members exprest the wish that the Words of the Songs had been put into their hands, for their memories had sometimes faild them. As the Musical Evening will, no doubt, be repeated every May while the Society lasts, the Committee thought that all Shakspere's Songs and Lines which have b.en set to Music, had better be printed, with a List of the Composers who have set them, and the Voices which are to sing them, so that the 'Book of the Words' might be a permanent one, and suit all the changing yearly Programs.

Accordingly, our Conductor, Mr. James Greenhill, com-piled,—from Alfred Roffe's *Handbook of Shakspere Music*, 1878, and other sources,—a draft List of the Songs and Composers, and I added the Words, from the revises of the *Old-Spelling Shakspere* edited by Mr. Stone and myself, and from the Quartos and First Folio.[1] The draft 'List' has been checkt by the Rev. W. A. Harrison and me with, and enlarged from, the Shakspere entries in the British Museum Catalog of 'Authors whose words have been set to Music,' many volumes of music, Chappell's Catalogs, &c.,[2] and has been revised by Mr. Wm. Chappell and others.[3] Mr. Edward

[1] Some context, or a short statement. has been given, in most cases, to show how and why each Song was brought in.

[2] In some instances we have been unable to ascertain the exact date when a piece was composed or published ; and the date given in the List must be taken as only approximately correct. But in very many more we have discovered the precise year—and had it been th ught necessary could have added the month and day—when a piece was first given to the world. Genest's 'Account of the English Stage' (10 vols., 1832), and Sir G. Grove's excellent 'Dictionary of Music and Musicians' have been of great service to us in this respect.

[3] Mr. Fry, of Novello and Co., has been good enough to look over our proofs.

Flügel of Leipzig has been so kind as to send a list of the
German settings. I have also compiled a 'Contents' of such
Collections of Shakspere Music as I have been able to get
hold of. Tho' still incomplete, the 'List' is no wise so
ridiculously imperfect as the entries of Shakspere Music in
the British Museum. Whether the Museum has only the
Shakspere Music catalogd, or its Catalog is desperately
behindhand, the result is equally lamentable, and does little
credit to the Museum Authorities.

Readers will note how the Musicians have naturally
found more material for their art in Shakspere's Comedies,
than in his Histories, Tragedies, and Poems; how, of these
Comedies, the *Midsummer Night's Dream* (15), the *Tempest* (13), *Twelfth Night* (9), and *As you like it* (7), have had
most pieces from them set; and how the following Songs
have proved the most attractive ones :[1]

1. Take, oh take those Lips away (*Meas. for Meas.*)   set 30 times.
2. Fletcher's ' Orpheus with his Lute' (*Henry VIII.*)   ,, 22 ,,
3. Marlowe's ' Come live with me' (*Pass. Pilgr.*),
      including ' To shallow Rivers' (*Merry Wives*) ...   ,, 19 ,,
4. It was a Lover and his Lass (*As you like it*)   ...   ,, 1? ,,
5. Who is Sylvia? (*Two Gentlemen*) ...   .   ,, 13 ,,
6. O Mistris mine (*Twelfth Night*)   ...   .   ,, 17 ,,
7. Sigh no more, Ladies (*Much Ado*) ...   .   ,, 15 ,,

Of the Poems, the spurious ones in the *Passionate Pilgrim*
have drawn to them more composers than Shakspere's own
non-dramatic work. Marlowe's " Come live with me' has
been set 19 times, to the 6 times of Shakspere's 18th Sonnet,
" Shall I compare thee to a Summer's Day ?"

                                                  F. J. F.

9 *April, 1884.*

---

[1] After writing the above, and correcting the proofs up to the *Merchant*, I turnd to Roffe's book in the British Museum on April 10—
Mr. Greenhill has had my copy for the last 18 months—and I was rather
shockt to find that Roffe had given the extracts too, so that our book
looks like a piracy of his. But my part was done independently; and
Mr. Greenhill's compilation from Roffe was a necessity. Every cataloguer
must use his foregoers' work, and add to it, so far as he can. Such
merit and usefulness as are in the present book must therefore be set
down as flowing from Roffe's example, though we have really worat
hard to add to his material. Our additions of settings to his list are
stard (*). But these stars do not represent the fresh dates and details
which we have inserted in Roffe's entries, or our corrections of his
mistakes.

THE following is a 'Contents' of the chief Collections of Shakspere Music. Of Dr. Kemp's 'Musical Illustrations of Shakspere' and many other books, no fit details are given. These books are not in the British Museum.—F. J. F.

1659—83. JOHN PLAYFORD. 'Select Ayres and Dialogues for one, two, and three voyces; to the theorbo-lute or basse-viol. Composed by John Wilson, Charles Colman (Doctors in Music), Henry Lawes, William Lawes, Nicholas Lancare, William Webb (Gentlemen and Servants to his late Majesty [Charles I.] in his publick and private musick). And other excellent masters of musick.' [This is in six parts, published in 1659, 1669, 1676, 1679, 1681, and 1683; it contains between three and four hundred songs, yet only two settings of words by Shakspere!]

1. Take, oh take those lips away, (*Measure for Measure*,) with the second verse, Hide, O hide those Ills of snow. (Fletcher, *The Bloody Brother.*) Dr. John Wilson
... ... Book I, page 1.
2. Where the bee sucks there suck I. (*Tempest.*) Robert Johnson; harmonized for three voices by Dr. Wilson Book I, p. 97.

A supplementary sheet, printed in 1670 ('the rare separately-paged sheet inserted in some copies of Book I.' W. H. Husk, in Grove's 'Dict. of Music'), contains the following:[1]

1. Come unto these yellow sands. (*Tempest.*) Solo, Soprano. Composed by John Banister, 1667 1
5. Full fathom five. (*Tempest.*) Solo, Soprano. Composed by John Banister, 1667 4

[1] The other pieces in this 'rare sheet' are: No. 2. 'Dry those eyes' (Solo for Ariel, Dryden's version). J. Banister. No. 3. 'Go thy way; why should'st thou stay?' (Duet for Ariel and Ferdinand, Dryden's version.) J. Banister. This is the celebrated *Echo Song* which so 'mightily pleased' Mr. Pepys that he 'got Mr. Banister to prick down the notes,' and 'Mr. Harris to repeat the words while I writ them down' [see Pepys' Diary, Nov. 7th, 1667; Jan. 6th, May 7th, May 11th, 1668]. No. 4. 'Adieu to the pleasures and follies of Love.' (Solo for Dorinda, Dryden's version.) James Hart, 1667.

6. Where t o Bee sucks. (*Tempest.*) Sung in the Machines' by
    Ar   spirits. Composed by Pelham Humfrey, 1667   4

1660. JOHN WILSON. "Cheerfull Ayres or Ballads. First
    composed for one single voice, and since set for three
    voices." Contains 69   and a   them:

(2. From the faire Lavinian shore.)
4. Full fathome five (*Tempest*). R. Johnson[2] [writer of the air].
5. Where the bee sucks (*Tempest*). R. Johnson [writer of the air].
(6. When love with unconfined wings.)
33 Lawne as white as driven snow (*Winter's Tale*). (See the late Dr.
    E. F. Rimbault's *Who   Jack Wilson?* 1846, p. 12-14.)

1673. HENRY PURCELL. The music in the Comedy of
    The Tempest 177   N   F   This is Davenant
    and Dryden's v.   f   revised by Thos.
    Shadwell, a produced a. an   t Duke's
    Theatre, Dorset Gardens. It   : 14 pieces. The
    settings   Shakspere's   e:

3. Come unto these yellow sands,) Solo, Soprano.
   Hark! hark! the watch-dogs, &c. } Chorus, S.A.T.B.
4. Full fathom   &c.   ) Solo, Soprano.
   Sea-Nymphs hourly: &c. } Chorus, S.A.T.B.

[The following pieces are set to Dryden's, Davenant's, and Shad-
well's   :—1. 'Where does the black Fiend . . ?' Trio, B.B.B. and
Chorus S.A.T.B. 2. 'Arise ye subterranean winds.' Solo, B. 5. 'Dry
those eyes.' Duet, S.S. 6. 'Kind fortune smiles.' Solo, S. 7. 'Dear,
pretty youth.' Solo, S.   'Great Neptune.' Duet, S.B. 9. 'The Nereids
and Tritons shall sing.' Chorus, S.A.T.B.   'Æolus, appear!' Solo,
B. 11. 'Your awful voice.   Solo, T.   'Halcyon days.' Solo, S.
13. 'See, the heavens smile.'   B. 14. No stars   shall hurt
you from above.' Duet, S.B.,   Chorus S.A.T.B.]

---

[1] Compare Dryden's lines, prologue for the opening of the New Theatre
in Drury Lane, 26th March, 1674, after the burning of the old one:
        "'Tis to be feared—
        That, as a fire the former house o'erthrew,
        Machines and *tempests* will destroy the new.'

[2] Robert Johnson was a celebrated performer on the lute, a young
Wilson (born, 1594) may have been his pupil. He wrote the music for
Middleton's *Witch*, as well as Shakspere's *Tempest*. Rimbault, p. 9-10.
Tho' John Wilson could not have composed the original music to 'Take,
oh take, those lips away!' (*Meas. for Meas.*) he may have been the 'Boy'
who sang it (p. 25 below). Later in his life, he did   it.—*Rimbault*,
p. 3-5.

1740. DR. THOMAS AUGUSTINE ARNE.   The Music in the Comedy of *As You Like It*, in Score (published (?) 1780, Oblong Folio).

1. When Daisies pied. (*Love's Labour's Lost.*) Sung in the character of Celia.   Solo, Soprano, Key of G.   2
2. Under the Greenwood Tree. (*As You Like It.*) Sung in the character of Amiens.   Solo, Tenor, Key of F.   4
3. Blow, blow, thou Winter Wind. (*As You Like It.*) Sung in the character of Amiens.   Solo, Tenor, Key of B♭   ...   7
4. Tell me where is Fancy bred? (*Merch. of Venice.*) Solo, Soprano.   Sung by Mrs. Clive.   Key of D minor   ...   8

1741. DR. T. A. ARNE.   The Songs in *As You Like It* . . . To which are added the Songs in *Twelfth Night* . . . . Contains the four Songs given above with the addition of:

7. Come away, come away, Death. (*Twelfth Night.*)   Solo, Tenor   16

1742. Dr. T. A. ARNE.   The Songs and Duets in the Blind Beggar of Bethnal Green[1] . . .

11. The Owl, Written by Shakespear in (*Love's labour lost*), it is a description of Winter, as the Cuckoo Song is of the Spring. When Isicles hang on the wall   15

17 . . DR. T. A. ARNE.   The Second Volume of Lyric Harmony . .

PAGE

5. Ariel's Song in the *Tempest*. 'Where the Bee sucks.'[2]   Solo   185
14. On Cloe Sleeping, taken from Shakespear. One of her Hands, one rosy Cheek lay under. (*Rape of Lucrece.* st. 56, 'Her lillie hand, her rosie Cheeke lies vnder.')   Solo   197

1745. J. F. LAMPE.   *Pyramus and Thisbe;* A Mock-Opera.   The Words taken from Shakespeare, as it is Perform'd at the Theatre-Royal in Covent-Garden. Set to Musick by Mr. I. F. Lampe.

---

[1] The *Merchant of Venice* Song named in the continuation of the Title is the spurious ' To keep my gentle Jesy '.
[2] The ' Song from Shakespear's *Cymbeline*,' on p. 187, is the spurious ' To fair Fidele's grassy Tomb.'

1745. THOMAS CHILCOT. Twelve English Songs, with
their Symphonies. The Words by Shakespeare and
other Celebrated Poets. Set to Musick by Thomas
Chilcot, Organist of Bath. London. John Johnson.

1755. JN. CHRISTOPHER SMITH. The *Fairies*. An Opera.
The words taken from Shakespear, and Set to Music by
Mr. Smith.

1756. JN. CHRISTOPHER SMITH. The *Tempest*. An Opera.
The Words taken from Shakespear, &c.   Set to Music
by Mr. Smith.

1762. JOSEPH VERNON. The New Songs in the Panto-
mime of *The Witches*, the celebrated Epilogue in the
Comedy of *Twelfth Night*, a Song in *The Two Gentlemen
of Verona* . . . a favourite French Air [2] sung in the
Comedy of *Twelfth Night* by Mrs. Abington. (1770,
Folio).

1807. FRANCIS HUTCHINSON. A Collection. (Not in
Brit. Mus)

[1] Theodore Aylward's 'Six Songs in Harlequin's Invasion, Cymbeline,
and Midsummer Night's Dream, &c.,' 1770, contains only one genuine song
'Hark, the Lark,' sung by Mr. Vincent.
[2] The French Air (D'une manière imparfaite), with translation by H.
Kelly, Esq., p. 2.

b

1812. *Musica Antiqua,* 2 vols, ed. J. Stafford Smith.

Willow Song in *Othello,* by Pelham Humphrey, Composer to the King, 1673. Solo, S. ii. 171.

Fare-well, deere love, (quoted in *Twelfth Night,*) by Robert Jones, 1601. Song, in 4 Parts. ii. 204.[1]

1814 (?). Dr. J. Kemp.   Musical Illustrations of Shakspere. (Not in Brit. Mus.)

Lady, by yonder **blessed Moon.** (*Romeo and Juliet.*) Duet, S.T. ab. 1799.

A Lover's **eyes** will gaze an Eagle blind. (*L. L. Lost.*) Solo, T. ab. 1799. Cello accompaniment.

Hamlet's Letter. Doubt thou the Stars **are fire.** (*Hamlet.*) Solo, T. 1814. Cello and P. F. accompaniment.

Willow Song. A poor soul sat sighing. (*Othello.*) Solo, S. 1807.

1816. Wm. Linley. Shakspeare's Dramatic Songs. 2 vols.

INDEX TO THE FIRST VOLUME.

---

[1] In Henry Smith's 'Six Canzonets for the Voice . . . the Words selected from Shakespeare,' &c., 1816, Congreve's two lines, "Music hath charms to soothe the savage breast, To soften rocks and bend the knotted Oak" (*Mourning Bride,* I. i. 1-2) are assigned to Shakspere.

b 2

[*Appendix.*] The Music in *Macbeth* as it is now performed on the Stage. Newly arranged in three parts, and a Piano Forte accompaniment by Mr. Samuel Wesley, p. 69-79. (As the words are not Shakspere's, the names of the Songs, &c. are not given here.[1])

1816. HENRY R. BISHOP. The Overture, Songs, Duetts, Trios, Quartetts and Chorusses in Shakspeare's *Midsummer Night's Dream*, as revived at the Theatre Royal, Covent Garden. [5 Pieces altered from Arne, Smith, Battishill, Dr. Cooke and Handel; the rest composed by H. R. B.]

2. By the simplicity of Venus' doves. Solo. S. 8
8. Trip away, make no stay. Part of the Chorus, 'Spirits, advance,' for S.S.A.T.B.... 31
9. O happy fair. Solo, T. Sung by Mr. Sinclair 40
11. Flower of this purple dye. J. C. Smith, arranged by Bishop. Solo, Tenor or Baritone 48

---

[1] The spurious song "O bid your faithful Ariel fly" is included in Linley's Collection. It was composed by Thos. Linley, Junr., 1777. The words are attributed to Dr. Laurence ('Shakspere Vocal Magazine'). The *Tempest* was brought out at Drury Lane in 1777, the year after Garrick retired. Garrick transferred his share of the theatre to Sheridan. Sheridan's wife was the sister of Thos. Linley, who thus became composer of the music for the theatre. Is it not likely that Sheridan may have written those words?

Since writing the above I find, catalogued in Bohn's 'Lowndes,' and in Halliwell's 'Shakesperiana': *The Tempest*. Altered by R. B. Sheridan. *The Songs only.* with music by T. Linley, Jun. London, 1-76, 8° (1777, S. Halliwell). 1778, 12°. I have not seen a copy of any Edition of this book: there are none in the Museum Library. But the fact that Sheridan altered the Songs in *The Tempest* seems to confirm my conjecture.—W. A. H.

¹ Altered to, 'In Theseus' house,' &c.

1821. HENRY R. BISHOP. The Overture, Songs, Duetts,
Glees and Chorusses, in Shakspeare's Play of the *Two
Gentlemen of Verona*, as performed at the Theatre Royal,
Covent Garden.

[1] No. 4 is ' Come o'er the brook, Bessé, to me ' (*Lear*), with a spurious
continuation, set as a Glee for 4 Voices, S.,A. or S.2, T.B., p. 22. The
burden, p. 26 and 31, is from Dr. Calcott.

1821. CHARLES E. HORN. Songs, Duets, &c., in *The Tempest*, as performed at the Theatre Royal, Covent Garden. (Not in Brit. Mus.)

Shall I compare thee to a summer's day? (*Sonnet* 18.) Duet, S.C.
Take all my loves. (*Sonnet* 40.) Solo, T. or B.
Being your slave, what should I do? (*Sonnet* 57.) Solo.[1]

1823. CHARLES E. HORN. Songs, Duets, Chorusses, &c., in *The Merry Wives of Windsor*, as performed at the Theatre Royal, Drury Lane. (Not in Brit. Mus.)

I know a bank. (*M. N. Dream.*) Duet, S.C.
All that glitters is not gold. (*Merchant of Venice.*) Duet, S.C.
Blow, blow, thou winter wind. (*As You Like It.*) Song, T. Sung
  by Braham.
Crabbed age and youth. (*Pass. Pilgrim.*) Song.
Even as the sun. (*Venus and Adonis.*) Song, S.
It was a lording's daughter. (*Pass. Pilgrim.*) Song, S.
When it is the time of night. (*M. N. Dream.*) Solo, S.
Trip, trip, away. (*M. N. Dream.*) Chorus of Fairies. S.T.B.

1824. HENRY R. BISHOP. The Whole of the Music in *As you like it*, as performed at the Theatre Royal, Covent Garden [&c.]. The Three Songs composed for the above Play, by Dr. Arne. The poetry Selected entirely from the Plays, Poems, and Sonnets of Shakspeare.

(1. Overture) ... ...
2. Whilst inconstant Fortune smiled[2] (*Passionate Pilgrim*, 20)
   Duetto, S.C. 10
3. Ah[3] me! what eyes hath Love put in my head (*Sonnet* 148).
   Solo, M.-S. 15

---

[1] Follows the spurious 'Kind fortune smiles.' (Dryden and Davenant, *The Tempest.*) Duet, S.T.
[2] 'Whilst . . find,' l. 29-34, 6 lines; then l. 51-8, 'She (*for* He) that is . . . foe,' 8 lines.
[3] O.—Shakspere. The last 2 lines of the Sonnet are not set.

1839. GEORGE NICKS. Ophelia's Airs in Shakspeare's
    Play of *Hamlet*, as they were wont to be sung at
    Covent Garden Theatre by a highly popular and dis-
    tinguished vocalist [*i. e.* Miss Stephens, afterwards
    Countess of Essex]. Dedicated with permission to the
    Countess of Essex.

    [The traditional airs arranged with accompaniments by G. Nicks.]

1843. FELIX MENDELSSOHN BARTHOLDY. The Music to
    Shakspere's *Midsummer Night's Dream*. This is all
    instrumental with the exception of :

3. You spotted snakes with double tongues. Duet S.S., and Chorus
    S.S.A.A.

12. Through the house give glimmering light. Chorus S.S.A.A., with
    Solo for S. 'First rehearse this song .   bless the place.'

    [1] Art.—Shakspere.

1847 (?). Shakspere Songs, edited by Charles Jefferys. Jefferys and Nelson.

1. Blow, blow thou winter Wind (*As you like it*). Tenor Solo. Dr. Arne.
2. Under the Greenwood Tree (*As you like it*). Tenor Solo. Dr. Arne.

ab. 1850. J. REEKES. Six Shakspere Songs. (Not in B. Mus.)

1. O Mistress mine. (*Tw. Night.*) Song.
2. Shall I compare thee to a Summer's day? (*Sonnet* 18, lines 1—3, and 9.)
3. Full many a glorious Morning. (*Sonnet* 33.) Solo.
4. Farewell, thou art too dear. (*Sonnet* 87.) Solo.
5. If Love have left you twenty thousand tongues. (*Venus and Ad.* st. 130.) Solo, A. or B.
6. Wilt thou be gone. (*Romeo and Juliet.*[1]) Solo.

1862. A. S. SULLIVAN. The Music to Shakespeare's *Tempest.*

		PAGE
2. Come unto these yellow sands. Solo, Soprano	}	14
Hark, hark, the watch-dogs bark. &c. Chorus, S.A.T.B.	}	
Full fathom five. Solo, S.	}	17
Sea-Nymphs hourly ring, &c. Chorus, S.A.T.B.	}	
3. While you here do snoring lie. Solo, Soprano...		22
9. Honour, riches, marriage blessing. Duet S.S., with Chorus for S.A.T.B. ...		63
12. Where the bee sucks. Solo, Soprano ...		100

[The remaining numbers consist of instrumental music.]

1864. JOHN CAULFIELD. A Collection of the Vocal Music in Shakespeare's Plays. 2 vols. J. Caulfield.

Vol. I. *The Tempest.*

[2]Come unto these yellow sands. Solo. Purcell ... 1
Hark, hark! the watch dogs bark. Chorus, S.A.T.B. Purcell ... 3
Full fathom five. Solo. Purcell ... 4

---

[1] J. L. Hatton's 'Overture and Music incidental to Shakspere's Play of K. Henry VIII,' 1855, consists of 6 pianoforte pieces; and no. 7, Fletcher's 'Orpheus with his Lute' set as a Duet for Soprano and Contralto.

B. Isaacson's 'Favorite Airs in Shakespeare's K. Henry V.', 1858, is a set of 12 pianoforte bits of old airs and new music.

Bishop's Music to the *Tempest* is the pianoforte score.

[2] Before this, is Garrick's "Thou soft flowing Avon," set by Arne.

J.

[1] Follow, the spurious 'O bid your faithful Ariel fly' (p. 20); Symphony and Grand Chorus descriptive of a Storm and Shipwreck, composed by Thos. Linley, Junr. (p. 27); Grand Chorus, 'Arise ye Spirits of the Storm' (S.A.T.B.), (p. 30); 'Kind Fortune smiles,' Solo, H. Purcell (p. 48); 'Dry those eyes,' Solo, H. Purcell (p. 55); 'Where does the black Fiend,' Solo and Chorus 'In Hell,' H. Purcell (p. 57, 58); 'The owl is abroad,' Solo, J. Smith (p. 62); Grand Masque, 'Great Neptune,' H. Purcell, duet (p. 65).

[2] Two spurious songs follow: '**Haste Lorenzo**' (p. 110), and '**To keep my gentle Jessy,**' p. 116.

[3] 'The annexed Piece ('Which is the **Properest Day to Drink**') is at present performed in the place of the Catch before mentioned,' p. 143-7.

1864.   *Shakspeare Vocal Album (and Magazine[1]).*

    [1] This is the Album in separate Songs, but with the same paging.

[1] 'Sweet Anne Page' ('With thee fair summers joys appear') follows, p. 42. Then Wm. Ball's 'Light o' Love,' p. 113.
[2] 'Thou soft flowing Avon,' Garrick's Ode to Shakspere, set by Arne, follows, p. 1.
[3] 'The Warwickshire lad,' Jubilee Music, 1769. Song and Chorus; Dibdin, is on p. 115.

1865. The Music in Shakspeare's *Tempest*, by Purcell, Arne, Smith and Linley. New Edition, with additions by Dryden, &c. London. C. Lonsdale. [I give only the genuine pieces, as usual.]

1866 (?). Chappell's Musical Magazine. Edited by E. F. Rimbault. No. 47. — Thirteen Standard Songs of Shakspeare. Price 1s.

[1] See note, p. xx.

1864. Choral Songs. (S.A.¹T.B., ... by G. A. MACFARREN.
Novello and Co. (Thirteen of em : the first by Fletcher ;
the next 6 by Shakspere.)

No. 1. "Orpheus with his Lute" (by Fletcher). *Henry VIII.*, p. 1.
  „ 2. Song of Winter. "When Icicles hang by the Wall." *Love's
      Labour's Lost*, p. 5.
  „ 3. "Come away, come away, Death!" *Twelfth Night*, p. 9.
  „ 4. Song of Spring. "When Daisies pied." *Love's Labour's Lost*.
      (A fresh p. 1—5)
  „ 5. "Who is Sylvia?" *Two Gentlemen of Verona*, p. 20.
  „ 6. "Fear no more the Heat o' the Sun." *Cymbeline*, p. 24.
  „ 7. "Blow, blow, thou Winter Wind." *As you like it*, p. 3 ?.

1869. Eight Shakspere Songs, set to Music in Four Parts,
by G. A. MACFARREN. Novello's Part-Song Book.
Second Series. Book XV. Price 1s. 4d.

NO.
124. "Sigh no more, Ladies." *Much Ado.*
125. "You spotted Snakes." *Mids. Night's Dream.*
126. "Take, O take those Lips away." *Meas. for Measure.*
127. "It was a Lover and his Lass." *As you Like it.*
128. "O Mistress mine." *Twelfth Night.*
129. "Under the Greenwood Tree." *As you like it.*
130. "Hark the Lark." *Cymbeline.*
131. "Tell me where is Fancy bred." *Merch. of Venice.*
   [In later numbers of this 2nd Series of Novello's Part-Song Book,
    are two Part-Songs by Richard Reay :]
146. "As it fell upon a Day." *Pass. Pilgrim;* by Richard Barnfield.
      Treble, A.T.B !
149. "Take, Oh take those Lips away." *Meas. for Measure.* Treble,
      A.T.B.

18 . . Sir H. R. Bishop's Glees and Choruses. A Selection,
publisht by Novello.

   7. "Who is Sylvia?" (*Two Gent. of Verona.* Key of G. S.A.T.B. 2d.
  15. "What shall he have?" (*As you like it.*) Key of E flat.
                                                    A.T.T.B. 2d.
  18. "Come, thou monarch." (*Antony and Cleopatra.*) Key of D.
                                                         A.T.B. 2d.
  33. "Good night, good rest." (*Pass. Pilgr.* Key of C. S.A.T.B. 2d.
  58. "Blow, blow, thou winter wind." (*As you like it.*) Key of G.
                                                              S.A.T.B. 2d.

   ¹ Or 2nd Soprano. These Songs also appear in Novello's Part-Song Book,
1st Series.

18 . . Novello's Secular Music. Glees, Madrigals, or Part-Songs, for Four Voices (S.A.T.B. unless otherwise expressed). 1½d. each.

124. "Full Fathom five." (*Tempest.*) S. solo and Chorus.   Purcell.
124. "Come unto these yellow sands." (*Tempest.*) Purcell.
67. "Hark, the Lark." (*Cymbeline.*)   Dr. Cooke.
81. "Sigh no more, Ladies." (*Much Ado.*) S.S.A.T.B. Stevens.
275. „   „   „   „   „   „   (S.A.T.B.) Macfarren.
254. "Tell me where is Fancy bred." (*Merchant.*) Mrs. M. Bartholomew.
49. "The cloud-capt Towers." (*Tempest.*) Stevens.
246. "Who is Sylvia?" (*Two Gent. of Verona.*) G. A. Macfarren.
64. "Ye spotted Snakes." (*Mids. N. Dream.*) R. J. S. Stevens.

18 . . . JOHN PARK, D.D. Songs composed and in part written by the late Rev. John Park, D.D., St. Andrews. With introductory notice by Principal Shairp, LL.D., St. Andrews; published 1876. (Not in Brit. Mus. Among the Contents are :

Sigh no more, ladies. (*Much Ado.*)   52
Under the greenwood tree. (*As You Like It.*)   ...   77
Come away, come away, death! (*Twelfth Night.* ...   82
When daisies pied. (*Love's Labour's Lost.*)...   ...   159
Orpheus with his lute. (*King Henry VIII.*)   245

1878. SIMPSON, Richard (the late : Member of the New Shakspere Society's Committee). *Sonnets of Shakspeare,* selected¹ from a Complete Setting, *and Miscellaneous Songs.* London. Stanley Lucas, Weber and C.

SONNETS.

¹ The selection, from a great number of songs submitted to her, has been kindly made by Mrs. Macfarren, wife of the eminent Professor, and Principal of the Royal Academy of Music. ' Notice ' by Mrs. Simpson. April 1878.

MISCELLANEOUS SONGS.[1]

* * * * *

Of the following books of Shakspere Music given in
Bohn's *Lowndes :—*

Dr. W. Boyce's Masque in the *Tempest* is not in the British Museum.
S. Arnold's *Macbeth* consists of instrumental music only.

For the following (imperfect) list of German and other
foreign Shakspere music, I am indebted to Mr. Ewald
Flugel of Leipzig.

1. Schumann, the last Clown's song, 'When that I was a little tiny
   Boy.' (*Twelfth Night.*) A flat, 6 8, in Opus 127.

2. Schumann, Opus 21. Novellette, No. 3 : 'When shall we three
   meet again?' (*Macbeth.*)

3. Franz Schubert and T. Kücken wrote music for 'Hark, the Lark.'
   (*Cymbeline.*)

4. Henry Hugo Pierson (Opus 63) : " Drei Gedichte von W. Shakspere
   für eine tiefe Stimme." Leipzig, Rieter—Biederman. (1) 'Tell
   me where is fancy bred?' (*M. of Venice.*) (2) 'Who is Sylvia?'
   (*Two Gentlemen of Verona.*) (3) 'Fear no more the heat o' the
   sun.' (*Cymbeline.*)

5. Mendelssohn (Opus 61) made a composition of the whole *Midsummer Night's Dream.* (Partitur und Orchesterstimmen.)

6. Schwanbeyer, Duetto from *Romeo* ('Per quel ch'or,' 'Bei Luna's
   Schimmer'). Berlin, 1851. Damköhler's Printing House.

7. Alvensleben, G. von—'From a drama of Shakspere's' in his Opus 4.

[1] I give only the Shakspere ones.

The following I take from 'Oscar Paul,'[1] Die Tonkunst
im Zusammenhange mit Shakespeare, 1864,' written for the
23rd of April, for the Shakspere Festivities.[2]

We have whole opera-settings of

8. *Romeo*, by Zingarelli, Vaccai, Bellini, Gounod 1867, Marquis D'Ivry
1871.
9. *Othello*, by Rossini. Produced in 1816.
10. *Macbeth*, by Chelard, Verdi, and Taubert.
11. *Merry Wives*, by Nicolai, Balfe (Falstaff) 1845 (there's also an
opera 'Falstaff,' *a* by Adam, and *b* by Salieri).
12. *Coriolanus*, by Niccolini.
13. *Amlete*, by Francesco Gassarini, Venice, 1705. Words by Apostolo
Zeno. Produced in London as a Pasticcio in 1712. (See Burney's
Hist. of Music, vol. iv, p. 231.) By Buzzola; and by Ambroise
Thomas, 1868.
14. *Tempest*, by Reichardt; by Zumsteg (with the title, 'Die Geister-
insel'); by Jullien; by Halévy (version by Scribe originally
intended for Mendelssohn).
15. *Taming of the Shrew* (Der Widerspänstigen Zähmung), by Her-
mann Götz, pub. 1875.

Parts of Shakspere's plays have been composed.

16. Parts of *Macbeth* by Gallus.
17. Parts of the *Tempest* by Taubert; by Alphonse Duvernoy (poème
symphonique pour soli, chœurs, et orchestre), 1880.
18. Parts of *As You Like It*, by Tausch.
19. Song in *Cymbeline* ('Horch, Horch, die Lerch'), by Schubert.

Orchestra-compositions:

20. Dramatic Symphony to *Romeo*, by Berlioz.
21. Overture to *Romeo* by Steibelt, and one by Ilinski.
22. Overture to *Hamlet*, by Gade, Liszt, and Joachim; Mannsfeldt-
Pierson is author of the funeral march in *Hamlet*.
23. Overture to the *Tempest*, by J. Rietz, J. Hager, and Vierling.
24. „ „ *Macbeth*, by Spohr, and by Pearsall.
25. „ „ *Lear*, by Berlioz.
26. „ „ *Cæsar*, by Schumann.
27. „ „ *Two Gentlemen of Verona*, by Street.
28. „ „ *King John*, by Radecke.
29. „ „ *Coriolanus*, by Bernh. Anselm Weber.
30. „ „ *Othello*, by Christ. Muller.
31. „ „ Music for the Entr'actes of *Othello*, by Emil Titl (for
the performances of the Burgtheater, Vienna).

---

[1] With additions by Mr. W. Barclay Squire.
[2] An article scarcely to be got in England.

1

All's Well that Ends Well.

Act I. Scene iii. lines 67—75.

"WAS THIS FAIRE FACE THE CAUSE, QUOTH SHE?"

[The scene is laid in the palace of Count Bertram, at Rousillon. There are present the Countess. Bertram's mother, her steward, and the clown Lavache.]

Steward. May it pleafe you, Madam, that hee bid *Hellen* come to you : of her I am to fpeake.
Counteffe of Roffillion (to the Clowne. LAVATCH). Sirra! tell my gentlewoman I would fpeake with her; *Hellen,* I meane.   66

Clowne. [sings] "*Was this faire face the caufe,*" *quoth fhe,*   67
   "*Why the* Grecians *fack'd* Troy?
Fond done, done fond!
   Was this King Priams *ioy?* '   70

With that fhe fighëd as fhe ftood,   [*bis.* 71
  And gaue this fentence then :
"*Among nine bad, if one be good,*
Among nine bad, if one be good,
  There's yet one good in ten."   75

Counteffe. What! "one good in tenne"? you corrupt the fong, firra!   77
Clowne. One good woman in ten, Madam; which is a purifying ath'fong : would God would ferue the world fo all the yeere! we'e'd finde no fault with the tithe woman, if I were the Parfon. "One in ten," quoth a! And wee might haue a good woman borne but one[1] euerie blazing ftarre, or at an earthquake, 'twould mend the Lotterie well : a man may draw his heart out, ere a plucke one.   84

[For the verse (l. 58—61) which comes before the passage quoted above, see p. 2.]
WM. LINLEY, A.D. 1816. Solo : Tenor or Bass. The 'Dramatic Songs of Shakspere,' by Wm. Linley.

    ' ore = over.

B

All's Well, Act I. Scene iii. lines 58—61.

"FOR I THE BALLAD WILL REPEATE."

Counteſſe. Wilt thou euer be a foule-mouth'd and calumnious
knaue?
Clowne. A Prophet I, Madam; and I ſpeake the truth the next
waie :   57

> *For I the Ballad will repeate,*   58
> *Which men full true ſhall finde ;*
> *Your marriage comes by deſtinie,*
> *Your Cuckow ſings by kinde.*   61

Counteſſe. Get you gone, ſir! Ile talke with you more anon.

[No setting of this verse is known.]

Anthony and Cleopatra.

Act II. Scene vii. lines 120—125.

SONG.

"COME, THOU MONARCH OF THE VINE."

[The triumvirs, Octavius Cæsar, Mark Antony, and Lepidus, with
their followers, have been banqueting with Sextus Pompeius,[1] on
board his galley. Before they part, Enobarbus, a friend of Antony,
proposes that they should " daunce now the *Egyptian* Backenals,
And celebrate our drinke."]

Enobarbus. All take hands!
[*To* Musicians.] Make battery to our eares with the loud Muſicke!
¶[2] The while Ile place you : then the Boy ſhall ſing :
The holding,[3] euery man ſhall beare as loud,
As his ſtrong ſides can volly.

[*Musicke Playes.* ENOBARBUS *places them hand in hand.*

The Song.

> *Come, thou Mouarch of the Vine,*
> *Plumpie Bacchus with pinke eyne!*   121
> *In thy Fattes our Cares be drown'd,*
> *With thy Grapes our haires be Crown'd :*   123
> *Cup vs, till the world go round,*
> *Cup vs, till the world go round!*   125

THOS. CHILCOT, about 1750. Solo, Tenor, or Bass by transposition.
Chilcot has left out the fifth line. Caulfield's Collection, 1864.

---

[1] Son of Pompey the Great.
[2] '¶' marks that the Speaker addresses some fresh person.
[3] *holding,* burden.

Another. Name unknown, 1759. See Roffe, p. 3.

WM. LINLEY, about 1815. Solo, Boy, with Chorus for Treble (Boy), Alto, Tenor, and Bass. Linley's 'Dramatic Songs of Shakspere,' 1816.

SCHUBERT (d. 1828). Solo, Tenor or Bass. A verse added in German and English. 'Shakspere Vocal Album (1864);'[1] and 'Shakspere Vocal Magazine,' 1864, p. 118.

SIR H. BISHOP, 1837. Chorus for three male voices. Composed for the *Comedy of Errors*. Novello. Arranged for Soprano, Contralto, Tenor, and Bass (Lonsdale's 'Shakspere Vocal Album,' 1864, p. 226. Now publisht by Augener, Newgate St.).

Ditto, rearranged by Hatton, 1862. Chorus, S.A.T.B. 'Shakspere Vocal Album,' 1864, and Ashdown.

WEISS, 1863. Bass Solo.

𝕬𝖘 𝖄𝖔𝖚 𝕷𝖎𝖐𝖊 𝕴𝖋.

Act II. Scene v. lines 1—8, 34—39.

"UNDER THE GREENE WOOD TREE."

[Sung by Amiens to the melancholy Jaques and his mates with the banisht Duke "in the Forreſt of *Arden*, and a many merry men with him; and there they liue like the old *Robin Hood* of *England:* they ſay many yong Gentlemen flocke to him euery day, and fleet the time carelesly, as they did in the golden world."— I. ii. 105—109.]

Enter AMYENS, IAQUES, *& others.*

Song.

Amyens.   *Vnder the greene wood tree,*
        who loues to lye with mee,   2
    And turne his merrie Note
        vnto the ſweet Birds tnrote,
    Come hither ! come hither ' come hither :
        Heere ſhall he ſee
        No enemie,
    But Winter and rough Weather.

    *   *   *   *   *   *

        Song.   [*Altogether heere.*

Who doth ambition ſhunne,
    and loues to liue i' th Sunne ;   35
Seeking the food he eates,
    and pleas'd with what he gets,   37
Come hither ! come hither ! come hither !
    Heere ſhall he ſee, &c.

[1] Not the piano-forte solo volume 'The Shakspere Album, or Warwickshire Garland.' London : Lonsdale and Longmans, 1862; 26, Old Bond St

Dr. T. A. ARNE, 1740. Solo, Tenor.[1]
MARIA HESTER PARK, about 1790. Three voices.
STAFFORD SMITH. about 1792. Glee for four voices.
*EDWARD SMITH BIGGS, about 1800. Three voices.
WM. LINLEY, *Shakspere's Dram. Songs*, 1816. (Chorus only to Arne's
 Song.) Chorus: "Who doth ambition shun?" for S.S.B., or
 T.T.B., to follow Dr. Arne's Song.
SIR HENRY BISHOP, 1824.[2] Dr. Arne's melody arranged for four male
 voices, and in this form introduced into the *Comedy of Errors.*
*G. A. MACFARREN, 1869. S.A.T.B. Part-Song. Novello.
*DR. JOHN PARK, 1876. Song.
*H. W. WAREING, 1878. S.A.T.B. Part Song. Novello.

<hr>

As You Like It, Act II. Scene vii. lines 173—189.

"BLOW, BLOW, THOU WINTER WINDE!"

Duke Senior (to Old ADAM, *and his young Master,* ORLANDO, *at
their Meal in the Forrest of* Arden). Welcome! fall to! I wil not
trouble you
As yet, to queſtion you about your fortunes.
[3]¶ Giue vs ſome Muſicke! ¶and, good Cozen, ſing!   172

Song.

 Amyens. Blow, blow, thou winter winde' 173
   Thou art not ſo vnkinde
    As mans ingratitude; 175
   Thy tooth is not ſo keene,
   Becauſe thou art not ſeene,
    Although thy breath be rude. 178
  Heigh ho! ſing, heigh ho! vnto the greene holly :
 Moſt Frendſhip is fayning ; moſt Louing, meere folly : 180
  Then, heigh ho, the holly!
  This Life is moſt iolly. 182

  Freize, freize, thou bitter ſkie! 183
  That doſt not bight ſo nigh
   As benefitts forgot ; 185
  Though thou the waters warpe,
  Thy ſting is not ſo ſharpe
   As freind remembred not. 188
  Heigh ho! ſing, &c.

[1] **Roffe** has, in error, entered as a setting of Shakspere's words, an old
ballad in an Ashmole MS., mentioned by Chappell, *Pop. Mus.*, ii. 539, 541.
The words are given by Chappell at p. 541.
[2] **He** also arranged Dr. Arne's Melody for Voice and Piano in his 'The
whole of the Music in *As you like it.*' 1824. p. 34—7.
[3] '¶' marks that the Speaker addresses some fresh person.

DR. T. A. ARNE, 1740. Tenor, or Bass by transposition (ed. 1854, 1856, &c.).
JOHN DANBY, about 1785. Three Tenors and one Bass. Arne's Melody harmonized.
R. J. S. STEVENS, about 1790. Glee, S.A.T.B. Novello.
WM. LINLEY, 1816. "Heigh ho" Chorus, to follow Arne's Song. Linley's 'Dramatic Songs of Shakspere,' 1816.
*C. E. HORN, 1823. Song, T. Sung by Braham in the operatized *Merry Wives of Windsor*.
SIR HENRY BISHOP, 1824.[1] Four male voices, and S.A.T.B. Introduced in the operatized *Comedy of Errors*. Arne's Melody harmonized, and the burthen from Stevens's Glee. Novello; also S.A.T.B. Novello.
SAMUEL WEBBE, about 1830. Glee for five voices.
HON. MRS. DYCE SOMBRE. Contralto or Bass Song, without the burthen 'Heigh ho'.
*MRS. A. S. BARTHOLOMEW (*first* MOUNSEY), 1857. Part Song, S.A.T.B. 'Six four-part Songs,' No. 3. Novello.
AGNES ZIMMERMANN, 1863. Song. Novello.
*G. A. MACFARREN, 1864. Part Song, S.A.T.B. Novello. 'Choral Songs,' No. 7.
R. SCHACHNER, 1865. Part Song. Addison and Lucas.

As You Like It, Act III. Scene ii. lines 81—8, 142—7.

"FROM THE EAST TO WESTERNE IND."

[Rosalind, drest as a young man, finds stuck on a tree in the Forest of Arden, some verses praising her, written by her lover Orlando. She reads them to the Clown, Touchstone, and the peasant, Corin.]

From the *Eaſt to weſterne Inde*,
no *iewel is like* Roſalinde. 82
Hir worth, being mounted on the winde,
through all the world beares Roſalinde. 84
All the pictures faireſt linde,
are but black to Roſalinde. 86
Let no face bee kept in mind,
but the faire of Roſalinde! 88

* * * * *

[Thus F. Roſalinde *of manie parts*, 142
by Heauenly Synode was deuis'd ;
Of manie faces, eyes, and hearts,
to haue the touches deereſt pris'd. 145
Heauen would that ſhee theſe gifts ſhould haue,
and I to liue and die her ſlaue. 147

*SIR ARTHUR S. SULLIVAN, 1865. Solo, Soprano. Called 'Rosalind.' Metzler & Co.

[1] He also arranged Dr. Arne's Melody for Voice and Piano in his 'The whole of the Music in *As You Like It*.' 1824. p. 51.

As You Like It, Act IV. Scene ii. lines 10—17.

"WHAT SHALL HE HAVE, THAT KIL'D THE DEARE?"

GLEE OR PART-SONG.

Enter IAQUES *and* Lords, *like* Forresters.

Iaques. Which is he that killed the Deare?
A Lord. Sir, it was I.
Iaques. Let's prefent him to the Duke, like a *Romane* Conquerour! and it would doe well to fet the Deares horns vpon his head, for a branch of victory. ¶ Haue you no fong, Forrefter, for this purpofe?   6
A Lord. Yes, Sir.
Iaques. Sing it! 'tis no matter how it bee in tune, fo it make noyfe enough.   9

Muficke.

Song.

A Lord. *What fhall he haue, that kild the Deare?*
   His Leather fkin, and hornes to weare!   11
     [Then fing him home : the reft fhall beare this burthen.
   Take thou no fcorne to weare the horne!
   It was a creft ere thou waft borne :   13
   Thy fathers father wore it,
   And thy father bore it :   15
   The horne, the horne, the lufty horne,
   Is not a thing to laugh to fcorne!   [Exeunt.

JOHN HILTON, about 1652. Round for four Bass voices. In Charles Knight's 'Shakspere.'
HENRY CAREY, 1723, or 1730. Solo. In 'Love in a Forest,' known as "The Huntsman's Song."
DR. PHILIP HAYES, about 1780. Three voices.
R. J. S. STEVENS, about 1790. Four male voices.
J. STAFFORD SMITH, about 1792. Glee : One Alto, Two Tenors, One Bass. In Caulfield's Collection.
WM. LINLEY, 1816. Two Sopranos and One Bass. An arrangement of J. S. Smith's Glee. Linley.
SIR HENRY BISHOP, 1824. Four male voices. A.T.T.B., in the operatized *Comedy of Errors*. In 'Shakspere Vocal Album' (1864), p. 219—for S.C.T.B. Pub. by Chappell.
*E. EDGAR, 1881. 'The horn, the horn.'

As You Like It, Act V. Scene iii. lines 14—31.

"IT WAS A LOVER, AND HIS LASSE."

[To the Clowne, (Touchstone,) and his country-wench, Audrey, whom he is about to marry.]

Enter two Pages.

1. *Page.*   Wel met, honeft Gentleman!
Clowne.   By my troth, well met!   Come, fit, fit, and a fong!
2. *Page.*   We are for you: fit i'th' middle!   8
1. *Page.*   Shal we clap into't roundly, without hauking, or
fpitting, or faying we are hoarfe? which are the onely prologues
to a bad voice.
2. *Page.*   I faith, y'faith! and both in a tune, like two gipfies on
a horfe.   13

                            Song.

It was a Louer, and his laſſe,
    With a hey, and a ho, and a hey nonino,
That o're the greene corne frild did paſſe,   16
    In the ſpring time, the onely pretty ring time,
    When Birds do ſing, hey ding a ding, ding :
    Sweet Louers loue the ſpring.   19

Betweene the acres of the Rie,
    With a hey, and a ho, & a hey nonino,
Theſe prettie Country folks would lie,   22
    In ſpring time, &c.

This Carroll they began that houre,
    With a hey, and a ho, & a hey nonino,
How that a life was but a Flower   26
    In ſpring time, &c.

And therefore take the preſent time'
    With a hey, & a ho, and a hey nonino ;
For Loue is crown'd with the prime   30
    In ſpring time, &c.

Clowne.   Truly, yong Gentlemen, though there was no great
matter in the dittie, yet y' note was very vntunable.   33
1. *Page.*   You are deceiu'd, Sir ; we kept time, we loft not our
time!
Clowne.   By my troth, yes : I count it but time loft, to heare
fuch a foolifh fong.   God buy[1] you! and God mend your voices!
¶ Come, *Audrie!*   [*Exeunt.* 38

MORLEY, 1600.   Solo.   In Chappell's 'Music of the Olden Time,' pp.
    204 and 704, and C. Knight's 'Shakspere'.   (Sung by Mr. Wilbey
    Cooper at the Crystal Palace, 23 April, 1859.—Rofle.)
R. J. S. STEVENS, 1786.   Glee, S.S.A.T.B.   Novello.
WM. LINLEY, 1816.   Duet, S.C.
SIR HENRY BISHOP, 1824.   Soprano Solo.   Sung by Miss M. Tree in
    the operatized *Comedy of Errors.*—Rofle.
S. REAY, 1862.   Madrigal.   Novello.
EDWARD LODER, 1864.   Part Song.
*F. STANISLAUS, 1868.   Solo, Soprano or Tenor.   Ashdown.
*G. A. MACFARREN, 1869.   Part Song, S.A.T.B.   Novello.

                    [1] *buy* = be with.

8   AS YOU LIKE IT.

*H. HILES, 1870. S.A.T.B. Novello.
*C. H. HUBERT PARRY, 1874. 'Spring Song.' 'A Garland,' No. 2. Contralto. Sung by Madame Ant. Sterling. Boosey.
*M. B. FOSTER, 1876. Solo, Contralto. Alfred Phillips. Kilburn.
*J. MEISSLER, 1877.
*OTTO PEINIGER, 1878. Song. Two Ditties, No. 2. Lucas & Weber.
*C. LAHMEYER, 1881. 'In the spring time.'
*D. DAVIES. Part Song. First sung May 7, 1883, at the Highbury Philharmonic Society.
*DR. J. C. BRIDGE, Nov. 1883. Part Song, S.A.T.B. Novello.
*B. LUARD SELBY. Part Song. Novello.
*J. BOOTH. Part Song. Novello.
*MICHAEL WATSON. Part Song, S.A.T.B. Ashdown.

As You Like It, Act. V. Scene iv. lines 101—8.

"THEN IS THERE MIRTH IN HEAVEN."

[Rosalind is the Duke's daughter, and is to wed Orlando. To the Duke, Orlando, and their fellows,]

Enter HYMEN, ROSALIND, *and* CELIA.

Still Muficke.

Hymen. *Then is there mirth in heauen,*
When earthly things made eauen
    Attone together.   103
Good Duke, receiue thy daughter !
Hymen *from Heauen brought her,*
    (Yea, brought her hether,)   106
That thou mightft ioyne hir hand with his,
Whofe heart within his bofome is.   108

DR. T. A. ARNE, 1740. Song.
SIR HENRY BISHOP, 1824. Song. Sung by Master Longhurst in the operatized *As You Like It*, p. 73.
    In his setting of the operatized *Two Gentlemen of Verona*, 1821, Sir H. Bishop has, at p. 81-91, first a Soprano Solo, of the first four lines of Sonnet 25, then a Chorus made up of lines 104-5 above, part of the Hymen song below,[1] and then a duet, one Soprano taking the first four lines of *Sonnet* 25, the other, the first four of *Sonnet* 97. See *Sonnet* 97, below.

As You Like It, Act V. Scene iv. lines 134—9.

"WEDDING IS GREAT JUNO'S CROWNE."

[To the 4 couples about to wed,—Orlando and Rosalind, Oliver and Celia, the Shepheard and Phebe, and the Clowne Touchstone and Audrey,—Hymen says :]

---
[1] Good Duke ! receive thy Daughter !
Hymen, from heaven brought her.
Such Union is great Juno's crown :
To Hymen, honour and renown !

Here's eight that muſt take hands,
To ioyne in *Hymens* bands, 122

* * * * * *

Whiles a Wedlocke Hymne we ſing,
Feede your ſelues with queſtioning ; 131
That reaſon, wonder may diminiſh
How thus we met, and theſe things finiſh ! 133

Song.

Wedding is great Iunos *crowne :* 134
O bleſſed bond of boord and bed !
'Tis Hymen *peoples euerie towne ;*
High wedlock then be honorëd ! 137
Honor, high honor and renowne,
To Hymen, *God of euerie Towne !* 139

THOMAS CHILCOT, about 1740. Solo.
WM. LINLEY, 1816. Song. Linley's 'Dram. Songs of Shakspere.'
*B. TOURS, 1882. Part Song. Unpublished.

Comedy of Errors.

Act II. Scene ii. lines 187—191.

"OH, FOR MY BEADS! I CROSSE ME FOR A SINNER."

[This is not a song, but two couplets and a half of rymed verse. The slave Dromio of Syracuse, not able to underſtand how he is mistaken for his twin-brother slave of Ephesus (of whom he has never heard), or how his master—Antipholus of Syracuse—is supposed to be that master's twin-brother of Ephesus, of whose existence he has never been told, declares that he and his Master must be in ' Fairie-land ' :]

Luciana. Dromio, goe bid the ſeruants ſpred for dinner !
Syr. Dromio. [*aside*] Oh, for my beads ! I croſſe me for a ſinner.
This is the Fairie land : oh, ſpight of ſpights !
We talke with Goblins, Owles, and Sprights ; 189
If we obay them not, this will inſue :
They'll ſucke our breath, or pinch vs blacke and blew. 191

DR. KEMP, d. 1824. Solo, Tenor, in Dr. K.'s 'Illustrations of Shakspere.'

Cymbeline.

Act II. Scene iii. lines 21—27.

"HEARKE! HEARKE! THE LARKE AT HEAVEN'S GATE SINGS."

[The foolish lout, Prince Cloten, serenades the perfect Imogen, (wife of Posthumus,) with whom he fancies he is in love.]

Cloten. I would this Muficke would come! I am aduifed to giue her Muficke a mornings; they fay it will penetrate.

Enter Mufitians.

Come on! tune! If you can penetrate her with your fingering, fo; wee'l try with tongue too: if none will do, let her remaine; but Ile neuer giue o're. Firft, a very excellent good conceyted thing; after, a wonderful fweet aire, with admirable rich words to it; and then let her confider.

Song.

Hearke! *hearke! the Larke at Heauens gate fings,*   21
    and Phœbus 'gins arife,
His Steeds *to water at thofe Springs*
    on chalic'd Flowres that lyes;   24
And winking Mary-buds begin to ope their Golden eyes.
With euery thing that pretty is[1]*, my Lady fweet, arife!*
    Arife, arife!   27

THOMAS CHILCOT, about 1750. Solo.
THEODORE AYLWARD, 1770. Solo. (Key of Eb; from lower B to upper Ab.) Sung by Mrs. Vincent.
DR. BENJAMIN COOKE, 1792. Glee for S.A.T.B. Novello.
K. F. CURSCHMAN (d. 1841). Solo. Publ. 1851.
FRANZ SCHUBERT (d. 1828). Solo. Publ. 1842, 1851, 1856, &c. In Chappell's 'Thirteen Standard Songs of Shakspere,' No. 11.
*T. KÜCKEN. Part Song. S.A.T.B. Novello.
*F. MOCHRING, 1865. 'Horch, horch, die Lerch', im Aether blau.' '6 Gesänge,' No. 4.
*HENRY LESLIE, 1867. An arrangement of Dr. Cooke's Glee for S.S.A.A. Novello.
*G. A. MACFARREN, 1869. Part Song. S.A.T.B. Novello.
*R. EMMERICH, 1874. 'Horch, horch, die Lerch', im Aether blau.' 'Fünf Gesänge,' &c. Op. 42, No. 1. Ständchen.
*E. H. THORNE. Part Song. S.S.C. Novello.

Cymbeline, Act IV. Scene ii. lines 258—281.

"FEARE NO MORE THE HEATE O' TH' SUN."

[Guiderius and Arviragus—seemingly peasant lads, but really the sons of King Cymbeline—sing over the apparently dead body of their unknown sister Imogen, disguised as a page, the Dirge which they had formerly sung over the corpse of their supposed mother Euriphile.]

Song.

Guiderius.   *Feare no more the heate o'th'Sun,*   258
       Nor the furious Winters rages!
       Thou thy worldly tafk hafl don,
       Home art gon, and tane thy wages.   261

[1] One of the song-writers, seeing that the plural *him* (hem) would ryme with 'begin' in l. 25, has, in spite of grammar, put *him* here.

	Golden Lads and Girles all muſt,	
	As Chimney-Sweepers, come to duſt.	263
Aruiragus.	*Feare no more the frowne o'th'Great!*	264
	Thou art paſt the Tirants ſtroake.	
	Care no more to cloath and eate!	
	To thee, the Reede is as the Oake :	267
	The Scepter, Learning, Phyſicke, muſt	
	All follow this, and come to duſt.	269
Guiderius.	*Feare no more the Lightning flaſh,*	270
Aruiragus.	*Nor th'all-dreaded Thunderſtone!*	
Guiderius.	*Feare not Slander, Cenſure raſh ;*	
Aruiragus.	*Thou haſt finiſh'd Ioy and Mone'*	273
Both.	*All Louers young, all Louers muſt*	
	Conſigne to thee, and come to duſt.	275
Guiderius.	*No Exorciſor harme thee!*	
Aruiragus.	*Nor no witch-craft charme thee!*	277
Guiderius.	*Ghoſt vnlaid forbeare thee!*	
Aruiragus.	*Nothing ill come neere thee!*	279
Both.	*Quiet conſumation haue ;*	
	And renownèd be thy graue!	281

DR. T. A. ARNE, (? ab. 1740). Solo. Sung by Mr. Lowe.
Name unknown. ? 1746. See Geneste, vol. iv. p. 193. Solo. In G
  major. Caulfield's Collection.
DR. BOYCE, 1758. (? Solo, or Glee. See Warren's 'Life of Boyce.')
  Called 'The Dirge in *Cymbeline*.'
*DR. NARES, d. 1783. Glee for A.T.B. Warren's 'Collection of Glees,
  &c.' Vol. II. and Cramer.
DR. NARES, d. 1783, and W. LINLEY, 1816. Trio for equal voices.
*G. A. MACFARREN, 1864. S.A.T.B. Choral Songs, No. 6. Novello.
*F. M. HAYES, 1881. 'The Dirge of Fidele.'
*JAMES GREENHILL, 1884. Part Song, S.C.T.B. *In Memoriam* Miss
  TEENA ROCHFORT SMITH, died Sept. 4, 1883.

Hamlet, Prince of Denmark.

Act II. Sc. ii. ll. 116—119. (Qo. 2, sig. E 4.)

"DOUBT THOU THE STARRES ARE FIRE."

[Hamlet's Letter to Ophelia.]

Letter.
Doubt thou the Starres are fire ;   116
Doubt that the Sunne doth moue ;
Doubt Truth to be a lyer ;
But neuer doubt I loue!   119

W. TINDAL, 1786. Op. 5. Solo Tenor. With an accompaniment
for Flute, Violin, and Violoncello. 'Eight Ancient Ballads,' No. 8.
(A 2nd verse added, not by Shakspere.)

R. J. S. STEVENS, 1790. Solo. With an accompaniment for two Flutes,
    two Violins, and one Bass.
Ditto. The same melody harmonized as a Glee.
J. FISIN, 1800 (?). Solo. 'Ten Songs,' No. 3. With an added verse.
C. DIGNUM, ab. 1800. Solo Tenor. (With a 2nd verse by Dr. Moore.)
M. KELLY, ab. 1800. Soprano Solo. Composed for Miss Abrams. 'Shak-
    spere Vocal Album,' p. 56. (The lines are enlarged, and a verse is
    added. Line 1 is, 'Doubt, O most beautiful, that the stars are fire,'
    &c. &c.)
WM. RUSSELL. ab. 1806 (1808, B. Mus. Cat.). Solo Tenor. Dedicated
    to Mr. J. P. Kemble.
DR. J. KEMP, 1814. Tenor. Accomp. for Violoncello and Piano.
    'Musical Illustrations of Shakspere,' by Dr. Kemp.
EDMUND KEAN. See Proctor's Life of E. Kean.—Roffe, p. 26.
SIR JOHN STEVENSON. Glee for two Tenors and one Bass.
J. DAVY, 1820. Duet for equal voices.
J. PARRY. 1824. Tenor Recitative and Air. Sung by Braham in the
    operatised *Merry Wives of Windsor.*

Hamlet, Act III. Scene ii. lines 282-5.

"WHY, LET THE STROOKEN DEERE GOE WEEPE."

[After the Play-scene, when the guilty Claudius has rusht from
the Hall, Hamlet says (Quarto 2, sign. H 3) :]

> " *Why, let the strooken Deere goe weepe,*   282
>   *The Hart vngauled play ;*
>   *For some must watch, while some must sleepe*
>   *Thus runnes the World away.*"   285

M. P. KING, 1803. Glee for three voices, unaccompanied.

SNATCHES OF OPHELIA'S SONGS. (IV. ii. Qo. 2, sign. K. 4.)

Hamlet, Act IV. Scene v. lines 23-30, 35. 37-39. (Qo. 2, sign. K. 4.)

"HOW SHOULD I YOUR TRUE LOVE KNOW?"

Shee sings.

Ophelia [mad]. *How should I your true **Loue know**,*   23
                    from another one ?
                By his Cockle hat and staffe,
                    and his Sendall shoone.   26
        *   *   *   *   *
                He is dead and gone, Lady !   27
                    he is dead and gone !
                *At his head, a grasgreene **turph** ;*
                    at his heeles, a stone.   30
        *   *   *   *   *

White his shroud as the mountaine snow   35
Larded all with sweet flowers;   37
Which beweept to the ground did go
With true-loue showers.   39

*Old Melody. In Chappell's 'Music of the Olden Time,' p. 236. Linley's 'Dramatic Songs,' &c., Vol. ii. p. 50. Caulfield, Vol. ii. p. 83. Charles Knight's *Shakspere.* George Nicks, 'Ophelia's Airs in *Hamlet,*' as sung by Miss Stephens. *Chappell's 'Thirteen Standard Songs of Shakspere,' No. 13.
SIR J. STEVENSON. 1789. Glee for two Sopranos and one Bass.
M. V. WHITE, 1882. Solo. 1876 (?) (Known as "Ophelia's Song.") Boosey.

<hr>

"THEY BORE HIM BARE-FASTE ON THE BEERE."

Hamlet, IV. ii.   (Qo. 2, sign. K. 4.)   Song.

They bore him bare-faste on the Beere,   164
(Hey non, nony; nony, hey nony! [Fo. 1])
And in his graue rain'd many a teare   166

*   *   *   *   *

Old Melody, in Caulfield. Knight. G. Nicks. Chappell's 'Songs.'
*W. Linley, 1816. Song. Linley's 'Dramatic Songs,' &c., Vol. ii. p. 51.

<hr>

"BONNY SWEET ROBIN."

Hamlet, IV. ii.   (Qo. 2, sign. K. 4.)   Song.

For bonny sweet Robin *is all my ioy.*   187

*   *   *   *   *

Old Melody. See Chappell's 'Popular Music,' p. 233, to be found in
*ANTHONY HOLBORNE'S 'Cittharn Schoole,' 1597.
*QUEEN ELIZABETH'S 'Virginal Book.'
*WILLIAM BALLET'S 'Lute Book.'
[Repeated in Caulfield, Linley, C. Knight, G. Nicks. *Chappell's 'Thirteen Songs.']

<hr>

"AND WILL A NOT COME AGAIN?"

Hamlet, IV. ii.   (Qo. 2, sign. L. 2.)   Song.

And wil a not come againe?   190
And wil a not come againe?
No, no! he is dead!
Goe to thy death bed!
He neuer will come againe!   194

His beard was as white as snow,   195
Flaxen was his pole.
He is gone, he is gone!
And we caft away mone.
God a mercy on his foule!   199

*Old Melody. "The tune entitled *Merry Milkmaids* in 'The Dancing Master,' 1650." (Chappell, p. 237.)
[Caulfield, Linley, C. Knight, G. Nicks. Chappell's 'Thirteen Songs.']
SIR JN. A. STEVENSON, 1800 (?). Glee, S.S.B.

Hamlet, IV. v. 48—55, 58—65.   Song.

"TO-MORROW IS S. VALENTINE'S DAY."

To morrow is S. Valentines day,   48
    All in the morning betime ;
    And I a mayde, at your window,
      To be your Valentine.   51
Then vp he rose, and dond his close,   52
    and dupt the chamber doore ;
    Let in the maide, that out a maide,
      neuer departed more.   55

   *   *   *   *   *

By Gis,[1] and by Saint Charitie,   58
    alack, and fie, for shame !
Young men will doo 't, if they come too 't ;
    by Cock,[2] they are to blame !   61
Quoth she, ' *Before you tumbled me,*   62
      you promisd me to wed.'
(He anfwers.) ' *So would I a done, by yonder funne,*
      And thou hadst not come to my bed.'   65

Old air in Chappell's ' Popular Music,' p. 227.
*Old Melody. ' Quaker's Opera,' 1728.
*Cobbler's Opera, 1729. (See Chappell, p. 227.)
[Repeated in Linley, Caulfield, C. Knight, G. Nicks. Chappell's
    'Thirteen Songs.']

Hamlet, Act V. Scene i. lines 69—72, 79—82, 102—5. (Qo. 2, sign. M. 2.)

STANZAS FOR GRAVE-DIGGER.

Song.

Clowne.   In Youth, when I did loue, did loue,   69
      Me thought it was very sweet,
      To cóntract, ô, the time ; for, A ! my behoue,
      O, me thought, there was nothing a meet.   72

   *   *   *   *   *

      But Age, with his stealing steppes,   79
      hath clawed me in his clutch,
      And hath shipped me into the land,
      as if I had neuer been fuch.   82

   *   *   *   *   *

[1] *Gis* is a contraction for *Jesus.*   [2] God.

A pickax, and a fpade, a fpade,   102
for and a fhrowding fheet;
O, a pit of Clay for to be made
for fuch a gueft is meet.   105

Chappell's ' Music of the Olden Time,' vol. i. p. 201.
Name unknown.   Caulfield's Collection, vol. ii. p. 90.

King Henry the Fourth.

PART I.

Act III. Scene i. lines 214,[1] 216, 217.   (Quarto 1, sign. F. 3.)

"SHE BIDS YOU ON THE WANTON RUSHES."

[Lord Mortimer speaks lovingly to his sweetheart, the daughter
of his fellow-oppoſer of Henry IV., Owen Glendower, who can only
speak Welſh.   She answers him, and her father interprets her answer
to her lover.]

The Ladie fpeakes againe in Welfh.

Mortimer.   O, I am ignorance itfelfe in this.

Glendower.   She bids you on the wanton ruthes lay you downe,
And reſt your head vpon her lap,   215
And fhe will fing the fong that pleafeth you,
Charming your bloud with pleafing heauineſſe;
Making fuch difference twixt wake and fleepe,   218
As is the difference betwixt day and night,
The houre before the heauenly harueſt teeme
Begins his golden progreſſe in the eaſt.   221

*L. J. ROGERS, 1878.   Part Song, S.A.T.B.   Novello

King Henry the Fourth.

PART II.

Act IV. Scene iv. lines 81-2, with 2 other bits.

"HEALTH TO MY SOUERAIGNE."

Weftmerland (to HEN. IV.).   Health to my Soueraigne, and new
   happineſſe
Added to that [that I am to deliuer . . .]
. . . an Oliue Branche, and Lawrell Crowne [3 *Henry VI.*. IV. vi. 34]
A Foe to Tyrauts, and my Countries Friend [Cato, in *Julius Cæsar*,
   V. iv. 5].

**WILLIAM SHIELD, 1809.   A Cento for three voices.   In 'A Cento,'
   p. 2, calld 'The King.   A Cento taken from the Works of
   Shakespeare.'*

¹ Line 215 is not set.

Act V. Scene iii. lines 18—23, 35—9, 48—50, 56, 7, 77—9, 134. (Quarto 1,
sign. K. 2.)

"DO NOTHING BUT EATE, AND MAKE GOOD CHEERE."

Scilens. [*somewhat cupshotten*] A, sirra (quoth-a) we shall

[*sings*] *Do nothing but eate, and make good cheere,*   18
      And praise God for the merry yeere,
      When flesh is cheape, and Females deare,
      And lusty Laddes roame here and there   21
        So merely ;
        And euer among, so merily !   23

    *   *   *   *

Scilens. *Be merry, be merry ! my Wife has all '*   35
      For women are Shrowes, both short and tall,
      'Tis merry in Hall, when Beards wagge[1] all !   37
        And welcome merry Shrouetide !
      Be mery ! be mery !   39

    *   *   *   *

Scilens. *A Cup of Wine, thats briske and fine,*   48
      And drinke vnto the Leman mine !
        And a mery heart liues long-a.   50

    *   *   *   *

      Fill the Cuppe, and let it come !
      Ile pledge you a mile to the[2] bottome.   57
      Silens. Do me right,   77
        and dub me Knight !
          Samingo !   79

    *   *   *   *

Falstaffe. Carry Master *Scilens* to bed !   134

Anonymous. Solo and Chorus in three parts. In Caulfield's Collection ;
  l. 22-3 omitted.
*W. LINLEY, 1816. Tenor Solo, with l. 22-3 and the two following
  snatches, l. 35-9, 48-50. Linley's 'Sh.'s Dramatic Songs,' ii. 34-6.
*SIR H. R. BISHOP, 1820. Introduced in operatized *Twelfth Night.*

𝕶𝖎𝖓𝖌 𝕳𝖊𝖓𝖗𝖞 𝖙𝖍𝖊 𝕰𝖎𝖌𝖍𝖙𝖍.

Act III. Scene i. lines 3—14

"ORPHEUS WITH HIS LUTE MADE TREES."

By John Fletcher. (III. i. is part of the Fletcher portion of
Henry VIII. Shakspere wrote only $1168\frac{1}{2}$ of the 2822 lines of the
play. The rest are Fletcher's.)

   [1] *Hall .. wagge*] F. hal .. wags Q.   [2] *to the* Quarto. *tee th'* Folio.

Enter QUEENE, *and her* Women *as at worke.*

Queene. Take thy Lute, wench! My Soule growes fad with
troubles!
Sing, and difperfe 'em, if thou canft : leaue working!

Song.

Orpheus *with his Lute made Trees,*   3
And the Mountaine tops that freeze,
Bow themfelues when he did fing.   5
To his Muficke, Plants and Flowers
Euer fprung ; as Sunne and Showers
There had made a lafting Spring.   8

Euery thing that heard him play,   9
Euen the Billowes of the Sea,
Hung their heads, & then la ly.   11
In fweet Muficke is fuch Art, [tha.]
Killing care, & griefe of heart,
Fall afleepe, or hearing, dye.   14

DR. ARNE? (ab. 1740). Song. Caulfield's Collection.
DR. M. GREENE, 1741.* [1742 in B. Mus. Catal.] Song. 'A Cantata
   and four Englifh Songs,' by Dr. Greene.
THOMAS CHILCOT (? ab. 1750). Song.
MATTHEW LOCKE (? ab. 1755).
J. CHRISTOPHER SMITH, 1755. In ' The Fairies.'
R. J. S. STEVENS (? ab. 1790). Glee for five voices.
LORD MORNINGTON. Died 1781. Four-part Madrigal.
THOMAS LINLEY, November, 1788. Song. Sung by Mrs. Crouch.
   Music destroyed at the burning of Drury Lane Theatre.
W. LINLEY, 1816. Song, Soprano.
SIR HENRY BISHOP, 1820. Duet, Soprano and Contralto. Originally
   sung by Misses Greene and M. Tree in *Twelfth Night.* 'Shakspere
   Vocal Album' (1864), p. 197. In Chappell's 'Popular English
   Duets,' ed. Na. Macfarren, No. 5.
JOHN L. HATTON, 1855. Duet, Soprano and Contralto.
VIRGINIA GABRIEL, 1862. Song. 'Shakspere Vocal Album,' p. 150.
*E. B. GILBERT, 1863. Part Song, S.A.T.B. Chappell's 'Vocal
   Library,' No. 25.
SIR G. A. MACFARREN, 1864. Four-part Song, S.A.T.B. 'Choral
   Songs,' No. 1. Novello.
SIR ARTHUR SULLIVAN, 1865. Song, Soprano or Tenor. Metzler.
E. D. HEATHCOTE, 1866. Song.
*ALWYN, W. C., 1875. Song.
*DR. JOHN PARK, 1876. Song.
*E. LASSEN, 1877. Song. German translation.
*R. PAYNE, 1881 to 1882. Duet or Part Song. [Rogers, a country
   publisher.]
*E. ASPA. Song. Novello.
*G. BENSON. Part Song, A.T.T.B. Novello.

                                                              C

King Lear.

Act I. Sc. iv. lines 181-184, 191-194, 217, 218, 235, 236.

FOUR SNATCHES SUNG BY THE FOOL.

Foole.   1. *Fooles had nere lesse grace in a yeere;*   181
For wisemen are growne foppish,
And know not how their wits to weare,
Their manners are so apish.   184

2. *Then they for sodaine ioy did weepe,*   191
And I for sorrow sung,
That such a King should play bo-peepe,
And goe the Foole among.   194

3. *He that keepes nor crust, nor crum,*
Weary of all, shall want some.   218
4. *The Hedge-Sparrow fed the Cuckoo so long,*
That it's had it[1] *head bit off by it young.*   236

(The two alternates, "The lord that counsell'd thee," ll. 154—
161, which are only in the Quarto, have not been set. They are
said, not sung, in the play.)

Numbers 1, 2, 3, 4. In Caulfield's Collection. Numbers 1 and 2, by
W. LINLEY, 1816, in L's. 'Dramatic Songs of Sh.' ii. 47-9.

Lear, Act II. Scene iv. lines 48—53, 79—86.

TWO SNATCHES FOR THE FOOL.

1. *Fathers that weare rags,*   48
do make their Children blind ;
But Fathers that beare bags,
shall see their Children kind.   51
Fortune, that arrant Whore,
Nere turns the key to th' Poore.   53

2. *That Sir, which serues and seekes for* **gaine**,   79
And followes but for forme,
Will packe, when it begins to **raine**,
And leaue thee in the storme.   82
But I will tarry : the Foole will stay ;
And let the wiseman flie :
The knaue turnes Foole that runnes away ;
The Foole no knaue, perdie!   86

In Caulfield's Collection.

---

[1] 'it' was one of the Elizabethan substitutes for the A.Sax. genitive neuter *his*.

Lear, Act III. Scene iv. lines 125-9.

"ST. WITHOLD FOOTED THRICE THE WOLD¹."

[Sung by Edgar when personating a 'Bedlam'.]

Edgar. *S. Withold footed thrice the old ;*
He met the Night-Mare, and her nine-fold :   126
  Bid her alight,
  And her troth-plight ; ²   128
And, aroynt thee, Witch! aroynt thee!

SIR HENRY BISHOP, 1819.   Duet, two Tenors.   Sung in the *Comedy of
Errors* by Mr. Pyne and Mr. Durusett.

𝕷𝖔𝖛𝖊'𝖘 𝕷𝖆𝖇𝖔𝖚𝖗'𝖘 𝕷𝖔𝖘𝖙.

Act IV. Scene ii. lines 95-108.

"IF LOVE MAKE ME FORSWORNE, HOW SHALL I SWEARE TO LOVE?"

[NATHANIEL reads BEROWNE'S 6-measure Sonnet to ROSALIN.]

If Loue make me forfworne, how fhall I fweare to loue ?   95
  Ah! neuer fayth could hold, yf not to beautie vowed.
Though to my felfe forfworne, to thee Ile faythfull proue ;
  Thofe thoughts to me were Okes, to thee like Ofiers bowed.   98
Studie his byas leaues, and makes his booke thine eyes,   99
  Where all thofe pleafures liue, that Art would comprehend.
If knowledge be the marke, to know thee fhall fuffife
  Well learned is that tongue, that well can thee commend ;   102
All ignorant that foule, that fees thee without wonder ;   103
  Which is to mee fome prayfe, that I thy partes admire :
Thy eie, Ioues lightning beares : thy voyce, his dreadful thunder,
  Which, not to anger bent, is mufique, and fweete fier.   106
  Celeftiall as thou art, Oh pardon loue this wrong,
  That finges heauens prayfe, with fuch an earthly tong.   108

JOHN MAJOR, about 1820.   Solo, Tenor.   'Shakspere Vocal Album,'
p. 108.
R. HUGHES, about 1840.   Solo, Bass.   Sung by Mr. Bland.

¹ *Old*, Folio 1.   ² sweetheart, groom.

C 2

Love's Labour's Lost, Act IV. Sc. iii. ll. 25—40, 58—71.

[The two following Sonnets do not seem to have been set.]

The KING reades his Sonnet, to be sent to the PRINCESSE.

"*So sweete a kiſſe, the golden Sunne giues not*   25
  To thoſe freſh morning dropps vpon the Roſe,
As thy eye-beames, when their freſh rayſe haue ſmot
  The night of dew, that on my cheekes downe floures.   28
Nor ſhines the ſiluer Moone one halfe ſo bright,   29
  Through the tranſparent buſome of the deepe,
As doth thy face, through teares of mine, giue light :
  Thou ſhinſt in euerie teare that I do weepe ;   32
No drop, but, as a Coach, doth carrie thee ;   33
  So ridſt thou triumphing in my wo.
Do but beholde the teares that ſwell in me,
  And they, thy glorie, through my griefe, will ſhew :   36
But do not loue thy ſelfe ! then thou will keepe
  My teares for gloſſes, and ſtill make me weepe.   38
O Queene of queenes ! how farre dooſt thou excell,
  No thought can thinke, nor tongue of mortal tell !"   40

───────

[LONGAVILL reades his Sonnet, to be ſent to MARIA.]

"*Did not the heauenly Rhetorique of thine eye,*   58
  Gainſt whom the world cannot holde argument,
Perſwade my hart to this falſe periurie ?
  Vowes for thee broke, deſerue not puniſhment.   61
A Woman, I forſwore ; but I will proue,   62
  Thou being a Goddeſſe, I forſwore not thee.
My Vow was earthly ; thou, a heauenly Loue !
  Thy grace being gainde, cures all diſgrace in mee.   65
Vowes are but breath ; and breath a vapoure is :   66
  Then thou, faire Sunne, which on my earth dooſt ſhine,
Exhaiſt this vapour-vow ; in thee it is :
  If broken then, it is no fault of mine :   69
If by mee broke, What foole is not ſo wiſe,
  To looſe an oth, to winn a Parradiſe ?"   71

───────

Love's Labour's Lost, Act IV. Scene iii. Lines 99—118.   (Also in
                  The Paſſionate Pilgrim.)

"ON A DAY (ALACKE THE DAY!")

[DUMAINE reades his Sonnet.]

  "*On a day, (alacke the day !)*
   Loue, whoſe Month is euer May,   100

Spied a blossome passing faire,
Playing in the wanton aire :   102
Through the Veluet leaues, the wind,
All vnseene, can passage finde ;   104
That the Louer, sicke to death,
Wish himselfe the heauens breath.   106
' Ayre,' (quoth he), ' thy cheekes may blow ;
Ayre, would I might triumph so !   108
But, alacke, my hand is sworne,
Nere to plucke thee from thy thorne :   110
Vow, alacke, for youth vnmeete,
Youth so apt to pluck a sweete !   112
Do not call it sinne in me,
That I am forsworne for thee ;   114
Thou, for whom Ioue would sweare,
Iuno but an Æthiop were ;   116
And denie himselfe for loue,
Turning mortall for thy loue.' "   118

THOMAS CHILCOT, 1750. Solo.
DR. T. A. ARNE (?ab. 1750). Solo. Caulfield's Collection.
JN. CHRISTOPHER SMITH, 1755. Solo, Contralto. In "The Fairies."
WILLIAM JACKSON. Three male voices.
T. LYON. about 1790. Four voices. 'Six Canzonets' (1795 ?).
M. P. KING. Duet, Tenor and Bass, or Soprano and Bass. Commences,
    " Do not call it sin in me."
JOHN BRAHAM. (See Roffe, p. 36.)
SIR HENRY BISHOP, 1821. Duet, S.C. Sung by Misses M. Tree and
    Hallande, in Two Gent. of Verona. 'Shakspere Vocal Album'
    (1864), p. 176.
W. P. STEVENS, 1852. Glee for four male voices.
*T. D. SULLIVAN, 1864. Quartette for Treble voices.
*ELLA, 1870. Song.
W. H. CUMMINGS, 1875. Part Song, S.A.T.B. Ashdown and Parry.
*C. H. HUBERT PARRY, about 1874. Song. 'A Garland,' No. 1. Boosey.
KELLOW J. PYE, 1879. 'To be sung in G, by a Tenor Voice.' (With
    "Good Night ! Good Rest !" in 'Two little Songs,' from the
    Passionate Pilgrim.)

_____

Love's Labour's Lost, Act IV. Scene iii. lines 318—29.

"A LOVER'S EYES WILL GAZE AN EAGLE BLINDE."

[Part of Berowne's speech, to prove to his Companions the wisdom
of breaking their vow to forswear the company of Women for three
years.]

    A Louers eyes will gaze an Eagle blinde ;
    A Louers eare will heare the lowest sound,
    When the suspitious head of theft is stopt.   320

Loues feeling, is more soft and senfible
Then are the tender hornes of Cockled Snayles.
Loues tongue, proues daintie Bachus groffe *in tafte.*
For Valoure, is not Loue a Hercules,   324
Still ciyming trees in the Hefperides?
Subtil as Sphinx; *as fweete and muficall*
As bright Appolos *Lute, ftrung with his haire.*
And when Loue fpeakes, the voyce of all the Goddes   328
Make heauen drowfie with the harmonie.

DR. KEMP, 1814. Solo with Violoncello accompaniment. Dr. Kemp's
'Illustrations of Shakspere.'
JOHN PARRY, 1824. Song. Sung by Mr. Braham in the *Merry Wives*
of Windsor.

Love's Labour's Lost, Act V. Scene ii. lines 877—912.

"WHEN DASIES PIED, AND VIOLETS BLEW."

[Sung after the show of the 'Nine Worthies' had been presented
before the King and the Princess.]

Re-enter all.

Braggart (ARMADO). This fide is *Hiems,* Winter ; This, *Ver,* the
Spring : The one maynteined by the Owle, th'other by the Cuckow.
❧ *Ver,* begin !

The Song.

Spring.

When Dafies pied, and Violets blew,   877
    And Ladi-fmockes all filuer white,
And Cuckow-budds of yellow hew,
    Do paint the Meadowes with delight,   880
The Cuckow then, on euerie tree,
Mocks married men ; for thus finges hee :   882
                                  Cuckow !

Cuckow, Cuckow ! *O word of feare,*
Vnpleafing to a married eare !   885
When Shepheards pipe on Oten Strawes,   886
    And merrie Larkes are Ploughmens Clockes,
When Turtles tread, and Rookes, and Dawes,
    And Maidens bleach their fummer fmockes,   889
The Cuckow then, on euerie tree,
Mockes married men ; for thus finges hee :   891
                                  Cuckow!

Cuckow, cuckow ! *O word of feare,*
Vnpleafing to a married eare !   894

RICHARD LEVERIDGE, 1725?, 1727. Solo. On a sheet in a vol. in
Brit. Mus. Lib. G 4¼ ; with the title 'The Cuckoo.'

DR. T. A. ARNE, 1740. Solo, Soprano. Sung by Mrs. Clive in *As You Like It*. 'Shakspere Vocal Album' (1864), p. 14.
JOHN STAFFORD SMITH, 1784. Glee for three male voices.
G. A. MACFARREN, 1864. Part Song, S.A.T.B. Novello. 'Choral Songs,' No. 4.
*RICHARD SIMPSON, about 186—; published 1878. Stanley Lucas.
*DR. JOHN PARK, 1876. Song.

"WHEN ISACLES HANG BY THE WALL."

Winter.

When Isacles hang by the wall,   895
  And Dicke the Sheepheard blowes his naile,
And Thom beares Logges into the hall,
  And Milke coms frozen home in paile,   898
When Blood is nipt, and wayes be fowle,
Then nightly singes the staring Owle,   900
                      Tu-whit, to-who!
  A merrie note,
  While greasie Ione doth keele the pot.   903

When all aloude the winde doth blow,   904
  And coffing drownes the Parsons saw,
And Birdes sit brooding in the Snow,
  And Marrians *nose lookes red and raw;*   907
When roasted Crabs hisse in the bowle,
Then nightly singes the staring Owle,   909
                      Tu-whit, to-who!
  A merrie note,
  While greasie Ione doth keele the pot.   912

DR. T. A. ARNE (ab. 1740?). Solo, Tenor or Bass. In 'Shakspere Vocal Album,' p. 75.
JOHN PERCY, composer of *Wapping Old Stairs*, d. 1797. Glee.
G. A. MACFARREN, 1864. Part Song, S.A.T.B. Novello. In 'Choral Songs,' No. 2.

Macbeth.

Act I. Scene i. lines 1—11.

"WHEN SHALL WE THREE MEET AGAINE?"

Thunder and Lightning.   Enter three Witches.

1. hen shall we three meet againe?
    In Thunder, Lightning, or in Raine?   2
    2. When the Hurley-burley's done,
    When the Battaile's loft, and wonne.
    3. That will be ere the set of Sunne.   5

1. Where the place?
2.   Vpon the **Heath.**
3. There to meet with *Macbeth.*   :
1. I come, *Gray-Malkin!*
2.   *Padock* calls.
3.   **Anon**!
All. Faire is foule, and foule is faire;
Houer through the fogge and filthie ayre!   [*Exeunt.*   11

M. P. KING, 1780. [1810, 1851, 1857, B. Mus. Cat.] Glee, S.S.B.
SAMUEL WEBBE. Two Baritones and one Bass.
*WILLIAM HORSLEY. Trio, S.S.B. Novello. Also as **a Song.** Cramer
    & Co.

Macbeth, Act IV. Scene i. lines 1—47.

"ROUND ABOUT THE CALDRON GO."

Thunder.   Enter the three Witches.

1. Thrice the brinded Cat hath mew'd.
2. Thrice, and once the Hedge-Pigge whin'd.
3. *Harpier*[1] cries, " 'tis time, 'tis time!"

1. Round about the Caldron go!
In, the poyſond Entrailes, throw!   5
Toad, (that vnder cold ſtone,
Dayes and Nights, ha's, thirty **one,**   7
Sweltred Venom, ſleeping got,)
Boyle thou firſt i'th'charmèd pot!   9
    All. Double, double, toile and trouble;
Fire burne, and Cauldron bubble!   11
    2. Fillet of a Fenny Snake,
In the Cauldron, boyle and bake!   13
Eye of Newt, and Toe of Frogge,
Wooll of Bat, and Tongue of Dogge;   15
Adders Forke, and Blinde-wormes Sting,
Lizards legge, **and** Howlets wing;   17
For a Charme of powrefull trouble,   18
Like a Hell-broth, boyle and bubble!
    All. **Double,** double, toyle and trouble;
Fire burne, and Cauldron bubble!   21
    3. Scale of Dragon, Tooth of Wolfe,
Witches Mummey, Maw and Gulfe   23
Of the rauin'd ſalt Sea ſharke;
Roote of Hemlocke, digg'd i'th'darke   25
Liuer of Blaſpheming Iew;
Gall of Goate, and Slippes of Yew,   27

[1] ? *Harpier* (Rom. type in F.) = Harper.

Sliuer'd in the Moones Ecclipse;
Nofe of *Turke*, and *Tartars* lips;   29
Finger of Birth-ftrangled Babe,
Ditch-deliuer'd by a Drab,
Make the Grewell thicke, and flab.   32
Adde thereto a Tigers Chawdron,[1]
For th'Ingredience of our Cawdron.   34
All. Double, double, toyle and trouble;
Fire burne, and Cauldron bubble!   36
2. Coole it with a Baboones blood!
Then the Charme is firme and good.   38

Enter HECAT, *to*[2] *the other three* Witches.

Hecat. O, well done! I commend your paines,
And euery one fhall fhare i'th'gaines: 40
And now about the Cauldron fing,
Like Elues and Fairies in a Ring,
Inchanting all that you put in.   43
　　　　　[Muficke and a Song.   Blacke Spirits, &c.
2. By the pricking of my Thumbes,
Something wicked this way comes: 45
Open, Lockes!
Who euer knockes.   47

Enter MACBETH.

M. P. KING, about 1800. Glee in three parts. Beginning, "Round
about the Caldron go."

Macbeth, Act IV. Scene i. lines 127—132.

"COME, SISTERS, CHEERE WE UP HIS SPRIGHTS!"

A fhew of eight Kings, (the Eighth with a glaffe in his hand,) and
BANQUO *laft.*

Macbeth. Thou art too like the Spirit of *Banquo:* Down!
Thy Crowne do's feare mine Eye-bals! ¶ And thy haire
Thou other Gold-bound-brow, is like the firft:
A third, is like the former. ¶ Filthy Hagges!
Why do you fhew me this?———A fourth? Start, eyes!
What, will the Line ftretch out to'th'cracke of Doome?
Another yet? A feauenth? Ile fee no more!
And yet the eighth[3] appeares, who beares a glaffe,
Which fhewes me many more: and fome, I fee,   120
That two-fold Balles, and trebble Scepters carry.
Horrible fight! Now I fee 'tis true;

---

　　　　[1] entrails.　　　　[2] *and* F.　　　　[3] eight, Fo.

For the Blood-bolter'd *Banquo* ſmiles vpon me,
And points at them for his.   [*They vaniſh.*]   ¶ What! is this ſo?
  1. I, Sir, all this is ſo.   But why
Stands *Macbeth* thus amazedly?

¶ Come, Siſters! cheere we vp his ſprights,
And ſhew the beſt of our delights!   128
Ile Charme the Ayre to giue a ſound,
While you performe your Antique round;   130
That this great King may kindly ſay,
Our duties did his welcome pay.   [*Muſicke.* 132
                          [*The Witches Dance, and vaniſh.*

  Macbeth.   Where are they? Gone? Let this pernitious houre
Stand aye accurſëd in the Kalender!

M. P. KING, about 1800.   Glee for three voices, and Chorus.

𝕸easure for 𝕸easure.

Act IV. Scene i. lines 1—8.

"TAKE, OH, TAKE THOSE LIPS AWAY!"

[The Moated Grange at S. Lukes.]

Enter MARIANA, *and* Boy *ſinging.*

Song.

Take, oh, take thoſe lips away,   1
  that ſo ſweetly were forſworne!
And thoſe eyes, the breake of day;
  lights that doe miſlead the Morne!   4
But, my kiſſes bring againe,
                          bring againe;   6
Scales of loue, but ſeal'd in vaine,
                          ſeal'd in vaine!   8

[Mariana has been deſerted by her baſe lover Angelo, because her
fortune was loſt.]

DR. JOHN WILSON.   Song.   Published, 1659, in John Playford's 'Select
    Airs and Dialogues.'   Bk. I. page 1.   The song is called 'Love's
    Ingratitude.'
JOHN WELDEN, about 1707.   Solo.   Col. of New Songs by Welden.
I. E. GALLIARD, 1730.   In a volume of the 'Musical Miscellany.'
THOMAS CHILCOT, 1750.   Solo, Soprano.
Name unknown.   See Roffe, p. 44.
CHRISTOPHER DIXON, 1760.   [1760? B. Mus. Cat.] Song.   Two English
    Cantatas and Four Songs by C. S.
W. N., 1770.   In the Library of the Sacred Harmonic Society.

G. GIORDANI, 1780. Glee for four voices.
G. GIORDANI, 1780. The same adapted for one voice and harpsichord.
J. S. SMITH, 1780. Glee for A.T.B.
W. JACKSON, soon after 1780. Duet. (Twelve Canzonets, No. 7.)
W. TINDAL, 1785. Duet : Soprano and Tenor. Six vocal pieces, No. 2.
   (Op. prima.)
T. TREMAIN, 1786. Duet. Thirteen Canzonets for two voices.
SIR JOHN STEVENSON, about 1795. Glee for four voices.
*L. ATTERBURY, died 1796. Round. Bland's 'Glee Collect.,' p. 215.
HON. A. BARRY, 1810. Three-voice Glee.
WM. LINLEY, 1816. Solo, Treble. Linley's 'Dram. Songs of Shaksp.'
   Vol. I. p. 36.
SIR HENRY BISHOP, 1819. Song, Soprano. Sung by Miss Stephens
   in the operatized 'Comedy of Errors.'
W. GARDINER, 1838. See 'Music and Friends,' by W. G.
F. LANCELOTT, 1858. Round. 'Cyclopedia of Music,' No. 12.
ALFRED MELLON, 1864. Song, Bass. Sung by Mr. Santley.
*C. A. MACIRONE, 1864. Song. Shakspere Vocal Magazine, No. 70.
*G. A. MACFARREN, 1869. Part Song, S.A.T.B. Novello.
*S. REAY, 1869. Part Song, S.A.T.B. Novello's Part Song Book.
   (Bk. 18 ; No. 169.)
*E. N. GRAZIA, 1872. Song. Weekes.
*JAMES COWARD, 1872. Solo. Cramer.
*FRANZ HÖFFER, 1873. Song, Baritone. 'Seven Songs, &c.' No. 3.
   Lucas and Weber.
*C. H. H. PARRY, 1875. 'Three Trios,' &c., No. 3. Song.
*A. H. D. PRENDERGAST, 1878. Part Song, A.T.T.B. Novello.
*J. GREENHILL, 1883. Song, for Tenor or Soprano.
*F. H. COWEN, 1884. Song. Compass F to F. [Composed for the
   Shaksperian Show, May 29th, 1884. 'Shaksperian Show-Book,'
   p. 62-3.)

Merchant of Venice.

Act II. Scene vii. lines 65—73.

"ALL THAT GLISTERS IS NOT GOLD."

Morrocho. [*opens the Golden Casket*] O hell ! what haue wee
   heare ?
A carrion Death, within whofe emptie eye
There is a written fcroule ! Ile reade the writing : [1]   64

---

[1] The lines in the 'fhedule' of the Silver Casket opend by Arragon
(II. ix.), and those in the 'fcroule' of the Leaden Casket opend by Bassanio
(III. ii.) do not seem to have been set to music. They follow here :—

Arragon. . . What is here ?

      [Reads] *The fier feauen times tried this,*   II. ix. 62
            " Seauen times tried " that iudgement is,
            That did neuer choofe amis,
            Some there be that fhadowes kis ;   65
            Such haue but a fhadowes blis.

[Reads] *" All that glifters is not gold!"*
Often haue you heard that told;   66
Many a man his life hath fold,
But my outfide to behold;   68
Guilded timbers wormes infold!
Had you beene as wife as bold,   70
Young in limbs, in iudgement old,
Your aunfwere had not beene injcrold,
" Fareyouwell! your fute is cold!"   73

CHARLES HORN, 1823. Duet, S.C. Sung in the *Merry Wives of Windsor.*

Merchant of Venice, Act III. Scene ii. lines 63—72

"TELL ME, WHERE IS FANCIE BRED?"

Here Muficke.

A Song, the whilft BASSANIO comments on the Cafkets to himfelfe.

(1)
Tell me, where is Fancie bred?
Or in the hart, or in the head?
How begot, how nourifhed?   65
Replie! replie!

There be fooles aliue, Iwis,
Siluer'd o're; and fo was this.   68
Take what wife you will to bed,
I will euer be your heed;
So be gone! you are fped!   II. ix. 71

Arragon. Still more foole I fhall appeare
By the time I linger heere.
With one fooles head I came to woo,
But I goe away with two.
[To PORTIA] Sweet, adiew!

Baffanio.   Heeres the fcroule,
The continent and fummarie of my fortune!

(1)
[Reads] *You that choofe not by the view,*   III. ii. 131
Chaunce as faire, and choofe as true!
Since this fortune falls to you,
Be content, and feeke no new!   134

(2)
If you be well pleafd with this,   135
And hold your fortune for your bliffe,
Turne you where your Lady is,
And claime her with a louing kis!   138

A gentle fcroule! ¶ Faire Lady! by your leaue!   [*kisses her.*

(2)

It is engendred in the eyes;
With gazing fed; and Fancie dies
In the cradle where it lies!   69

(3)

Let vs all ring Fancies knell!
He begin it: Ding, dong, bell!
All. Ding, dong, bell!   72

DR. T. A. ARNE, 1740. Solo. Sung by Mrs. Clive in *As You Like It.*
   Caulfield's Collection.
SIR J. STEVENSON, 1798. Duet. Tenor and Bass. Arranged for two
   Trebles by Sir H. R. Bishop. ('Shakspere Vocal Magazine,' No. 40.)
R. J. S. STEVENS, 1800. Three Sopranos and One Tenor; instrumental
   Bass.
*REV. L. RICHMOND, about 1810 or 1820. Round.
WM. LINLEY, 1816. Duet, with Chorus. Linley's 'Dramatic Songs of
   Shakspere.'
JOHN HATTON, 1855 (and 1859). Solo and Ladies' Chorus. Sung by
   Miss Poole in the *Merchant of Venice.*
*M. BARTHOLOMEW (MRS. MOUNSEY). Part-Song. S.A.T.B. Novello.
*G. A. MACFARREN, 1869. Part Song, S.A.T.B. Novello.
*J. ARTHUR HARCOURT, 1872. Song, Soprano or Tenor. Williams.
*B. LUETZEN, 1877. Duettino. Brighton.
*C. PINSUTI, about 1880. Part Song. A.T.T.B. Novello.
*C. PINSUTI. The same arranged for S.C.T.B.
*J. G. CALCOTT, 1883. Part Song. S.S.C. Novello.

—

Merchant of Venice, Act V. Scene i. lines 1—22.

"IN SUCH A NIGHT AS THIS."

[Belmont. Portia's Park.]

Enter LORENZO *and* JESSICA.

Lorenzo. The moone shines bright. In such a night as this,
When the sweet winde did gently kisse the trees,
And they did make no noyse; in such a night,
Troylus (me thinks) mounted the *Troian* walls,   4
And sigh'd his soule toward the *Grecian* tents
Where *Cressed* lay that night.
   Jessica.   In such a night,
Did *Thisbie* fearefully ore-trip the dewe,
And saw the Lyons shadow, ere him selfe,   8
And ranne dismayed away.

Lorenzo.   In fuch a night,
Stoode *Dido*, with a willow in her hand,
Vpon the wilde fea banks, and waft her Loue
To come againe to *Carthage.*
   Ieffica.   In fuch a night,   12
Medea gathered the inchanted hearbs
That did Renew old *Efon.*
   Lorenzo.   In fuch a night,
Did *Ieffica* fteale from the wealthy *Iewe*,
And, with an vnthrift Loue, did runne from *Venice*,   16
As farre as *Belmont.*
   Ieffica.   In fuch a night,
Did young *Lorenzo* fweare he lou'd her well,
Stealing her foule with many vowes of faith,
And nere a true one!
   Lorenzo.   In fuch a night,   2.
Did pretty *Ieffica* (like a little fhrow,)
Slander her Loue; and he forgaue it her.

SIR A. S. SULLIVAN, 1865. Duet for Soprano and Tenor. introduced
   into the Cantata of *Kenilworth.*
*C. GARDNER, 1878. Duet, Soprano and Baritone. Lucas and Weber.

Merchant of Venice, Act V. Scene i. lines 54-65.

"HOW SWEET THE MOONE-LIGHT SLEEPES
UPON THIS BANKE!"

[Lorenzo to Jessica, in Portia's park, by moonlight.]

How fweet the moone-light fleepes vpon this banke!
Heere will we fit, and let the founds of muficke
Creepe in our eares. foft ftilnes, and the night,   56
Become the tutches of fweet harmonie.
Sit, *Ieffica*! looke how the floore of Heauen
Is thicke inlayed with pattens of bright gold!
There's not the fmalleft orbe which thou beholdft,   60
But, in his motion, like an Angell, fings,
Still quiring to the young eyde Cherubins:
Such harmonie is in immortall foules!
But whilft this muddy vefture of decay   64
Dooth grofly clofe it in, we cannot heare it.

JOHN PERCY. Died, 1797. Solo.
CHARLES DIGNUM. 1800. Duet : Soprano, Tenor. In a volume of
   Mr. Dignum's compositions.
THOMAS HUTCHINSON, 1807. Duet : Soprano, Tenor.
M. P. KING, 1825 (?). Trio for three voices. Chappell, New Bond
   Street.

MISS E. NAYLOR, 1845. Duet.
*SIR A. S. SULLIVAN, 1865. Recitative for Tenor before the Duet for
   Soprano and Tenor, introduced into the Cantata of *Kenilworth.*
*HENRY LESLIE, 1866. Part Song. Novello.
*T. BLANCHARD. Song. Blockley, Junr., 3, Argyll Street, Regent Street.
*C. GARDNER, 1878. Duet, Soprano and Baritone. Lucas and Weber.
*J. G. CALCOTT, 1883. Part Song, S.C.T.B.B. First sung by Leslie's
   choir, Feb. 2, 1883.
*J. G. CALCOTT, 1883. The same arranged as a Trio, S.S.C. Patey
   and Willis.

Merchant of Venice, Act V. Scene i. lines 71—83.

"FOR DOE BUT NOTE A WILDE AND WANTON HEARD."

[Lorenzo, while sitting in Portia's park with Jessica in the moonlight,
   calls on the Musicians to play, and thus greet Portia on her
   home-coming from Venice.]

Come, hoe! and wake *Diana* with a himne!
With fweeteft tutches, pearce your Miftres eare,
And draw her home with mufique.   [*Play Mufique.* 68
  Ieffica. I am neuer merry, when I heare fweet mufique.
  Lorenzo. The reafon is, your fpirits are attentiue:

For doe but note a wilde and wanton heard
Or race of youthfull and vnhandled colts,   72
Fetching mad bounds, bellowing and neghing loud,
(Which is the hote condition of their blood;)
If they but heare perchance a Trumpet found,
Or any ayre of Mufique touch their ears,   76
You fhall perceaue them make a mutuall ftand,
Their fauage eyes turn'd to a modeft gaze,
By the fweet power of Mufique: therefore the Poet
Did faine that *Orpheus* drew trees, ftones, and floods;   80
Since naught fo ftockifh, hard, and full of rage,
But Mufique, for the time, doth change his nature:
The man that hath no Mufique in himfelfe,
Nor is not moued with concord of fweet founds,   84
Is fit for treafons, ftratagems, and fpoiles;
The motions of his fpirit are dull as night,
And his affections darke as *Erebus.*
Let no fuch man be trufted! marke the mufique!   88

T. COOKE, 1828. Part of this speech as a Solo, Tenor. Sung by
   Braham in the *Taming of a Shrew,* operatized. (See Geneste's
   English Stage, ix. 418.)

𝔐𝔢𝔯𝔯𝔶 𝔚𝔦𝔳𝔢𝔰 𝔬𝔣 𝔚𝔦𝔫𝔡𝔰𝔬𝔯.[1]

Act II. Scene ii. lines 186—7.

"LOVE LIKE A SHADOW FLIES, WHEN SUBSTANCE LOVE PURSUES."

[Ford, as Brooke, tells Falstaff, of his imaginary success-less pursuit of his own wife, whom he wishes Falstaff to try and corrupt.]

(181) "briefly, I haue purfu'd her, as Loue hath purfued mee, which hath beene on the wing of all occafions; but whattoeuer I haue merited, (either in my minde, or in my meanes,) meede (I am fure) I haue receiued none, vnletfe Experience be a Iewell that I haue purchafed at an infinite rate; and that hath taught mee to fay this:

> " Loue like a fhadow flies, when fulfiance Loue purfues,
> " Purfuing that that flies, and flying what purfues."   187

JOHN BRAHAM, 1824. Duet: Soprano and Tenor. Sung in *Merry Wives of Windsor*. (See the amusing account in Geneste's *English Stage*, ix. 234.)

EDWARD FITZWILLIAM, 1853. Solo. 'A Set of Songs.' No. 2.

Merry Wives, Act III. Scene i. lines 15—19. 21—24. (See *Pass. Pilgr.*)

"TO SHALLOW RIVERS."

[The Welsh Parson, Sir Hugh Evans, is waiting in vain in Windsor Park, near Frogmore, to fight a duel with the French physician, Dr. Caius, who has challenged him for backing his rival for the hand of 'sweet Anne Page'. To keep up his courage, he attempts to sing a snatch from Marlowe's song, *Come liue with me and be my loue*, (printed as Shakspere's by Iaggard in 1599; but given to Marlowe in *England's Helicon*, 1600) which, in the original, runs thus:

> "There will we fit vpon the Rocks,
> And fee the Shepheards feed their flocks.
> By fhallow Riuers, by whofe fals
> Melodious birds fing Madrigals.
> There will I make thee a bed of Rofes,
> With a thoufand fragrant pofes, &c.

In his nervous condition, Evans misquotes the words of the Song, and at last breaks down altogether. The mention of *Riuers*, however, recalls professional associations; so that, in his "trembling of minde," and with his "difpofitions to cry," he unconsciously mingles the sacred and the secular, by tacking on to Marlowe's verses the first line of the old metrical version of the 137th Psalm (*Super flumina*) —

---

[1] See O. Nicolai's *Die luftigen Weiber von Windsor*, komifche Oper nach Shakefpeares Lustfpiel, &c. 1853. folio.

" When we did sit in Babylon,
The rivers round about,
Then, in remembrance of Sion,
The tears for grief burst out."]

Euan. 'Pleſſe my ſoule! how full of Chollors I am, and trem-
pling of minde! I ſhall be glad if he haue deceiued me! How
melancholies I am! I will knog his Vrinalls about his knaues coſtard,
when I haue good oportunities for the orke! 'Pleſſe my ſoule!   14

[Sings] *To ſhallow Riuers, to whoſe falls,*
Melodious Birds ſings Madrigalls: 16
There will we make our Peds of Roſes,
And a thouſand fragrant poſies.   18
To ſhallow—

Mercie on mee! I haue a great diſpoſitions to cry—.

[Sings] *Melodious birds ſing Madrigalls:——*
When as I ſat in Pabilon:—   22
And a thouſand vagram Poſies.
To ſhallow, &c.

"Melody by an unknown author in a MS. as old as Shakspere's time."
(Sir John Hawkins's 'History of Music.') Reproduced in Charles
Knight's 'Shakspere.'

DR. JOHN WILSON, about 1600. This Melody is harmonized by Sir H.
Bishop, as "O by Rivers."

THOS. CHILCOT, about 1750. The whole Poem, *Come live with me, &c.*
(see *The Passionate Pilgrim*, below), set as a Song.

Name unknown, 1770. In the British Museum.

DR. SAMUEL ARNOLD, 1774. Song. Sung by Mr. Reinhold. In 'A
Collection of Songs sung at Vauxhall and Marylebone Gardens.'

DR. ARNE, 1777. Known as "A Favourite Scotch Air." Sung by Miss
Catley, in 'Love in a Village.'

SAMUEL WEBBE, about 1780. Glee for four male voices. A.T.T.B.

T. TREMAIN, 1786. Duet, two Sopranos, or two Tenors. 'A Book of
Canzonets,' by T. T.

F. DALBERG (Baron), 1790. Solo. 'Three English Songs and a Glee.'

THOMAS HUTCHINSON, 1807. Duet: Soprano and Contralto. Commences "Here will we sit." Hutchinson's Collection.

SIR HENRY BISHOP, 1819. Song. Sung by Miss Stephens in the
Comedy of Errors. 'Shakspere Vocal Album,' 1864.

*SIR H. R. BISHOP, 1820. As a Serenade for 5 Voices, S.S.A.T.B.
Adapted from Dr. Wilson and J. Saville, and introduced into the
operatized *Twelfth Night.* Shakspere's words freely altered.
Begins, *O, by rivers.*

W. TURNBULL, 1830. Song.

JOHN HATTON, 1855. Song, Tenor. Sung by Signor Mario.

JOHN HATTON. Part Song, S.A.T.B. Novello.

J. B. TURNER, 1859. Song.

DR. STERNDALE BENNETT, 1816—1875. Part Song. Mr. Hullah's
Collection. Hutchins and Romer.

Name Unknown. "To Shallow Rivers." Caulfield's Collection.

Merry Wives, Act V. Scene v. lines 92—8.

"FIE ON SINNEFULL PHANTASIE."

[Falstaffe, with a buck's head and horns on him, has come into Windsor Park to meet Mrs. Ford and Mrs. Page at Herne's Oak. Their friends, disguised as Fairies, &c, have surprised him, and he has thrown himself to the ground, face downwards. The Fairies have lighted their Tapers :]

> [*They put the Tapers to his fingers, and he starts.*
> *Falstaff.* Oh, oh, oh!
> *Queene* [Anne PAGE]. Corrupt, corrupt, and tainted in desire! 89
> About him, (Fairies,) sing a scornfull rime ;
> And as you trip, still pinch him to your time !   91

[*Here they pinch him, and sing about him, & the* Doctor *comes one way & steales away a* Fairy in White. *And* SLENDER *another way : he takes a* Fairy in Greene. *And* FENTON *steales* Misteris ANNE, *being in White.*

The Song.

> *Fie on sinnefull phantasie !   Fie on Lust, and Luxurie !*   92
> *Lust is but a bloudy fire, kindled with vnchaste desire,*
>   *Fed in heart whose flames aspire,*
>   *As thoughts do blow them higher and higher.*   95
> *Pinch him, (Fairies,) mutually !   Pinch him for his villanie !*
>   *Pinch him, and burne him, and turne him about,*
>   *Till Candles, & Star-light, & Moone-shine be out !*   98

[*A noise of hunting is made within ; and all the* Fairies *runne away.* FALSTAFFE *pulls off his bucks head, and rises vp. And enter* Master PAGE, Master FORD, *and their* Wiues, Master SHALLOW, *& Sir Hugh* EVANS.]

C. ADDISON, ? 1811. Solo up to the word "villanie," l. 96. Sung by Sir Hugh Evans, with Chorus for S.S.B., on the words, "Pinch him," &c. Caulfield's Collection.

Midsummer Night's Dream.

Act I. Scene i. lines 171—8, 182—5, 204—7, 234—9.

"BY THE SIMPLICITIE OF VENUS DOVES."

[Hermia loves Lysander, and he loves her. Demetrius also loves her ; and her father wishes to give her to him, as by the Athenian law he can. To prevent this, Lysander proposes to take Hermia to his widow-aunts', 7 leagues from Athens, and there marry her.]

Lysander. . . . If thou loueft mee, then,
Steale forth thy fathers houfe to-morrow night ;   164
And in the wood, a league without the towne,
(Where I did meete thee once with *Helena,*
To do obferuance to a morne of May,)
There will I ftay for thee.
    Hermia.   My good *Lysander!*   168
I fweare to thee, by *Cupids* ftrongeft bowe,
By his beft arrowe, with the golden heade,

By the fimplicitie of *Venus* doues,
By that which knitteth foules, and profpers loues,   172
And by that fire which burnd the *Carthage* queene,   [Dido.]
When the falfe *Troian* vnder faile was feene,   [Æneas] 174
By all the vowes that euer men haue broke,
(In number more then euer women fpoke,)   176
In that fame place thou haft appointed mee,
To-morrow truely will I meete with thee.   178
    Lysander. Keepe promife, loue! Looke, here comes *Helena!*

SIR HENRY BISHOP, 1816. Solo for Soprano. Sung by Miss Stevens,
   as Hermia, in *Midsummer Night's Dream.*

———

M. N. Dream, I. i. 182—5.

"O HAPPY FAIRE!
YOUR EYES ARE LOADSTARRES; AND YOUR
TONGUE'S SWEETE AIRE."

Enter HELENA *[in love with* DEMETRIUS, *who loves* HERMIA.]

Hermia. God fpeede, faire *Helena!* whither away?
Helena. Call you mee 'faire'? That 'faire' againe vnfay! 181
Demetrius loues your faire :
          ô happy faire!
Your eyes are loadftarres; and your tongue's fweete aire 183
More tunable then larke, to fheepeheards eare,
When wheat is greene, when hauthorne buddes appeare. 185
Sickneffe is catching : O, were fauour fo,
Your words Ide catch, faire *Hermia,* ere I goe ;   187
My eare fhould catch your voice, my eye, your eye,
My tongue fhould catch your tongues fweete melody! 189
Were the world mine, (*Demetrius* being bated,)
The reft ile giue to be to you tranflated.   191
O, teach mee how you looke ; and with what Art,
You fway the motion of *Demetrius* heart!   193

CHRISTOPHER SMITH, 1754. Solo, Soprano. In the operatized *M. N.
   Dream,* called 'Fairies.'

W. SHIELD, 1796 (?). No. 2 in 'Shakespears Duel[1] and Loadstars.' Glee for three voices, S.C.B. Also in 'Shakspere Vocal Magazine,' 1864, No. 43.

*SIR H. R. BISHOP, 1816. Solo, T., in the operatized *M. N. Dream.* Sung by Mr. Sinclair.

E. J. LODER, 1844. Solo, Soprano or Tenor, from lower D to upper G. No. 5 of a set of six 'Songs of the Poets,' by Loder.

EDWARD HINE. Solo, Soprano or Tenor, from lower D to upper G; key of E♭.

M. N. Dream, I. i. 204—7.

"BEFORE THE TIME I DID LISANDER SEE."

[Hermia promises Helena that she'll leave Athens (with Lysander), so that Demetrius—who loves her instead of Helena—shall be no longer tempted, by the sight of her, to refuse Helena his love.]

Hermia. Take comfort! he no more shall fee my face :
Lysander and my felfe will fly this place.   203

Before the time I did *Lifander* fee,
Seem'd *Athens* as a Paradife to mee.   205
O then, what graces in my loue doe dwell,
That hee hath turnd a heauen vnto a hell!   207

CHRISTOPHER SMITH, 1754. Song. In the 'Fairies.'

M. N. Dream, I. i. 234-9.

"LOVE LOOKES NOT WITH THE EYES, BUT WITH THE MINDE."

[Hermia and Lysander having gone. Helena soliloquises on Love's power and blindness, and laments her lover Demetrius's faithlessness in giving her up for Hermia.]

Helena. How happie some, ore otherf-me can be!
Through *Athens*, I am thought as faire as fhee.   227
But what of that? *Demetrius* thinkes not fo;
He will not knowe, what all but hee doe know.   229
And as hee erres, doting on *Hermias* eyes,
So I, admiring of his qualities.   231
Things bafe and vile, holding no quantitie,
Loue can tranfpofe to forme and dignitie.   233

Loue lookes not with the eyes, but with the minde;
And therefore is wingd *Cupid* painted blinde.   235
Nor hath loues minde, of any iudgement tafte;
Wings, and no eyes, figure vnheedy hafte.   237

[1] The Duel is, 'It was a lordlings Daughter.'—*Pass. Pilgrim.*

And therefore is loue faid to bee a childe,
Becaufe, in choyce, he is fo oft beguil'd.   2.9
As waggifh boyes, in game themfelues forfweare,
So the boy, Loue, is periur'd euery where.   241
For, ere *Demetrius* lookt on *Hermias* eyen,
Hee hayld downe othes, that he was onely mine.   243
And when this haile, fome heate from *Hermia* felt,
So he diffolued, and fhowrs of oathes did melt.   245

CHRISTOPHER SMITH, 1754. Solo. In the 'Fairies.'

M. N. Dream, II. i. 2—15.

"OVER HILL, OVER DALE.

[*A Wood neere Athens.*   April 30.]

Enter, a Fairie *at one doore, and* ROBIN GOODFELLOW (PUCKE) *at another.*

Rob. How now, fpirit? whither wander you?

Fairie.   Ouer hill, ouer dale,   2
          Thorough bufh, thorough brier,
       Ouer parke, ouer pale,
          Thorough flood, thorough fire,   5
       I do wander euery where,
       Swifter than the Moons fphere;   7
       And I ferue the Fairy Queene,
       To dew her orbs vpon the greene.   9
       The cowflippes tall, her Penfioners bee;
       In their gold coats, fpottes you fee   11
       Thofe be Rubies, Fairie fauours;
       In thofe freckles, liue their fauours.   13
       I muft goe feeke fome dew-droppes here,
       And hang a pearle in euery cowllippes eare.   15

Farewell, thou Lobbe of fpirits! Ile be gon.
Our Queene, and all her Elues, come here anon.   17

WM. JACKSON, 1770-5 (?). Glee for two Sopranos, one Tenor, and one
   Bass. This is the middle movement in his arrangement of Arne's
   Air "Where the bee sucks."
*T. COOKE, 1840. Florid Song. Ashdown.
EDWARD FITZWILLIAM, 1855. Solo, with **Clarionet Obbligato.** In
   'Songs for a Winter Night,' No. 3.
G. A. MACFARREN, 1856. Solo. Composed for and sung by Madame
   Viardot.
*W. WILSON, 1858. Duet. Sung by the Misses Brougham.
J. F. DUGGAN, 1862. Solo.
*J. HATTON. Part Song, S.A.T.B. Novello.

M. N. Dream, II. ii. 155—68, 249—53.

"THAT VERY TIME I SAW," &c.

Oberon. . . . My gentle *Pucke*, come hither! Thou remembreſt, 148
Since once I ſat vpon a promontory,
And heard a Mearemaide, on a Dolphins backe,
Vttering ſuch dulcet and harmonious breath,
That the rude ſea grewe ciuill at her ſong,   152
And certaine ſtarres ſhot madly from their Spheares,
To heare the Sea-maids muſicke.
   Puck.   I remember.
   Oberon. That very time, I ſaw, (but thou could'ſt not,)
Flying betweene the colde Moone and the earth,   156
Cupid, all arm'd: a certaine aime he tooke
At a faire Veſtall, throned by the weſt,
And looſ'd his loue-ſhaft ſmartly from his bowe,
As it ſhould pearce a hundred thouſand hearts;   160
But, I might ſee young *Cupids* fiery ſhaft
Quencht in the chaſt beames of the watry Moone;
And the imperiall Votreſſe paſſ'd on,
In maiden meditation, fancy-free.   164
Yet markt I, where the bolt of *Cupid* fell.
It fell vpon a little weſterne flower;
Before, milke white; now purple, with Loues wound,
And maidens call it, 'Loue-in-idleneſſe.'   168
Fetch mee that flowre! the herbe I ſhewed thee once.
The iewce of it, on ſleeping eyeliddes laide,
Will make, or man or woman, madly dote
Vpon the next liue creature that it ſees.   172
Fetch mee this herbe, and be thou here againe
Ere the *Leuiathan* can ſwimme a league!
   Puck. Ile put a girdle, round about the earth,
In forty minutes.   [*Exit.*

T. COOKE, 1840. Soprano. Sung by Madame Vestris. Called "Love
  in Idleneſs."

M. N. Dream, II. i. 249—58.

"I KNOW A BANKE, WHERE THE WILDE TIME BLOWES."

   Oberon [*to* PUCKE.] ¶ Haſt thou the flower there? Welcome,
wanderer!
   Puck. I, there it is!
   Oberon.   I pray thee, giue it mee.   248

I know a banke, where the wilde time blowes,
Where Oxlips, and the nodding Violet growes,   250
Quite ouercanopi'd, with lufhious woodbine,
With fweete mufke rofes, and with Eglantine: 252
There fleepes *Tytania*, fometime of the night,
Luld in thefe flowers, with daunces and delight;   254
And there the fnake, throwes her enammeld fkinne,
Weed, wide enough, to wrappe a Fairy in.   256
And, with the iuyce of this, Ile ftreake her eyes,
And make her full of hatefull phantafies.   258

JOHN PERCY, died 1797.   Soprano ; Flute Obbligato.
CHARLES E. HORN, 1824 (ed. 1856, 1858).   Duet for Soprano and
    Mezzo-Soprano.
*J. BARNETT, 1830.   Duet, Soprano and Mezzo-Soprano.

M. N. Dream, II. ii. 9—24, 66—83.
"YOU SPOTTED SNAKES, WITH DOUBLE
TONGUE."

Enter TYTANIA, Queene of Fairies, *with her trine.*

Queen.   Come, now a Roundell, and a Fairy fong!   1
Then, for the third part of a minute, hence!
Some to kill cankers in the mufk rofe buds;
Some warre with Reremife, for their lethren wings,   4
To make my fmall Elues coates; and fome keepe backe
The clamorous Owle, that nightly hootes and wonders
At our quaint fpirits: Sing me now a-fleepe!
Then to your offices, and let mee reft.   8

Fairies *fing.*

You fpotted Snakes, with double tongue,   9
Thorny Hedgehogges, be not feene!
Newts and blindewormes, do no wrong!
Come not neere our Fairy Queene!   12
Philomele, with melody,
Sing in our fweete Lullaby,
Lulla, lulla, lullaby! lulla, lulla, lullaby!

Neuer harme,   16
Nor fpell, nor charme,
Come our louely lady nigh!
So, good night, with lullaby!   19
1. *Fairy.   Weauing Spiders, come not heere*   20
Hence, you long legd Spinners! hence!
Beetles blacke, approach not neere!
Worme nor fnaile, doe no offence!   23
Philomele, with melody, &c.   [TITANIA *fleepes.*

2. *Fairy.* Hence, away! now all is well :
   One aloofe, ftand Centinell!   [*Exeunt* Fairies.

CHRISTOPHER SMITH, 1794. Solo, Soprano. Sung by Titania. In
   the 'Fairies.'
W. B. EARLE, 1794. Glee for four voices.
R. J. S. STEVENS, 1800(?). Four-voice Glee, S.A.T.B. Novello.
Name unknown. Solo.
MENDELSSOHN, 1843. Duet, Two Sopranos, with a Chorus of Sopranos
   and Altos. Novello.
*W. HILLS, 1865, &c. 'Vocal Trios,' &c., No. 4. Robert Cocks.
*J. MOUNT, 1879. 'The Fairies' Song.'
*G. A. MACFARREN, 1879. For four Ladies' voices, S.S.A.A. Novello.

M. N. Dream, II. ii. 66—83.

"THROUGH THE FORREST HAVE I GONE."

[Oberon sends Puck into the Forest to find a youth in **Athenian**
dress ('weedes'), Demetrius, that despises Helena who loves him.
Puck is to squeeze pansy-juice on Demetrius's eyes, so that he may
fall in love with Helena the moment he wakes. But Puck finds
Lysander near Hermia, both asleep; and, mistaking them for
Demetrius and Helena, squeezes the pansy-juice on Lysander's eyes.
(Lysander on waking sees Helena, and falls furiously in love with her,
to Hermia's great angerment.)]

Enter PUCKE.

Puck. Through the forreſt haue I gone ;
But *Athenian* found I none,   67
On whofe eyes, I might approue
This flowers force in ſtirring loue.   [*Sees* LYSANDER. 69
Night and filence! Who is heere?
Weedes of *Athens* he doth weare :   71
This is hee (my maſter faide)
Defpiféd the *Athenian* maide :   [*Sees* HERMIA. 73
And here the maiden, ſleeping found.
On the danke and dirty ground!   75
Pretty fowle! ſhe durſt not lye
Neere this lack-loue, this kil-curteſie.   [*Points to* LYSANDER. 77
" Churle! vpon thy eyes I throwe
All the power this charme doth owe :   79
When thou wak'ſt, let loue forbidde
Sleepe, his feat on thy eye lidde !   81
So awake, when I am gon ;
For I muſt now to *Oberon*.   [*Exit.* 83

MRS. J. B. GATTIE, 1825 ?). Solo, Canzonet.

M. N. Dream, III. i. 109—112, 114—117.

"THE WOOSELL COCK, SO BLACKE OF HEWE."

[Puck frightens Bottom's companions, and they run away.]

Bottom. Why doe they runne away? This is a knauery of them, to make mee afeard. 100

Re-enter SNOWTE.

Snowte. O *Bottom*, thou art chaung'd! What do I fee on thee?
Bottom. What doe you fee? You fee an Affe-head of your owne, Do you? [*Exit* SNOWTE.

Re-enter QUINCE.

Quince. Bleffe thee, *Bottom!* bleffe thee! Thou art tranflated. [*Exit.* 104
Bottom. I fee their knauery! This is to make an affe of mee; to fright me, if they could. But I wil not ftirre from this place, do what they can! I will walke vp and downe heere, and I will fing, that they fhall heare I am not afraide: 108

[*Sings*] *The Woofell cock, fo blacke of hewe,* 109
With Orange tawny bill,
The Throfile, with his note fo true,
The Wren, with little quill, 112

(*Tytania.* [*Waking*] What Angell wakes me from my flowry bed?)
Bottom [*Sings*]. *The Fynch, the Sparrowe, and the Larke,* 114
The plainfong Cuckow gray,
(*Whofe note, full many a man doth marke,*
And dares not anfwere, 'nay!') 117

For indeede, who would fet his wit to fo foolifh a birde? Who would giue a bird the ly, though hee cry 'Cuckow,' neuer fo?

(PURCELL probably set this; but his setting has been lost. Roffe, p. 60.)
Name unknown. Caulfield's Collection.
DR. C. BURNEY, 1762. Song. Roffe, p. 60.

M. N. Dream, III. i. 153, 154.

"AND PLUCK THE WINGS FROM PAINTED BUTTERFLIES."

[Titania commands her fairies to wait upon BOTTOM.]

Titania. Be kinde and curteous to this gentleman!
Hop in his walkes, and gambole in his eyes! 146
Feede him with Apricocks, and Dewberries,

With purple Grapes, greene figges, and Mulberries!
The hony bagges, fteale from the Humble-B.es;   149
And, for night tapers, croppe their waxen thighes,
And light them at the fiery Glowe-wormes eyes,
To haue my loue to bedde, and to arife;

And pluck the wings from painted Butterflies,   153
To fanne the Moone-beames from his fleeping eyes!
Nod to him, Elues, and doe him curtefies!   155

*SIR H. R. BISHOP, 1816.   Part of the Quartett, S.A.T.B., beginning
  'Welcome to this place.'

M. N. Dream, III. ii. 102—9.

"FLOWER OF THIS PURPLE DY."

[To remedy Puck's miftake of taking Lysander for Demetrius,
and to restore the latter's loue to Helena (from Hermia), Oberon,
finding Demetrius afleep in the wood, says to Puck :]

Oberon. About the wood, goe fwifter then the winde,
And *Helena* of *Athens*, looke thou finde!   95
All fancy-ficke fhe is, and pale of cheere,
With fighes of loue, that cofts the frefh blood deare.   97
By fome illufion, fee thou bring her here!
He charme his eyes, againft the doe appeare.   99
Robin. I goe, I goe! looke how I goe!
Swifter then arrow, from the *Tartars* bowe!   [*Exit.*   101

Oberon. Flower of this purple dy,   102
Hit with *Cupids* archery,
Sinke in apple of his eye!   [*Drops iuice into* DEMETRIVS *eyes.*
When his loue he doth efpy,   105
Let her fhine as glorioufly
As the *Venus* of the fky!   107
When thou wak'ft, if fhe be by,
Begge of her, for remedy.   109

CHRISTOPHER SMITH. 1754.   Solo. Sung by Oberon. 'The Fairies.'
*SIR H. R. BISHOP, 1816, arranged the above as a Solo for Baritone,
  and introduced it into the operatized *M. N. Dream.*

M. N. Dream, III. ii. 379—87, 394—99.

"LO,[1] NIGHT'S SWIFT DRAGONS CUT THE CLOUDS FULL FAST."

[Demetrius, on waking, falls violently in love with his old sweetheart Helena, with whom Lysander—under the influence of the pansy-

---

[1] *F 1,* Shakspere.

juice—is also in love. Lysander challenges Demetrius to fight for
Helena. Oberon bids Puck 'overcast the night,' and lead the rivals
apart and astray, and tire them out till they fall asleep. He'll then
cure Lysander, and give him back to Hermia. Puck answers:]

Puck. My Faiery Lord, this muft be done with hafte,

For Nights fwift Dragons cut the clouds full faft,	379
And yonder fhines *Auroras* harbinger;	
At whofe approach, Ghofts, wandring here and there,	381
Troope home to Churchyards: damnèd fpirits all,	
That in croffe-waies and floods haue buriall,	383
Already to their wormy beds are gone;	
For feare leaft day fhould looke their fhames vpon,	385
They wilfully themfelues exile from light,	
And muft for aye confort with black-browed night.	387

T. COOKE, 1840. Solo, Soprano. Sung by Miss Rainforth as 1st Fairy
in the *Midsummer Night's Dream.*

M. N. Dream, III. ii. 396—9.

"UP AND DOWN, UP AND DOWN."

[Puck assures Oberon that he'll mislead, and tire out, the angry
rivals for Helena's Love, Lysander (when under the charm) and
Demetrius:]

Puck. Vp & down, vp & down,	396
I will lead them vp & down!	
I am feard in field & town!	
Goblin, lead them vp & downe!	399

CHRISTOPHER SMITH, 1754. Solo. In the 'Fairies.'
DR. C. BURNEY, 1762. Solo.
T. COOKE, 1840. Solo, Soprano. Sung by Madame Vestris as 'Oberon,'
    compass from F to lower C.

M. N. Dream, V. i.

"A TEDIOUS BRIEFE SCENE OF YOUNG
PYRAMUS AND HIS LOVE THISBE;"
VERY TRAGICAL MIRTH.

Re-enter BOTTOM *as* PYRAMUS.

Thefeus. Pyramus drawes neare the wall: filence!	167
Pyramus. O grim-lookt night! o night, with hue fo blacke!	
O night, which euer art, when day is not!	
O night, O night! alacke, alacke, alacke!	
I feare my Thifbyes promife is forgot!	171

[To Snout *as* Wall.] *And thou, ô wall, ô sweete, ô louely wall,*
    That standst betweene her fathers ground and mine!
Thou wall, ô wall, O sweete and louely wall!
    Showe mee thy chinke, to blink through with mine eyne!   175
                    [Snout *holds up his hand, with his fingers* thus <
Thankes, curteous wall! Ioue shirld thee well, for this!
    But what see I? No Thisby doe I see.
O wicked wall, through whome I see no bliffe!
    Curst be thy stones, for thus deceiuing mee!   179

                Re-enter Flute *as* Thisby.
    *   *   *   *   *   *
    Thisby. My loue! thou art my loue, I thinke.
    Pyramus. Thinke what thou wilt, I am thy louers Grace;   193
And, like Limander, am I truyly still.
    Thisby. And I, like Helen, till the Fates me kill.   195
    Pyramus. Not Shafalus, to Procrus was so true.
    Thisby. As Shafalus to Procrus, I to you.   197
    Pyramus. O, kisse mee through the hole of this vilde wall!
    Thisby. I kisse the walles hole; not your lips at all!   199
    Pyramus. Will thou, at Ninnies tomte, meete me straight way?
    Thysby. Tide life, tyde death, I come without delay!   201

                    Enter Pyramus.
Pyramus. Sweete Moone, I thanke thee for thy sunny beams!
    I thanke thee, Moone, for shining now so bright;
    For by thy gratious, golden, glittering beames,
    I truft to take, of truest Thisby, sight.   266
                            [Sees her bloody Mantle.
        But stay: ô spight!
        But marke, poore knight,
        What dreadfull dole is here!   269
        Eyes, do you see?
        How can it bee?
    O dainty duck! o deare!   272
        Thy mantle good,—
        What! stain'd with blood?
    Approach, ye Furis fell,   275
        O Fates come, come!
        Cut thread and thrumme!
        Quaile, crush, conclude, and quell!   278

    Duke. This paffion, & the death of a deare friend, would goe
neere to make a man looke fad.
    Hyppolita. Befhrewe my heart, but I pitty the man.
    Pyramus. O, wherefore, Nature, didst thou Lyons frame?   282
    Since Lyon vilde hath here deflour'd my deare,
Which is—no, no!—which was, the fairest dame
    That liu'd, that lou'd, that lik't, that look't with cheere. 285

Come teares, confound!
Out, fword! and wound
The pappe of Pyramus: 288
I, that left pappe,
Where heart doth hoppe.
Thus dy I, thus, thus, thus! [Stabs himfelfe. 291
Now am I dead!
Now am I fled!
My foule is in the fky!   294
Tongue, loofe thy light!
Moone, take thy flight?
Now dy, dy, dy, dy, dy!   [Dies. 297

*   *   *   *   *   *
Re-enter THISBY. Sees Pyramus's Corpse.
*   *   *   *

Thifby. Afleepe, my loue?
  What? dead! my doue?
  O Pyramus, arife!   315
  Speake, fpeake! Quite dumbe?
  Dead! dead? A tumbe
  Mufi couer thy fweete eyes.   318
  Thefe lilly lippes,
  This cherry nofe,
  Thefe yellow cowflippe cheekes,   321
  Are gon! are gon!
  Louers make mone!
  His eyes were greene as leekes.   324
  O Sifters three,
  Come, come to mee,
  With hands as pale as milke!   327
  Lay them in gore,
  Since you hone fhore
  With fheeres, his threede of filke.   330
  Tongue, not a word!
  Come, trufty fword!
  Come, blade, my breaft imbrew! [Stabs herfelfe.
  And farewell, friends!
  Thus Thifby ends:
  Adieu, adieu, adieu!   [Dies. 336

1. 'And thou, O wall.' (l. 172—75, above). Song. Tenor, S.
2. 'O wicked wall!' (l. 178—9, above). Song.   „
3. 'Not Cephalus to Procris.' (l. 196—97, above). Duet, S.T.
4. 'Approach, ye Furies.' (l. 275—8, above). Song, Tenor, S.
5. 'Now am I dead.' (l. 292—7, above). Song.   „
5. 'These lily lips.' (l. 319—330, above). Song.   „
JOHN FREDK. LAMPE, 1745. Pyramus and Thisbe. A Mock Opera.

M. N. Dream, IV. i. 70-3.

"BE, AS THOU WAST WONT TO BEE!"

[Oberon, having received from Titania the little changeling boy
about whom they quarreld, and pitying her dotage upon Bottom,
removes the spell from her eyes.]

Enter ROBIN GOODFELLOW.

Oberon. Welcome, good *Robin!* Seest thou this sweete sight?
Her dotage, now I doe beginne to pittie;   46
For, meeting her of late, behinde the wood,
Seeking sweete fauours for this batefull Foole,   [*Bottom*]
I did vpbraid her, and fall out with her.
For fhe his hairy temples then had rounded   50
With coronet of frefh and fragrant flowers;
And that fame deawe, which fometime on the buddes
Was wont to fwell, like round and orient pearles,
Stood now within the pretty flouriets eyes,   54
Like teares that did their owne difgrace bewaile.
When I had, at my pleafure, taunted her,
And fhe, in milde tearmes, begd my patience,
I then did afke of her her changeling childe   58
Which ftraight fhe gaue mee, and her Fairy fent,
To beare him to my bower in Fairie land.
And now I haue the boy, I will vndoe
This hatefull imperfection of her eyes.   62
And, gentle *Puck,* take this transformed fcalpe
From off the heade of this *Athenian* fwaine,   [*Bottom*]
That, hee awaking when the other do,
May all to *Athens* backe againe repaire,   66
And thinke no more of this nights accidents,
But as the fearce vexation of a dreame.
But firft I will releafe the Fairy Qu_ene.   [*Muficke.* 69

Squeezes iuice on her Eyes.

¶ Be, as thou waft wont to bee!
    See, as thou waft wont to fee!   71
    Dians budde, ore *Cupids* flower,
    Hath fuch force, and blefled power.   73
Now, my *Titania!* wake you, my fweete Queen.'   [*She wakes.*
    Titania. My *Oberon!* what vifions haue I feene!
Me thought I was enamourd of an Affe.
    Oberon. There lyes your loue!

*JONATHAN BATTISHILL, 1763.
*SIR H. R. BISHOP, 1816. The same, adapted and arranged as a S lo,
    T. Sung by Duruset in the operatized *M. N. Dream.*

M. N. Dream, IV. i. 118, &c.

"MY HOUNDS ARE BRED OUT OF THE SPARTANE KINDE."

Enter THESEUS *and all his traine, with* HIPPOLITA *and* EGEUS.
May 1, Daybreak.

Thefeus. Goe, one of you! finde out the forrefter!
For now our obferuation is performde :
And fince we haue the vaward of the day,
My loue fhall heare the muficke of my hounds.   105
Vncouple! in the weflerne vallie let them goe!
Difpatch, I fay, and finde the forrefter!
                                    [*Exit one of the Traine.*
¶ Wee will, faire Queene, vp to the mountaines toppe,
And marke the muficall confufion   109
Of hounds and Echo in coniunction.
    Hippolita. I was with *Hercules* and *Cadmus* once,
When in a wood of *Creete* they bayed the Beare
With hounds of *Sparta :* neuer did I heare   113
Such gallant chiding! For, hefides the groues,
The fkyes, the fountaines, euery region neare
Seemd all one mutuall cry : I neuer heard
So muficall a difcord, fuch fweete thunder!   117
    Thefeus. My hounds are bred out of the *Spartane* kinde,
So flew'd, fo fanded ; and their heads are hung
VVith eares that fweepe away the morning deawe ;
Crooke-kneed, and deawlapt, like *Theffalian* Buls ;   121
Slowe in purfuit, but matcht in mouth like bels,
Each vnder each. A cry more tunable
Was neuer hollowd to, nor cheerd with horne,
In *Creete*, in *Sparta*, nor in *Theffaly!*   125
Iudge when you heare!

*SIR H. R. BISHOP, 1816. Chorus of Hunters, A.T.B. Begins : ' Hark!
Hark! each Spartan hound.' (Shakspere s lines, 118, 123, 124,
freely paraphrased.)

M. N. Dream, V. i. 358—369.

"NOW THE HUNGRY LYON ROARES."

[After Duke Theseus and his Bride, and all their guests have gone.]
Enter PUCKE.

Pucke. Now the hungry Lyon roares,   358
        And the wolfe behowls the Moone ;
    Whilft the heauie ploughman fnores,
        All with weary tafke foredoone.   361

Now the wafted brands doe glowe,
　　Whilſt the ſcriech-owle, ſcrieching lowd,
Puts the wretch that lyes in woe,
　　In remembrance of a ſhrowde.　　　　　365
Now [1] it is the time of night,
　　That the graues, all gaping wide,
Euery one lets forth his ſpright,
　　In the Churchway paths to glide.　　　　369
And wee Fairies—that doe runne
　　By the triple *Hecates* teame,
From the preſence of the Sunne,
　　Following darkeneſſe like a dreame—　373
Now are frollick　not a mouſe
Shall diſturbe this hallowed houſe.　　　　375
I am ſent with broome, before,
　　To ſweepe the duſt behinde the dore.　　377

Enter King *and* Queene *of Fairies, with all their* traine.

Oberon.　Through the houſe giue glimmering light,　378
　By the dead and drowſie fier :
Euery Elfe and Fairy ſpright,
　　Hop as light as birde from brier;　　　　381
And this dittie, after mee,
Sing, and daunce it trippingly.

Titania.　Firſt, rehearſe your ſong by rote,
To each word a warbling note.　　　　　　385
Hand in hand, with Fairy grace,
Will we ſing and bleſſe this place.　　　　387

Obꜱʀoɴꜱ *Song* [2]: *the Fairies repeat it &̃ daunce.*

Oberon.　Now, vntill the [3] breake of day,
　　Through this houſe each Fairy ſtray.　　389
　　To the beſt bride-bed will wee ;
　　Which by vs ſhall bleſſed be ;　　　　　391
　　And the iſſue there create,
　　Euer ſhall be fortunate :　　　　　　　393
　　So ſhall all the couples three,
　　Euer true in louing be :　　　　　　　395
　　And the blots of Natures hand,
　　Shall not in their iſſue ſtand.　　　　　397
　　Neuer mole, hare-lippe, nor ſcarre,
　　Nor marke prodigious, ſuch as are　　　399
　　Deſpiſed in natiuitie,
　　Shall vpon their children be.　　　　　401

---

[1] 'Now,' alterd to 'When,' by C. Horn.

[2] The Song is not giuen in Shakſpere's text ; only Oberon's ſpeech to his Fairies

[3] 'Now, vntill the,' alterd to 'Meet me all by' (see l. 409, below), by Biſhop.

With this field-deaw confecrate,
Euery Fairy take his gate,   403
And each feuerall chamber bleffe,
Through this palace with fweete peace;   405
And the owner of it bleft,
Euer fhall in fafety reft.   407
Trippe away! make no ftay!
Meete me all, by breake of day!   409

R. LEVERIDGE, 1727. Solos for 1st, 2nd, 3rd, &c., up to 8th Fairy,
and a Chorus to finish. May be found in his two volumes. Collec-
tion published, 1727.
DR. COOKE, about 1775. Five-part Glee. Begins, 'Hand in hand,'
l. 386 above. Novello.
R. J. S. STEVENS, about 1790? Glee for four voices, S.A.T.B., begins,
"Now the hungry lion."
CHRISTOPHER SMITH, 1794. Begins, 'Now, until the break of day.'
In the 'Fairies.'
W. LINLEY, 1816. Solo, Bass.
*SIR H. R. BISHOP, 1816. Solo, Tenor; with Chorus, S.S.A.A.T.B.
Begins 'In Theseu.' house give glimmering light'; and includes
lines 21-4. Sung in the operatized M. N. Dream.
*SIR H. R. BISHOP, 1816. Solo, Tenor. Begins, 'In the best Bride-
bed,' (lines 33, 34, 45, 46). Sung in M. N. Dream.
*SIR H. R. BISHOP, 1816. Chorus, S.S.A.T.B. The lines 'Trip away,'
&c. (408 and 409, above). This is part of Cooke's Glee, 'Hand in
hand,' arranged by Bishop and introduced into his Chorus, 'Spirits
advance,' sung in M. N. Dream.
SIR H. R. BISHOP, 1821. Quartett, A.T.T.B. Sung in Two Gentlemen
of Verona.
C. E. HORN, 1823. Song and Chorus. Sung in Merry Wives of
Windsor. Commences, 'When it is the time of night,' l. 360,
above.
MENDELSSOHN, 1843. Solo, S., and Chorus, S.S.A.A.

Much Ado about Nothing.[1]

Act III. Scene i. lines 57—68.

"SIGH NO MORE, LADIES, SIGH NO MORE."

The Song.[2]

Balthafer. Sigh no more, Ladies, figh no more!   57
Men were deceiuers euer:
One foote in fea, and one on fhore,
To one thing conftant neuer.   60

[1] See Hector Berlioz's Beatrice et Bénédict. Opéra ... imité de Shakspere. 1862. 8vo.
[2] Sung by 'Iacke Wilson,' a singer of the Burbages' Company, to which
Shakspere belongd. See Dr. Rimbault's pamflet 'Who was Jack Wilson?'
identifying the singer with the composer, Dr. John Wilson.

E

Then figh not fo, but let them go!   61
And be you blith and bonnie,
Conuerting all your foundes of woe,
Into ' hey nony, nony.'   64

Sing no more ditties, fing no moe,   65
Of dumps fo dull and heauy!
The fraud of men was euer fo,
Since fummer firft was leauy ;   68
Then figh not fo, &c.

DR. ARNE, about 1740. Song, Bass. For Mr. Beard, in *Much Ado
About Nothing.* 'Shakspere Vocal Album,' 1864.
CHRISTOPHER SMITH, 1794. Solo, S. For 'Oberon' in the 'Fairies.'
Caulfield's Collection.
R. J. S. STEVENS, 1790 (1800, 1846, &c.). Five-part Glee. S.S.A.T.B.
WM. LINLEY, 1816. Solo. Melody of Stevens's Glee as Solo.
SIR ARTHUR SULLIVAN, 1865. Solo, Tenor. Metzler.
*F. STANISLAUS, 1868. Solo : Tenor or Soprano. Ashdown.
G. A. MACFARREN, 1869. Part Song, S.A.T.B. Novello.
W. BALFE. Duet : Soprano and Contralto.
*G. BARKER. Solo. Robert Cocks.
*G. E. FOX, 1876. Solo, Baritone. **D to (upper) G.**
*DR. JOHN PARK, 1876. Solo.
*ETHEL HARRADEN, 1877. Solo, Mezzo-Soprano. Duff and Stewart.
*F. G. COLE, 1879. Tenor Solo : 'Composed expressly for his friend
Walter Allen.'
*MALCOLM LAWSON, 1880. Glee for Ladies' Voices, S.S.A.A, unac-
companied. With piano-forte accompaniment. Stanley Lucas,
Weber, & Co.
*H. C. HILLER, 1880.

Much Ado, V. ii. 24—7.

"THE GOD OF LOVE."

Margaret [to BENEDICKE]. Well, I will call *Beatrice* to you,
who I thinke hath legges.   [*Exit* MARGARITE.
Benedicke. And therefore wil come.   [*Sings.*

The God of loue
That fits aboue,   25
And knowes mee, and knowes me,
How pittiful I deferue . . .   27

I meane in finging ; but in louing, *Leander* the good fwimmer,
Troilus, the firft imploier of pandars, and a whole booke full of thefe
quondam carpet-mongers, whofe names yet runne fmoothly in the
euen rode of a blancke verfe, why, they were neuer fo truly turnd
ouer and ouer as my poore felfe in loue.

Anonymous. Caulfield's Collection.

Much Adoe, V. iii. 3—10.

"DONE TO DEATH BY SLANDEROUS TONGUES."

[A Church in Messina.]

Enter CLAUDIO,[1] PRINCE, *and three or four with tapers.*

Claudio. Is this the monument of *Leonato?*
A Lord. It is, my Lord.

CLAUDIO *reads his Epitaph on* HERO *from a Paper.*

> *Done to death by slanderous tongues,*   3
> *Was the* Hero *that heere lies:*
> *Death, in guerdon of her wronges,*
> *Giues her fame which neuer dies:*   6
> *So the life that dyed with shame,*
> *Liues in death with glorious fame.*   8
> *Hang thou there vpon the toomb,*
> *Praising hir when I am dead!*[2]   10

THEODORE AYLWARD, 1770. Glee for four voices. 'Elegies and Glees,'
  by T. A.

Much Adoe, Act V. Scene ii. lines 12—21.

"PARDON, GODDESSE OF THE NIGHT!"

Claudio. Now, Musick, sound, & sing your solemne hymne!   11

> Song. *Pardon! Goddesse of the Night!*
> *Those that slew thy virgin knight;*
> *For the which, with songs of woe,*
> *Round about her tombe they goe:*   15
> *Midnight! assist our mone!*
> *Help vs to sigh & grone,*
> *Heauily, heauily!*   18
> *Graues! yawne and yeeld your dead,*
> *Till death be vtterèd,*
> *Heauily, heauily!*[3]

DR. ARNE, about 1740. Solo for Soprano In Caulfield's Collection.
T. CHILCOT, about 1745. Solo. In 'Shakspere Vocal Album,' 1864
  (transposed into D minor).
W. LINLEY, 1816. Duet and Chorus. In Linley's ' Dramatic Songs of
  Shakspere.'

[1] Claudio has slanderd his loue Hero, and believes that his slanders have
kild her.
[2] Some Editors emend 'dead' to 'dumb.' But the emendation is only
a 'fancy' one, for ryme's sake.
[3] The Folio reads 'Heauenly, heauenly.'

E 2

Othello.

Act II. Scene iii. lines 71—5.

"AND LET ME THE CANNAKIN CLINKE, CLINKE!"

Iago. Some Wine, hoa! [*Sings.* 70

> *And let me the Cannakin clinke, clinke!*
> *And let me the Cannakin clinke!* 72
> *A Souldiers a man;*
> *Oh, man's life's but a span!* 74
> *Why, then let a Souldier drinke!*

Some Wine, Boyes!
Cassio. 'Fore Heauen, an excellent Song! 77
Iago. I larn'd it in *England;* where indeed they are moſt
potent in Potting. Your *Dane,* your *Germaine,* and your ſwag-belly'd
Hollander, (drinke, hoa!) are nothing to your *English.*[1] 80

*PELHAM HUMFREY, 1673. Song. Solo, Soprano. In *Musica Antiqua,*
ii. 171, ed. J. Stafford Smith. 1812.
Name Unknown. Caulfield's Collection.
W. LINLEY, 1816. Round for three male voices. In Linley's 'Dramatic
Songs of Shakspere.'

Othello, IV. iii. 34, &c.

"SONG OF 'WILLOUGH.'"

[Desdemona talks to her woman Æmilia, who is undressing her
to go to the bed in which Othello strangles her.]

Desdemona. My Mother had a Maid call'd *Barlarie:* 26
She was in loue; and he the lou'd prou'd mad,
And did forſake her. She had a Song of ' Willough ':
An old thing 'twas; but it expreſſ'd her Fortune,
And ſhe dy'd ſinging it. That Song, to night, 30
Will not go from my mind: I haue much to do,

---

[1] Iago's next song is an old English ballad, which has its own tune. The
music is in Caulfield's Collection (II. 68).
> *Iago.* Oh, sweet England!
> *King Stephen was and a worthy Peere,* 92
> *His Breeches coſt him but a Crowne;*
> *He held them Six pence all to deere,*
> *With that he cal'd the Tailor ' Lowne!'* 95
> *He was a wight of high Renowne,* 96
> *And thou art but of low degree:*
> *'Tis Pride that pulls the Country downe,*
> *And take thy auld Cloake about thee,* 99

Some Wine, hoa!

But to go hang my head all at one fide,
And fing it like poore *Barbarie.* Prythee, difpatch!

*　　*　　*　　*　　*　　*　　*

Defdemona [fings]. *The poore Soule fat finging, by a Sicamour tree.*
　Sing all a greene Willough !　　　　　　　　　35
Her hand on her bofome, her head on her knee ;
　Sing Willough, Willough, Willough !　　　　37
The frefh Streames ran by her, and murmur'd her moanes ;
　Sing Willough, &c.
Her falt teares fell from her, and foftned the ftones ;
　Sing Willough, &c.
(Lay by these.) *Willough, Willough !*　　　　　42
(Prythee, high thee! he'le come anon.)
Sing, all a greene Willough muft be my Garland.
Let no body blame him! his fcorne I approue.　　45
(Nay, that's not next. Harke! who is't that knocks?
Æmil. It's the wind.)
Defdemona. I call'd my Loue 'falfe Loue' : but what faid he then ?
　Sing Willough, &c.　　　　　　　　　　49
If I court mo women, you'le couch with mo men.

Ancient, 1600.[1] Solo, Contralto.　Chappell's ' Music of the Olden Time,'
　vol. i. p. 207.
SIGNOR GIORDANI, 1783. Solo.
*Anonymous. 'Willow! a Glee for four voices.' London, 1800 ?',
　folio.[2] S1, S2, S3, or Contra Alto, B.
J. MOREHEAD. Glee for three voices. Giordani. arranged by J. M.
JAMES HOOK, 1800. Solo, Mezzo-Soprano. Sung by Mrs. Jordan.
　'Shakspere Vocal Album.' 1864.
DR. I. KEMP, 1807. Song, Soprano. 'Vocal Magazine of Canzonets,'
　&c. &c., p. 100.
W. LINLEY, 1816. Solo. Linley's 'Dramatic Songs of Shakspere.'
SIR HENRY BISHOP, 1819. Solo. Sung in *Comedy of Errors,* by Miss
　Stevens.
SIR ARTHUR SULLIVAN, 1865. Solo, Contralto. Metzler.
*W. SHIELD set the introduction to this Song, beginning ' *My Mother
　had a maid called Barbara,*' but he did not go on with it, so as to
　include *Willow, Willow.* (See Linley, vol. ii. p. 24.)
*W. MICHAEL WATSON. Part Song. (Cross-reference in Brit. Mus.
　Catalogue, but no principal entry.)

---

　[1] The music of 'Willow, willow' is older than 1600. It is found in
Thomas Dallis's MS. 'Lute-book,' with the title 'All a greane willow.'
Dallis taught music at Cambridge; and his book, dated 1583, is now in the
Library of Trin. Coll., Dublin. (D. iii. 30.)
　[2] The singer is made a man. The words are much alterd: After 37
above, are

　　　He sigh'd in his singing, and after each groan,
　　　　O Willow, &c.
　　I'm dead to all pleasure, my true love is gone.
　　　　&c.　　　　　&c.

𝕽omeo and 𝕵ulief.

Act I. Scene v. lines 95—112. Quarto 2, ed. Daniel.

"IF I PROPHANE WITH MY VNWORTHIEST HAND."

Romeo [*to* IVLIET]. If I prophane with my vnworthieſt hand,
This holy ſhrine, the gentle ſin is this ;   95
My lips, two bluſhing Pylgrims, readie ſtand,
   To ſmoothe that rough touch, with a tender kis.   98
   Iuliet. Good Pilgrime, you do wrong your hand too much,
Which mannerly deuocion ſhowes in this ;
For Saints haue hands, that Pilgrims hands do tuch ;
And palme to palme, is holy Palmers kis.   102
   Romeo. Haue not Saints lips, and holy Palmers too?
   Iuliet. I, Pilgrim! lips that they muſt vſe in praire.
   Romeo. O then, deare Saint, let lips do what hands do!
They pray (grant thou) leaſt faith turne to diſpaire.   106
   Iuliet. Saints do not moue, thogh grant for praiers ſake.
   Romeo. Then moue not while my praiers effect I take   108
Thus from my lips, by thine, my ſin is purgd.
   Iuliet. Then haue my lips the ſin that they haue tooke.
   Romeo. Sin from my lips? ô treſpas ſweetly vrgd!
Giue me my ſin againe !
   Iuliet.   Youe kiſſe bith booke.   112

FRANCIS HUTCHINSON, 1807.   Duet, Soprano and Tenor.

Romeo and Juliet, II. ii. 107—24. Quarto 2, ed. Daniel.

"LADY! BY YONDER BLESSED MOONE I VOW."

   Romeo. Lady! by yonder bleſſed Moone I vow,[1]   107
That tips with ſiluer all theſe Fruite tree tops. . .
   Iuliet. O ſweare not by the Moone,—th'inconſtant Moone,
That monethly changes in her circled Orbe,—
Leaſt that thy Loue proue likewiſe variable.   111
   Romeo. What ſhall I ſweare by?
   Iuliet.   Do not ſweare at all !
Or, if thou wilt. ſweare by thy gracious ſelfe,
Which is the God of my Idolatrie,
And Ile beleeue thee.

[1] ſweare. Folio

Romeo.   If my hearts deare loue. . . .   115
Iuliet. Well, do not fweare! although I ioy in thee,
I haue no ioy of this contráct to night;
It is too rafh, too vnaduifd, too fudden,
Too like the lightning, which doth ceafe to bee   119
Ere one can fay, 'It lightens.' Sweete! goodnight!
This bud of Loue, by Sommers ripening breath,
May proue a bewtious Floure when next we meete.
Goodnight! goodnight! As fweete repofe and reft,
Come to thy heart, as that within my breft!   124

DR. J. KEMP, about 1790. Duet, Soprano and Tenor. Violoncello
   Obbligato. In 'Illustrations of Shakspere,' by Dr. J. Kemp.
DR. J. KEMP. Solo. Violoncello Ob. Begins, 'Love heralds should
   be thought.' 'Illustrations of Shakspere,' by Dr. J. Kemp.
HOWARD GLOVER, 1861. Song, Soprano. Called 'Sweet good night!'
   or Juliet's Song.
COUNTESS MARIE CORELLI, 1882. Recitative and Air. Called 'Romeo's
   good night!' Stanley Lucas.
(See W. S. STEVENS's 'Lyric Recitation of the Garden Scene in *Romeo
   and Juliet,* paraphrased from Shakspere,' 1821.)

Romeo and Juliet, III. v. 1—11.   Quarto 2, ed Daniel.

"WILT THOU BE GONE? IT IS NOT YET NEARE DAY."

[After their one night together, as husband and wife.]

Enter ROMEO *and* IULIET *aloft.*

Iuliet. Wilt thou be gone? It is not yet neare day: 1
It was the Nightingale, and not the Larke,
That pierft the fearefull hollow of thine eare;
Nightly fhe fings on yond Pomgranet tree: 4
Beleeue me, Loue, it was the Nightingale!
Romeo. It was the Larke, the Herauld of the Morne;
No Nightingale! Looke, Loue, what enuious ftreakes
Do lace the feuering Cloudes in yonder Eaft!   8
Nights Candles are burnt out, and Iocand Day
Stands tipto on the myftie Mountaine tops.
I muft be gone, and liue; or ftay, and die.   11

PERCY, 1785. Duet. Called 'The Garden Scene' in *Romeo and
   Juliet.*
J. REEKES, about 1850. Solo. J. Reekes, 'Six Songs from Shakspere.'

Taming of the Shrew.

Induction. **Scene ii.** lines 33—54.

"WILT THOU HAVE MUSICKE? HARKE! APOLLO PLAIES."

[The humourous Lord who has taken the drunkard Sly to his
house, and told his men to treat Sly as a Lord, says to him:]

Lord. Wilt thou haue Muficke? **Harke!** *Apollo* plaies, [*Mufick.*
And twentie caged Nightingales do fing: 34
Or wilt thou fleepe? Wee'l haue thee to a **Couch,**
Softer and fweeter then the luftfull bed 36
On purpofe trim'd vp for *Semiramis.*
Say thou wilt walke; we wil beftrow the ground:
Or wilt thou ride? Thy horfes fhall be trap'd,
Their harneffe ftudded all with Gold and Pearle. 40
Doft thou loue hawking? Thou haft hawkes will foare
Aboue the morning Larke: Or wilt thou hunt?
Thy hounds fhall make the Welkin anfwer them,
And fetch thrill ecchoes from the hollow earth. 44
  1. *Man.* Say thou wilt courfe; thy gray-hounds are as fwift
As breathëd Stags, I, fleeter than the Roe.
  2. *Man.* Doft thou loue pictures? we wil fetch thee ftrait
Adonis, painted by a running brooke, 48
And *Citherea* all in fedges hid,
Which feeme to moue and wanton with her breath,
Euen as the wauing fedges play with winde.
  Lord. Wee'l fhew thee *Io,* as fhe was a Maid; 52
And how fhe was beguilëd and furpriz'd,
As liuelie painted as the deede was done.

T. COOKE, 1828. Song. Sung by Mifs Fanny Ayton in *Taming of the
Shrew.*

Taming of the Shrew, Act II. Scene i. lines 167—77.

"SHOULD HE UPBRAID, I'LL OWN THAT HE PREVAIL."[1]

ALTERED FROM THE SPEECH BEGINNING, "SAY, THAT SHE RAILE."

[Baptista, the father of Kate the Shrew, speaks to Petruchio, who
wants to marry her:]

[1] The words in Bishop's song are as follows, the alterd ones being in italics:
  Should he upbraid, I'll own that he prevail,
  And sing as sweetly as the Nightingale.
  Say that *he* frown, I'll say '*his* looks I view
  As morning roses newly *tipt* with dew,'
  Say *he* be mute, I'll *answer with a smile,*
  And dance and play, and wrinkled Care beguile.

Signior *Petruchio*, will you go with vs,
Or fhall I fend my daughter *Kate* to you ?   164
 Petruchio. I pray you do !   [*Exit. Manet* PETRUCHIO.
      I will attend her heere,
And woo her with fome fpirit when fhe comes.

Say, that fhe raile ; why, then Ile tell her plaine,
She fings as fweetly as a Nightinghale :   168
Say, that fhe frowne ; Ile fay fhe lookes as cleere
As morning Rofes newly wafht with dew :
Say, fhe be mute, and will not fpeake a word ;
Then Ile commend her volubility,   172
And fay fhe vttereth piercing eloquence :

If fhe do bid me packe, Ile giue her thankes,
As though fhe bid me ftay by her a weeke :
If fhe denie to wed, Ile craue the day   176
When I fhall afke the banes, and when be married.
But heere fhe comes ; and now, *Petruchio*, fpeake !

Enter KATERINA.

Good morrow, *Kate !* for thats your name, I heare.

SIR H. R. BISHOP, 1821. Solo. Compofed for and sung by Miss M.
Tree in *The Two Gentlemen of Verona.*

𝕿empeſt.

Act I. Scene ii. lines 198—206.

"NOW I FLAM'D AMAZEMENT."

 Profpero [to ARIEL].   Haft thou, Spirit,   193
Performd to point, THE TEMPEST that I bad thee ?
 Ariel. To euery Article !
I boorded the Kings fhip. Now on the Beake,   196
Now in the Wafte, the Decke, in euery Cabyn,

I flam'd amazement. Sometime I'ld diuide,
And burne in many places ; on the Top-maft,
The Yards, and Bore-fpritt, would I flame diftinctly ;   200
Then meete, and ioyne. *Ioues* Lightning, the precurfers
O'th dreadfull Thunder-claps, more momentarie
And fight out-running, were not ; the fire, and cracks
Of fulphurous roaring, the moft mighty *Neptune*,   204
Seeme to befiege, and make his bold waues tremble,
Yea, his dread Trident fhake.

JN. CHRISTOPHER SMITH, 1756. Recitative in Smith's 'Tempest,'
 p. 12.

TEMPEST.

Tempest, Act I. Scene ii. lines 375—85.

"COME UNTO THESE YELLOW SANDS."

Enter FERDINAND; *&* ARIEL, *inuiſible, playing and ſinging.*

Ariel. [Song.] *Come vnto theſe yellow ſands,*
and then take hands; 376
Curtſied when you haue, and kiſt
the wilde waues whiſt! 378
Foote it featly heere and there,
and, ſweete Sprights, beare the burthen! 380
[Burthen, diſperſedly.] *Harke, harke! bough waugh!*
The watch-Dogges barke, bough waugh! 382
Ariel. *Hark, hark, I heare,*
the ſtraine of ſtrutting Chanticlere
cry, ' Cockadidle-dowe!' 385

JOHN BANISTER, 1667. Solo. Playford's 'Select Ayres, &c.'
HENRY PURCELL, 1673. Soprano Solo and Chorus, S.A.T.B.
JN. CHRISTOPHER SMITH, 1756. Solo. Smith's 'Tempest.'
SIR JOHN STEVENSON, 1798 (?). Glee for S.S.B. 4-hand Piano accompaniment.
*SIR ARTHUR S. SULLIVAN, 1862. Solo, S., and Chorus, S.A.T.B.
*RICHARD SIMPSON, 1878. Solo, MS. Lucas and Weber.

Tempest, Act I. Scene ii. lines 395—402.

"FULL FADOM FIVE THY FATHER LIES."

[Ariel's song tells Prince Ferdinand that his father is drownd. (He is, in fact, alive and well.)]

Ariel. [Song.] *Full fadom fiue thy Father lies:* 395
Of his bones are Corrall made:
Thoſe are pearles that were his eies,
Nothing of him that doth fade, 398
But doth ſuffer a Sea-change
Into ſomething rich & ſtrange: 400
Sea-Nimphs hourly ring his knell:
[Burthen:] *ding dang!*
Harke! now I heare them: ding-dong, bell! 402

ROBERT JOHNSON. Shakspere's time. Harmonized for three voices by Dr. Wilson. 'Cheerful Ayres or Ballads,' by Dr. Wilson.
JOHN BANISTER, 1667. Song, Soprano. Playford's 'Select Ayres, &c.' Arranged (C. or B.) with Chorus, S.A.T.B., by Edw. J. Loder. Lonsdale.
HENRY PURCELL, 1673. Soprano Solo and Chorus, S.A.T.B.
JN. CHRISTOPHER SMITH, 1756. Solo. Contralto or Bass.
*SIR ARTHUR SULLIVAN. 1862. Solo, S., and Chorus, S.A.T.B. Novello.
*C. H. HUBERT PARRY, 1874. Song, Contralto, C to E♭. 'A Garland,' &c., No. 5. Sung by Miss Antoinette Sterling. Boosey. Called "A Sea Dirge."

*A. M. WARREN, 1874. Solo, Bass. Weekes and Co.
*G. R. VICARS, June 1, 1883. Part Song. Novello.

Tempest, Act II. Scene i. lines 298—303.

"WHILE YOU HERE DO SNOARING LIE."

[Sebastian has arranged with Antonio, that when he (S.) raises his hand, Antonio shall kill the sleeping Gonzalo, while he, Sebastian, kills king Alonso, who lies asleep, too. Ariel, sent by Prospero, wakes Gonzalo, and frustrates the plot.]

Re-enter ARIELL, *innisible, with Musicke and Song.*

Ariel [to GONZALO *sleeping].* My Matter (through his Art) foresees the danger
That you (his friend) are in ; and sends me forth   296
(For else his proiect dies) to keepe them liuing.

[*Sings in* GONZALOES *eare.*

While you here do snoaring lie,
Open-ey'd Conspiracie
His time doth take.   300
If of Life you keepe a care,
Shake off slumber and beware !
Awake, awake !   303

DR. ARNE (?), 1746. Song. In Caulfield's Collection.
THOMAS LINLEY, 1777. Linley's 'Dramatic Songs of Shakspere.'
*SIR ARTHUR S. SULLIVAN, 1862. Solo, Soprano. (Music to *The Tempest*, p. 22.)

Tempest, Act II. Scene ii. lines 41, 42, 45—53.

"SNATCHES OF SONG FOR STEPHANO."
Sung by Mr. Bannister.

Enter STEPHANO *singing, & holding a larke Bottle of Sacke.*

Stephano.   I shall no more to sea, to sea,
            Here shall I dye ashore. . .

This is a very scuruy tune to sing at a mans Funerall : well, here's my comfort !   [*Drinkes.* 44
[*Sings.*] *The Master, the Swabber, the Boate-swaine & I,*   45
The Gunner, and his Mate,
Lou'd Mall, Meg, and Marrian, and Margerie,
But none of us car'd for Kate.   48
For she had a tongue with a tang,
Would cry to a Sailor ' goe hang !'   50
She lou'd not the fauour of Tar nor of Pitch ;
Yet a Tailor might scratch her where ere she did itch.
Then, to Sea, Boyes ! and let her goe hang !   53
This is a scuruy tune too : But here's my comfort !   [*Drinkes.*
Anonymous. Caulfield's Collection.

Tempest, Act II. Scene ii. lines 173-79.

"NO MORE DAMS I'LL MAKE FOR FISH."

[Caliban, Prospero's slave, made drunk by Stephano's sack,—made "a howling Monster, a drunken Monster," as Trinculo says,—swears to be Stephano's subject, and no longer serve Prospero.]

Caliban. *No more dams I'le make for fish,*
        Nor fetch in firing,
        At requiring,   175
        Nor scrape trenchering,
        Nor wash dish!   177
        Ban', ban', Ca .. calyban,
        Has a new Master. Get a new Man!   179

Freedome, high-day! high-day, freedome! freedome! high-day, freedome!

Jn. CHRISTOPHER SMITH, 1756. Solo, Bass. Smith's 'Tempest.' Caulfield's Collection.
J. W. HOBBS, 1861. Song, Bass. Called 'Caliban.'
J. F. DUGGAN, 1870. Tenor or Bass Song. Called 'Caliban.'

Tempest, Act III. Scene ii. lines 118, 19.

"FLOUT 'EM, AND COUT 'EM."

Caliban [*to* STEPHANO]. Thou mak'st me merry! I am full of pleasure!
Let vs be iocond! Will you troule the Catch   114
You taught me but whileare?
    Stephano. At thy requeſt, Monſter, I will do reaſon; any reaſon.
¶ Come on, *Trinculo!* let vs ſing!   117

          Sings.

Flout'em, and cout'em! and skout'em, and flout'em!
       Thought is free.

HENRY PURCELL, 1675. Round for three. Caulfield's Collection.

Tempest, Act III. Scene ii. lines 131-9.

"BE NOT AFFEARD! THE ISLE IS FULL OF NOYSES."

[Ariel invisible, plays, upon a tabor and pipe, the tune of 'the Catch' that Caliban and his two companions have just been trying to sing. Stephano and Trinculo are frightened, but are reassured by Caliban.]

Caliban. Art thou affeard? 129
Stephano. No, Monſter! not I!

Caliban. Be not affeard! the Iſle is full of noyſes,
Sounds, and ſweet aires, that giue delight, and hurt not:
Sometimes a thouſand twangling Inſtruments 133
Will hum about mine eares; and ſometime Voices,
That, if I then had wak'd after long ſleepe,
Will make me ſleepe againe; and then, in Dreaming,
The Clouds (methought) would open, and ſhew Riches 137
Ready to drop vpon me; that, when I wak'd,
I cri'de to dreame againe.

*J. F. DUGGAN, 1871. ('A second song for Caliban.') Solo, Baritone.
Sung by Santley.

Tempest, Act IV. Scene i. lines 44-8.

"BEFORE YOU CAN SAY, 'COME, AND GOE'."

[Ferdinand and Miranda are to witness a Masque of Proſpero's
Spirits.]

Proſpero [*to* ARIEL]. . . . Goe bring the rabble
(Ore whom I giue thee powre) here, to this place!
Incite them to quicke motion, for I muſt
Beſtow vpon the eyes of this yung couple [1] 40
Some vanity of mine Art: it is my promiſe,
And they expect it from me.
    Ariel.   Preſently?
    Proſpero. I! with a twincke!

Ariel. Before you can ſay 'come, and goe,' 44
And breathe twice, and cry 'ſo, ſo':
Each one, tripping on his Toe,
Will be here with mop and mowe.
Doe you loue me, Maſter? no? 48

JN. CHRISTOPHER SMITH, 1756. Solo. Smith's 'Tempest.'
THOS. LINLEY, 1777. Solo. Linley's 'Dramatic Songs of Shakspere.'

Tempest, Act IV. Scene i. lines 106—17.

"HONOR, RICHES, MARRIAGE-BLESSING."

IUNO *deſcends, & enters.*

Iuno [*to* CERES]. How do's my bounteous ſiſter? Goe with me
To bleſſe this twaine,[1] that they may proſperous be, 104
And honourd in their Iſſue!

    [1] Ferdinand and Miranda.

Iuno. *Honor, riches, marriage-bleſſing,*
   Long continuance, and encreaſing,   107
   Hourely toyes, be ſtill vpon you!
   Iuno ſings her bleſſings on you.   109

Ceres. *Earths increaſe, foyzon plentie,*
   Barnes and Garners, neuer empty,   111
   Vines, with cluſtiring bunches growing,
   Plants, with goodly burthen bowing: 113
   Spring come to you at the fartheſt,
   In the very end of Harueſt!   115
   Scarcity and want ſhall ſhun you,
   Ceres bleſſing ſo is on you.   117

SIGNORINA DE GAMBERINI, 1785 (?). Solo. Entitled. "The frien-ly
 wiſh from Shakspere." 'Twelve English and Italian Songs,' by
 Gamberini. No. 2. Brit. Mus. Lib.
WILLIAM LINLEY, 1816. Duet for two Sopranos.
T. S. COOKE, 1840 (?). Duet for two Sopranos. Novello.
H. VAN DEN ABEELEN, 1859. Duet. Known as "Homage to Shakspere."
 Ashdown and Parry.
*SIR ARTHUR S. SULLIVAN, 1862. Duet for Soprano and Contralto,
 with Chorus. 'Duet for two Sopranos,' 1863. Novello.

Tempest, Act IV. Scene i. lines 134—8.

"YOU SUN-BURN'D SICKLEMEN, OF AUGUST WEARY."

Re-enter IRIS.

Iris. You Nimphs, cald *Nayades,* of ye windring brooks,
With your ſedg'd crownes, and euer-harmleſſe lookes, 129
Leaue your criſpe channels, and on this greene-Land
Anſwere your ſummons! *Iuno* do's command!   131
Come, temperate Nimphes, and helpe to celebrate
A Contract of true Loue! be not too late!   133

Enter Certaine Nimphes.

¶ You Sun-burn'd Sicklemen, of Auguſt weary,
Come hether from the furrow, and be merry!   135
Make holly-day! your Rye-ſtraw hats put on,
And theſe freſh Nimphs encounter, euery one, 137
In Country footing!

Enter certaine Reapers *(properly habited) they ioyne with the*
 Nimphes, *in a gracefull dance; towards the end whereof,* PROS-
 PERO *ſtarts ſodainly, and ſpeakes; after which, to a strange*
 hollow and confuſed noyſe, they heauily[1] vaniſh.

FRANCIS HUTCHINSON, 1807. Glee for two Tenors and one Bass.
 Collection of Vocal Music by Hutchinson.

    [1] *heauily* = mournfully.

Act V. Scene ii. lines 152—6.

"THE CLOWD-CAPT TOWRES, THE GORGEOUS PALLACES."

Prospero [*to* FERDINAND]. Our Reuels now are ended. Thefe
  our actors
(As I foretold you) were all Spirits, and   149
Are melted into Ayre, into thin Ayre,
And, like the bafeleffe fabricke of this vifion,
The Clowd-capt Towres, the gorgeous Pallaces,
The folemne Temples, the great Globe it felfe,   153
Yea, all which it inherit, fhall diffolue,
And (like this infubftantiall Pageant faded)
Leaue not a racke behinde.
               We are fuch ftuffe
As dreames are made on; and our little life   157
Is rounded with a fleepe.

R. J. STEVENS, about 1795. Glee for six voices, S.A.T.T.B.B. Novello.

Tempest, Act V. Scene i. lines 1—8.

"NOW DO'S MY PROIECT GATHER TO A HEAD."

Before PROSPEROES *Cell*.
Enter PROSPERO (*in his Magicke robes*), *and* ARIEL.

Profpero. Now do's my Proiect gather to a head   1
My charmes cracke not; my Spirits obey; and Time
Goes vpright with his carriage. How's the day?
  Ariel. On the fixt hower; at which time, my Lord,   4
You faid our worke fhould ceafe.
  Profpero.   I did fay fo,
When firft I rais'd THE TEMPEST. Say, my Spirit,
How fares the King, and's followers?
  Ariel.   Confin'd together,
In the fame fafhion, as you gaue in charge, ...   8

JN. CHRISTOPHER SMITH, 1756. Recitative. Smith's 'Tempest.'

Act V. Scene i. lines 88—94.

"WHERE THE BEE SUCKS, THERE SUCK I."

[Prospero is about to present himself before King Alonso,
Antonio, and the rest.]

Prospero.   . . . . .   Ariell.
Fetch me the Hat, and Rapier in my Cell!   84
I will diſcaſe me, and my ſelfe preſent
As I was ſometime *Milliaine.*   Quickly, Spirit!
Thou ſhalt ere long be free.   87

[ARIELL *ſings, and helps to attire him.*

Where the Bee ſucks, there ſuck I ;
In a Cowſlips bell, I lie ;
There I couch when Owles doe crie ;
On the Batts backe I doe flie
    after Sommer merrily.   92
Merrily, merrily, ſhall I liue now,
Vnder the bloſſom that hangs on the Bow !   94

Proſpero.   Why! that's my dainty *Ariell!*   I ſhall miſſe thee;
But yet thou ſhalt haue freedome : ſo, ſo, ſo!

ROBERT JOHNSON. Shakspere's time. Harmonized for three voices,
    by Dr. Wilson. 'Cheerful Ayres,' by Dr. Wilson, Oxford, 1660.
    Playford's 'Select Ayres, &c.' I. 97. Printed in Hullah's 'Singers'
    Library,' No. 21, 1859.
PELHAM HUMFREY, 1657. Called "A Song in the machines, by Ariel's
    Spirits." Printed in Playford's 'Select Ayres, &c.'
PURCELL, 1673. Dr. Rimbault had it in MS.
DR. ARNE, 1746. Solo, Soprano. The same, harmonized for S.S.T.B.,
    by W. Jackson. Caulfield's Collection.
NICOLO PASQUALI, 1750. Solo. It alters "On the Batts backe I doe
    flie," l. 91, to "On the swallow's wings I fly." Twelve English Songs
    in Score, collected from several Masques, &c. No. II. 'A Song
    in the Tempest.'
JN. CHRISTOPHER SMITH, 1756. Solo. Smith's 'Tempest.'
*SIR ARTHUR SULLIVAN, 1862. Solo. Novello.

Troylus and Cressida.

Act IV. Scene iv. lines 15—18.

"O, HEART, HEAUIE HEART!"

[Troylus comes to Pandarus's house, to fetch his love Cressid, in
order to deliver her up to Diomed and the Greeks, who are to take
her to her father, Calchas, in the Grecian camp.]

Enter TROYLUS.

Creſ. O *Troylus, Troylus!*   [*Embracing him.*
Pan. What a paire of ſpectacles is here! let me embrace too!
' *Oh heart,*' as the goodly ſaying is ;   14

    ' *Oh heart, heauie heart,*
        Why ſigheſt thou without breaking ? '

where he anſwers againe;

> 'Becauſe thou canſt not eaſe thy ſmart
> By friendſhip, nor by ſpeaking':   18

There was neuer a truer rime! Let vs caſt away nothing, for we
may liue to haue neede of ſuch a Verſe! We ſee it, we ſee it!
How now, Lambs?   21

M. P. KING, 1810 (?).
*SIR H. R. BISHOP, 1810. Duet for Two Sopranos.

Twelfth Night.

Act I. Scene i. lines 1—15.

"IF MUSICKE BE THE FOOD OF LOVE, PLAY ON!"

The Dukes *Palace.*

Enter ORSINO, Duke *of* Illyria, CURIO, *and other* Lords; Muſicians
attending.

Duke.

IF Muſicke be the food of Loue, play on!   1
Giue me exceſſe of it, that, ſurfetting,
The appetite may ſicken, and ſo dye.
  That ſtraine agen! it had a dying fall: 4
O, it came ore my eare, like the ſweet ſound
That breathes vpon a banke of Violets,
Stealing, and giuing, Odour!—Enough; no more!
'Tis not ſo ſweet now, as it was before.   8
O ſpirit of Loue, how quicke and freſh art thou,
That, notwithſtanding thy capacitie
Receiueth as the Sea: nought enters there,
Of what validity, and pitch ſo ere,   12
But falles into abatement, and low price,
Euen in a minute! ſo full of ſhapes is Fancie,
That it alone is high fantaſticall.

JAMES CLIFTON, 1781. Solo. Reproduced in 'Shakspere Vocal Album,'
  1864.
SIR JOHN STEVENSON. Air, Contralto or Bass. Commences, 'That
  strain again,' l. 4. In a set of eight Songs and four Duets.
SIR J. STEVENSON and T. COOKE, 1828. Quartet. Opera, *Taming of
  the Shrew.*
A. MATTHEY, 1847. Canzonet.
CHARLES HORSLEY. Solo. Chappell, New Bond Street.
GEORGE BENSON, 1861. Glee.
*W. C. SALLE, 1863. Canzonet.

F

66   TWELFTH NIGHT.

Twelfth Night, Act I. Scene v. lines 254—262.

"MAKE ME A WILLOW CABINE AT YOUR GATE."

[Viola, drest as Duke Orsino's page, Cesario, takes her Master's
message of love to Olivia, who, not caring for him, falls in love with
his page Cesario-Viola. The latter says to Olivia:]

Viola. If I did loue you in my matters flame,
With such a suffring, such a deadly life,
In your deniall I would finde no fence;
I would not vnderstand it.
    Oliuia.   Why, what would you?   253

Viola. Make me a willow Cabine at your gate,
And call vpon my soule within the house;
Write loyall Cantons of contemn'd loue,
And sing them lowd, euen in the dead of night;   357
Hallow your name to the reuerberate hilles,
And make the babling Gossip of the aire
Cry out, ' *Oliuia!* ' O, you should not rest
Betweene the elements of ayre, and earth,   261
But you should pittie me!

JOHN BRAHAM, 1828. Solo, Tenor. Sung by himself in *Taming of the
Shrew.*

Twelfth Night, Act II. Scene iii. lines 36—41, 44-9.

"O MISTRIS MINE, WHERE ARE YOU ROMING?"

Sir Andrew. Excellent! Why, this is the best fooling, when
all is done. Now, a song!
   Sir Toby. Come on; there is sixe pence for you! Let's haue a
song!   31
   Sir Andrew. There's a testrill of me too! if one knight giue a …
   Clowne. Would you haue a loue-song, or a song of good life?
   Sir Toby. A loue song, a loue song!
   Sir Andrew. I, I! I care not for 'good life.' [Clowne *sings.* 35

        O *Mistris* mine, where are you roming?
        O, stay and heare! your true loue's coming,
          That can sing both high and low: 38
        Trip no further, prettie sweeting!
        Iourneys end in louers meeting,
          Euery wise mans sonne doth know.   41

   Sir Andrew. Excellent good, ifaith!
   Sir Toby. Good, good!   43

Clowne. *What is Loue? tis not heereafter ;*
Prefent mirth hath prefent laughter;
What's to come is ftill vnfure :   46
In delay there lies no plentie ;
Then come kiffe me, Sweet and twentie!
Youth's a fiuffe will not endure!   49
Sir Andrew. A mellifluous voyce, as I am true knight!

Anonymous, 1599 and 1611. Morley's 'Confort Leffons.' In Queen
Elizabeth's Virginal Book, p. 125, the melody is arranged by Byrd.
(Chappell, 'Music of the Olden Time,' vol. i. p. 209.)
R. J. S. STEVENS, 1785. Glee. Novello.
WILLIAM LINLEY, 1816. Solo. Linley's 'Dramatic Songs of Shakfpere.'
J. ADDISON, 1820. Solo, Tenor. In Caulfield, vol. i. p. 137.
ELIZABETH CRAVEN, MARGRAVINE OF ANSPACH. Madrigal for two
     voices.
J. MAJOR, 1856. ('Cyclopædia of Music,' No. 356.)   An adaptation of
     Elizabeth Craven's Madrigal. Duet.
J. REEKES, 1850 to 1860. Song. 'Six Songs from Shakspere.'
SIR ARTHUR S. SULLIVAN, 1866. Solo, Bass. Sung by Mr. Santley.
     Metzler.
*F. STANISLAUS, 1870. Song. Ashdown.
*G. A. MACFARREN, 1872. Part Song, S.A.T.B. (Foster's 'Choral
     Harmonist,' No. 4.)
*REV. C. E. HEY, 1877. Part Song : Soprano, Contralto, Tenor, Bass,
     in *Twelfth Night.* Patey and Willis.
*A. H. D. PRENDERGAST, 1878. Part Song, A.T.B. Stanley Lucas,
     Weber, and Co.
*H. W. WAREING, 1878. Part Song. Novello.
*J. MOUNT, 1879. Song.
*F. E. GLADSTONE, 1880. Song. Novello.
*L. CARROTT, 1881. Song. Stanley Lucas, Weber, and Co.
*E. T. DRIFFIELD. Part Song, A.T.T.B. Novello.

Twelfth Night, Act II. Scene iii.

"SNATCHES OF SONG FOR SIR TOBY."

Enter MARIA.

Maria. What a catterwalling doe you keepe heere! If my
Ladie haue not call'd vp her Steward *Maluolio,* and bid him turne
you out of doores, neuer truft me!   68
Toby. My Lady's a *Catayan,* we are politicians; *Maluolio's* a
Peg-a-ramfie, and [*sings*] '*Three merry men be wee.*' Am not I con-
fanguinious? Am I not of her blood! Tilly vally! 'Ladie ':
[*sings*] '*There dwelt a man in Babylon, Lady, Lady!*'   73
Clowne. Befhrew me, the knight's in admirable fooling!
Sir Andrew. I, he do's well enough if he be difpos'd, and fo
do I too : he does it with a better grace, but I do it more naturall.
Toby. [*sings*] '*O, the twelfe day of December,*' . . .   77
Maria. For the loue o' God, peace!

Enter MALUOLIO.

*   *   *   *   *   *   *   *   *

Maluolio. Sir *Toby*, I muſt be round with you! My Lady [86
bad me tell you, that, though ſhe harbors you as her kinſman, ſhe's
nothing ally'd to your diſorders. If you can ſeparate your ſelfe and
your miſdemeanors, you are welcome to the houſe; if not, and it
would pleaſe you to take leaue of her, ſhe is very willing to bid you
farewell.   91
Toby.   [*sings*] ' *Farewell, deere heart! ſince I muſt needs be gone.'*
(*Maria.*   Nay, good Sir *Toby!*)
Clowne.   [*sings*] ' *His eyes do ſhew his dayes are almoſt done.'* 94
(*Maluolio.*   Iſ't euen ſo?)
Toby.   ' *But I will neuer dye.'*
Clowne.   Sir *Toby*, there you lye.   97
(*Maluolio.*   This is much credit to you.)
Toby.   ' *Shall I bid him go?'*
Clowne.   ' *What and if you do?'*   100
Toby.   ' *Shall I bid him go, and ſpare not?'*
Clowne.   ' *Oh, no, no, no, no, you dare not!'*   102

In Caulfield's Collection, vol. i. p. 147.   Composer unknown.
*ROBERT JONES, 1601 (12th from the 1st Book).   Song, in four Parts.
    In *Muſica Antiqua*, vol. ii. 204, ed. J. Stafford Smith, 1812. Cald
    ' Farewell, dear Heart!'

Twelfth Night, Act II. Scene iv. lines 51—66.

"COME AWAY! COME AWAY, DEATH!"

Re-enter CURIO & Clowne (FESTE).

The Duke. [to FESTE]   O, fellow, come! the ſong we had laſt
        night!
¶ Marke it, *Ceſario!* it is old and plaine;
The Spinſters and the Knitters in the Sun,
And the free maides that weaue their thred with bones,   45
Do vſe to chaunt it: it is ſilly ſooth,
And dallies with the innocence of loue,
Like the old age.
Clowne.   Are you ready, Sir?   49
Duke.   I; prethee, ſing!   [*Muſicke.*

The Song.

Clowne. Come away! come away, Death!   51
        And in ſad cypreſſe let me be laide;
    Fye, away! fie, away,[1] *breath!*
    I am ſlaine by a faire cruell maide: 54

---

[1] Editors generally read ' *Fly away . . . fly away.'*

My ſhrowd of white, ſtuck all with Ew,   55
 O, prepare it!
My part of death, no one ſo true
    did ſhare it.   58
Not a flower, not a flower ſweete,   59
 On my blacke coffin, let there be ſtrewne;
Not a friend, not a friend greet
My poore corpes, where my bones ſhall be throwne! 62
A thouſand thouſand ſighes to ſaue,   63
 lay me, ô, where
Sad true louer neuer find my graue,
 to weepe there!   66

DR. ARNE, 1741. Solo, T. Sung by Mr. Lowe. 'Shakspere Vocal
  Album.'
R. J. S. STEVENS, 1790. Glee. Novello.
MARIA HESTER PARK, 1790. Solo. Inscribed to Dr. Parsons.
By a Lady (anonymous). Solo.
WILLIAM LINLEY, 1816. Solo, Bass. Linley's 'Dramatic Songs of
  Shakspere.'
*SAMUEL WEBBE, JUN., 1830. Glee.
*J. BRAHMS, born 1833. Part Song for female voices, with accompani-
  ment for two horns and harp. Opus 17. Published with English
  words, 1884. Novello. (It is older in Germany.)
G. A. MACFARREN, 1864. Glee, S.A.T.T.B. Novello.
*DR. JOHN PARK, 1876. Solo.

Twelfth Night, Act II. Scene iv. lines 110—115.

"SHE NEVER TOLD HER LOVE."

[Viola, as the page Cesario, says to her master, Orsino, Duke of
Illyria:]

My Father had a daughter lou'd a man,
As it might be, perhaps, were I a woman,
I ſhould your Lordſhip.
    Duke.   And what's her hiſtory?   109
    Viola. A blanke, my Lord.

                    She neuer told her loue,
But let concealment, like a worme i'th budde,
Feede on her damaſke cheeke: ſhe pin'd in thought;
And, with a greene and yellow melancholly,   113
She ſate like Patience on a Monument,
Smiling at greefe.

HAYDN, 1790. Solo. Dedicated to Lady C. Bertie. (Canzonets, 2nd
  set, No. 4.)
DR. HARRINGTON of Bath, about 1790. Terzetto. Called 'Viola's
  account of her own concealed love,' in *Twelfth Night.* Book of
  Dr. Harrington's Compositions.

GEORGE NICKS, 1842. Duet for two Sopranos. Robert Cocks.
EDWARD L. HIME, 1856. Glee for four male voices.
*A. C. ROWLAND, 1874. Part Song, S.S.T.B. Lamborn Cock.

Twelfth Night, Act III. Scene i. lines 147—162.

"CESARIO! BY THE ROSES OF THE SPRING."

[Olivia, scorned by the page Cesario-Viola, with whom she is in
love, first speaks to herself, and then to Viola, as Cesario:—]

Olivia. *(aside)* O, what a deale of scorne lookes beautifull
In the contempt and anger of his lip!   144
A murdrous guilt shewes not it selfe more soone
Then loue that would seeme hid : Loues night is noone!)   146

Cesario! by the Roses of the Spring,
B. maid-hood, honor, truth, and euery thing,   148
I loue thee so, that, maugre all thy pride,
Nor wit, nor reason, can my pashion hide !   150
Do not extort thy reasons from this clause,
For that I woo, thou therefore hast no cause ;   152
But, rather, reason thus with reason fetter :
Loue sought, is good : but, giuen vnsought, is better !   154
    Viola. By innocence I sweare, and by my youth,
I haue one heart, one bosome, and one truth,   156
And that no woman has : nor neuer none
Shall mistris be of it, saue I alone !   158
And so adieu, good Madam ! neuer more
Will I my Maisters teares to you deplore !   160
    Olivia. Yet come againe ! for thou perhaps mayst moue
That heart, which now abhorres, to like, his loue.   [*Exeunt.* 162

SIR HENRY BISHOP, 1820. Duet. Altered from Winter. Sung by
    Misses Greene and Tree, in the operatised *Twelfth Night.*

Music for the Clowne's Snatches, in lines 72-9 and 118-121, is
given in Caulfield, I. 153 ; but his Song, which ends IV. ii., does not
seem to have been set [yet of course it has been].

Clowne. [*advances & sings*] Hey, Robin ! iolly Robin !
Tell me how thy Lady does !
Maluolio. Foole !   74
Clowne. My Lady is vnkind, perdie.
Maluolio. Foole !
Clowne. Alas, why is she so ?
Maluolio. Foole, I say !   78
Clowne. She loues another . . . Who calles, ha ?

[Malvolio, having been made to believe that Olivia loves him, is bound in a dark room as a madman. He calls to the Clown, Feste, whom he hears singing. Malvolio wishes to write to Olivia, in proof of his sanity, and Feste promises to be the bearer of the letter.]

Clowne. [*sings*] *I am gone, fir;*   118
            And anon, fir,
         Ile be with you againe,   120
            In a trice,
            Like to the old Vice,
         Your neede to fuftaine;   123

         Who, with dagger of lath,   124
         In his rage and his wrath,
            Cries, ' ah, ha!' to the Diuell: 126
         Like a mad lad,
            ' Paire thy nayles, dad;
            Adieu, good man Diuell!'   129

         Twelfth Night, Act V. Scene i. lines 378—396.

"WHEN THAT I WAS AND A LITTLE TINË BOY."

[When all the other Players have left the Stage, the Clowne, Feste, winds up the Play with this Song:]

Clowne *fings*.

When that I was and a little tinë[1] boy,   378
   with hey, ho, the winde and the raine,
A foolifh thing was but a toy,   380
   for the raine, it raineth euery day.

But when I came to mans eftate,   382
   with hey, ho, &c.
Gainft Knaues and Theeues men fhut their gate.   384
   for the raine, &c.

But when I came, alas! to wiue,   386
   with hey, ho, &c.
By fwaggering could I neuer thriue,   388
   for the raine, &c.

But when I come vnto my beds,   390
   with hey, ho, &c.
With tofpottes ftill had drunken heades,   392
   for the raine, &c.

         [1] *tinë* = tiny.

A great while ago **the world began,**   394
hey, ho, &c.
But that's all one ; **our** *Play is done ;*   396
and wee'l striue to pleafe you euery day.   [*Exit.*

J. VERNON, 1763. Solo, Tenor. In 'The new Songs, &c.', No. 2.
Composed by Vernon, and sung by him in *The Twelfth Night* at
Drury Lane, October 19th, 1763. (Wrongly attributed by Linley
to Fielding.) Linley's 'Dramatic Songs of Shakspere.' 'Handbook
of Standard English Songs.' R. Cocks.
SIR J. STEVENSON, 1834. Glee, S.A.T.B.
*RICHARD SIMPSON, 1878. Solo, Baritone. Lucas and Weber.
*J. L. HATTON, 1848. Solo, T., with four-part Chorus for male voices;
gained the prize given by the Melodists' Club. Williams, Berners St.
*SCHUMANN. Solo. Augener, Newgate St.

Two Gentlemen of Verona.

Act I. Scene iii. lines 84—87.

"OH, HOW THIS SPRING OF LOVE RESEMBLETH."

[Protheus is found by his father Antonio, reading a letter from his
love Julia, whom he wants his father's consent to marry. Askt
whose letter it is, Protheus shams that it is one from his friend
Valentine, describing how happily he gets on at the Emperor's court.
On this, Antonio resolves to send Protheus at once to the Court, to
join Valentine, and thus separate him from Julia. Protheus, caught
in his own trap, thus soliloquises :]

Protheus. Thus haue I shund the fire, for feare of burning,
And drench'd me in the sea, where I am drown'd.
I fear'd to shew my Father *Iulias* Letter,   80
Least he should take exceptions to my loue ;
And, with the vantage of mine own excufe,
Hath he excepted moft again'tt my loue.

Oh, how this fpring of loue refembleth   84
The vncertaine glory of an Aprill day,
Which now fhewes all the beauty of the Sun,
And by and by a clowd takes all away !   87

SIR HENRY BISHOP, 1819. Solo. Sung by Miss M. Tree, in the
Operatised *Comedy of Errors.*

Two Gentlemen of Verona, Act II. Scene vii. lines 33—38.

"HINDER NOT MY COURSE."

[Julia resolves to go to the Emperor's court, after her lover
Protheus. Her maid Lucetta tries to prevent her, and counsels her
to wait at home till Protheus returns. Julia answers :]

Iulia. Oh, know'ſt thou not, his looks are my ſoules fuod?
Pitty the dearth that I haue pinëd in,   16
By longing for that food ſo long a time!
Didſt thou but know the inly touch of Loue,
Thou wouldſt as ſoone goe kindle fire with ſnow,
As ſeeke to quench the fire of Loue with words!   20
- *Lucetta.* I doe not ſeeke to quench your Loues hot fire,
But qualifie the fires éxtreame rage,
Left it ſhould burne aboue the bounds of reaſon.
Iulia. The more thou dam'ſt it up, the more it burnes :   24
The Current, that with gentle murmure glides,
(Thou know'ſt,) being ſtop'd, impatiently doth rage;
But, when his faire courſe is not hindered,
He makes ſweet muſicke with th'enameld ſtones,   28
Giuing a gentle kiſſe to euery ſedge
He ouer-taketh in his pilgrimage;
And ſo, by many winding nookes, he ſtraies,
With willing ſport, to the wide Occin.   32

Then let me goe, and hinder not my courſe!
Ile be as patient as a gentle ſtreame,
And make a paſtime of each weary ſtep,
Till the laſt ſtep haue brought me to my Loue;   36
And there Ile reſt, as, after much turmoile,
A bleſſéd ſoule doth, in *Elizium!*

M. M. ALLNAT, 1860.   Song.   In 'Two Songs, &c.'

Two Gentlemen of Verona, Act IV. Scene ii. lines 38–52.

"WHO IS SILVIA? WHAT IS SHE?"

[Julia, having reacht the Emperor's city, in man's attire, is taken
by her Host to hear her faithless lover Protheus serenade Silvia, the
love of his friend Valentine, to whom he has turnd traitor, in order
that he may win Silvia for himself.]

Song.

Who is Siluia? what is ſhe,   38
  That all our Swaines commend her?
Holy, faire, and wiſe is ſhe: 40
  The heauen ſuch grace did lend her,
That ſhe might admiréd be.   42
Is ſhe kinde as ſhe is faire?   43
  For beauty liues with kindneſſe.
Loue doth to her eyes repaire,   45
  To helpe him of his blindneſſe,
And, being help'd, inhabits there.   47

Then to Siluia let vs sing,   48
  That Siluia is excelling :
She excels each mortall thing,   50
  Vpon the dull earth dwelling !
To her let vs Garlands bring !   52

RICHARD LEVERIDGE, 1727. Solo. Reproduced in 'Shakspere Vocal
    Album,' 1864, and Caulfield's Collection, 1864, with Chorus for T.T.B.
    'The New Songs, &c.', No. 7.
J. VERNON, 1762. Solo, Tenor ('Key of F, ranging up to B♭.'—Roffe).[1]
R. J. S. STEVENS, 1810 (?). Glee.
WILLIAM LINLEY, 1816. Solo. Linley's 'Dramatic Songs of Shakspere.'
SIR H. BISHOP, 1820. Pasticcio. Morley, 1595; Raven-croft, 1614.
    Novello. In the Operatised *Twelfth Night.* Glee for five voices.
SIR HENRY BISHOP, 1821. Concerted Piece. Pasticcio. 'By the sim-
    plicity,' an air in 'Midas'. In the Operatised *Two Gentlemen of
    Verona.* Glee for S.A.T.T.B.
*JOSEPH ELLIOTT, 1825 (?). Glee. A.T.T.B. Cramer & Co.
SAMUEL WEBBE, JUNR., 1830. Glee for five voices.
FRANZ SCHUBERT, 1826. Solo, Baritone. Op. 106, No. 4. Litolff, v. 107.
    'Shakspere Vocal Album,' 1864.
J. F. DUGGAN, 1854. Duet, Soprano and Bass.
~GEORGE A. MACFARREN, 1864. Part Song, S.A.T.B. 'Choral Songs,'
    No. 5.
*MISS M. A. MACIRONE. Part Song. S.A.T.B. Ashdown.
*LIONEL S. BENSON, 1873. Duet : Soprano, Contralto, or Tenor and
    Bass. Stanley Lucas and Weber.
*W. H. HOWELLS. Part Song, S.A.T.B. Lamborn Cork.
*C. S. HEAP. Part Song, S.A.T.B. Stanley Lucas and Weber.
*R. H. WAITHMAN, 1882. Part Song. Weekes.
*ISIDORE DE SOLLA, June, 1883. Solo. Stanley Lucas & Co.
*WALTER MACFARREN. Sept. 15, 1883. Part Song, S.C.T.B. 'The
    Lute.' Patey and Willis.
*W. J. YOUNG. Nov. 1883. Part Song. S.A.T.B. Novello.

Winter's Tale.[2]

Act IV. Scene iii. lines 1—12.

"WHEN DAFFADILS BEGIN TO PEERE."

[A Road near the Shepheards Cottage.]

Enter AUTOLICUS, singing.

When Daffadils begin to peere,
  With (heigh !) the Doxy ouer the dale,
Why, then comes in the sweet o'the yeere,
  For the red blood raigns in y' winters pale.   4

Composed by Vernon for himself, and sung by him in the character of
Thurio at Drury Lane Theatre, December 27th, 1762. (See Genest.)
    [2] See M. Bruch's '*Hermione*, grosse Oper . . . nach Sh.'s *Wintermärchen*,'
&c. 1872, folio.

The white fheete bleaching on the hedge,
With (hey!) the fweet birds, O, how they fing!
Doth fet my pugging[1] tooth an edge;
For a quart of Ale is a difh for a King!   8
The Larke, that tirra-Lyra chaunts,
With (heigh!) the Thrufh and (hey!) the Iay!
Are Summer fongs for me and my Aunts,
While we lye tumbling in the hay.   12

DR. WM. BOYCE, about 1759. Song. In Linley's ' Dramatic Songs
    of Shakspere,' and Caulfield, II. 46.
*H. W. WAREING, Mus. Bac. S.A.T.B. Novello.
*MISS C. A. MACIRONE. S.A.T.B. Novello.

Winter's Tale, Act IV. Scene ii. lines 15—22.

"BUT SHALL I GO MOURNE FOR THAT, MY DEERE."

Autolycus. . . . I haue feru'd Prince *Florizell*, and in my time
wore three pile ; but now I am out of feruice :   14

But fhall I go mourne for that, (my deere?)   15
The pale Moone fhines by night :
And when I wander here and there,
I then do moft go right.   18

If Tinkers may haue leaue to liue,   19
and beare the Sow-fkin Bourget,
Then my account I well may giue,
and in the Stockes auouch it.   22

My Trafficke is ' fheetes ' : when the Kite builds, looke to leffer
Linnen ! My Father nam'd me *Autolicus;* who, being (as I am)
lytter'd vnder *Mercurie*, was likewife a fnapper-vp of vnconfidered
trifles. With Dye and drab, I purchaf'd this Caparifon ; and my
Reuennew is the filly Cheate. Gallowes, and Knocke, are too
powerfull on the Highway. Beating and hanging are terrors to mee!
For the life to come,—I fleepe out the thought of it.   29

Anonymous. Caulfield's Collection, vol. ii. p. 52.
J. F. LAMPE, 1748. Solo, S. or M.S. British Museum. G. 306,
    piece 251.

Winter's Tale, Act IV. Scene iii. lines 119—122.

"JOG-ON, JOG-ON, THE FOOT-PATH WAY."
(SNATCH OF SONG.)

[Autolycus has shammd illness, and robd the Clowne, the old
Shepherd's son, who takes leave of him :]

[1] thieving.

Clowne. Then fartheewell! I muſt go buy Spices for our ſheepe-
ſhearing.   113
Autolycus. Proſper you, ſweet ſir! [*Exit* Clo.] Your purſe is
not hot enough to purchaſe your Spice. He be with you at your
ſheepe-ſhearing too! If I make not this Cheat bring out another,
and the ſheerers proue ſheepe, let me be vnrold, and my name put
in the booke of Vertue!   118

        Song. *Iog-on, Iog-on, the foot-path way,*   119
           And merrily hent the Stile-a!
           A merry heart goes all the day!
           Your ſad, tyres in a Mile-a.   [*Exit.* 122

Anonymous. This tune is in the 'Dancing Maſter' (1650 to 1698),
called *Jog on.* Also in Q. Elizabeth's 'Virginal Book,' p. 416, with
the name of *Hanskin.* It is an Air with variations by Richard
Farnaby. (Chappell's 'Music of Olden Time,' p. 211.)
Anonymous. Snatch. Caulfield's Collection.
Dr. Boyce, about 1759. The centre of his 'When Daffodils.'
Miss C. A. Macirone, 1860. Part Song, S.A.T.B. Novello.

Winter's Tale, Act IV. Scene iv. lines 217—229.

"LAWNE, AS WHITE AS DRIVEN SNOW."

[The Old Shepherd's Servant deſcribes to him and his Clowne-
ſon, to his ſuppoſed daughter Perdita, and their gueſts at their Sheep-
ſhearing, the goods and the ſinging of Autolycus, diſguiſed as a
Pedler:]

Servant. Hee hath Ribbons of all the colours i'th Rainebow; [205
Points, more then all the Lawyers in *Bohemia* can learnedly
handle, though they come to him by th'groſſe; Inckles,[1] Caddyſſes,[2]
Cambrickes, Lawnes: why, he ſings em ouer, as they were Gods,
or Goddeſſes! you would thinke a Smocke were a ſhee-Angell, he
ſo chauntes to the ſleeue-hand, and the worke about the ſquare
on't.   210
Clowne. Pre'thee bring him in! and let him approach ſinging.
Perdita. Forewarne him, that he vſe no ſcurrilous words in's
tunes!   [*Exit* Servant. 213
Clowne. You haue of theſe Pedlers, that haue more in them then
you'd thinke (Siſter!)
Perdita. I, good brother, or go aboute to thinke.   216

       Enter Autolicus *ſinging.*

      Lawne, as white as driuen Snow;
      Cypreſſe, blacke as ere was Crow;   218
      Gloues, as ſweete as Damaſke Roſes;
      Maſkes for faces, and for noſes;   220

[1] *Inckles,* tapes.   [2] *Caddyſſes,* worsted lace.

Bugle-bracelet, Necke-lace Amber,
Perfume for a Ladies Chamber ;   222
Golden Quoifes and Stomachers,
For my Lads to giue their deers ;   224
Pins, and poaking-stickes of steele ;[1]
What Maids lacke, from head to heele :   226
   Come buy of me, come! come buy! come buy!
   Buy, Lads! or elfe your Lafses cry :
                     Come, buy!

Dr. WILSON, 1660. Solo.
Anonymous. Solo. Caulfield's Collection.
Dr. BENJAMIN COOKE, 1780 (?). Glee.
*E. S. BIGGS, 1800 (?). Solo, Tenor. 'Here's lawn as white.'
THOS. HUTCHINSON, 1807. Song. 'Vocal Collection' of Mr. Hutchinson.
WILLIAM LINLEY, 1816. Song, Tenor. Linley's 'Dramatic Songs of
   Shakspere.'
*CARL NESTOR. Song. Baritone.

Winter's Tale, Act IV. Scene iv. lines 291—302.

"GET YOU HENCE, FOR I MUST GOE!"

[Autolycus, Mopsa (with whom the Clowne is in love), and her
friend Dorcas, sing a Ballad together :]

Autolycus. This is a merry ballad, but a very pretty one!   281
Mopsa. Let's haue some merry ones!
Autolycus. Why, this is a passing merry one, and goes to the tune
of '*Two maids wooing a man*' there's scarse a Maide westward, but
she sings it : 'tis in requesit, I can tell you!   285
Mopsa. [*looking at it*] We can both sing it : if thou'lt beare a
part, thou shalt heare; 'tis in three parts.
Dorcas. We had the tune on't, a month agoe!
Autolycus. I can beare my part, you must know 'tis my occupa-
tion : Haue at it with you!   290

Song.

Aut.	*Get you hence, for I must goe!*	
	Where, it fits not you to know.	292
Dor.	*Whether ?*	
Mop.	*O, whether ?*	
Dor.	*Whether ?*	
Mop.	*It becomes thy oath full well,*	
	Thou to me thy secrets tell.	295
Dor.	*Me too! Let me go thether !*	296
Mop.	*Or thou goest to th' Grange, or Mill ;*	
Dor.	*If to either, thou dost ill.*	298

[1] To stiffen the curls of their Ruffs on.

Aut.   *Neither!*
Dor.   *What, neither?*
Aut.   *Neither!*
Dor.   *Thou haſt ſworne, my Loue to be,*
Mop.   *Thou haſt ſworne it more to mee!*   301
Both.   *Then whether goeſt? Say whether?*   302

DR. WM. BOYCE, about 1759. Trio. Linley's 'Dramatic Songs of
Shakspere.' Also in Caulfield, II. 60.

Winter's Tale, Act IV. Scene iv. lines 309—314.

"WILL YOU BUY ANY TAPE?"

[AUTOLYCUSES Song.]

Will you buy any Tape, or Lace for your Cape?   309
   My dainty Ducke, my deere-a?
Any ſilke, any Thred, any Toyes for your head,
      Of the new'ſt, and fin'ſt, fin'ſt weare-a!   311
Come to the Pedler! Money's a medler,
That doth vtter all men's ware-a.   [*Exit.* 314

Anonymous. Solo. Caulfield's Collection.
DR. BOYCE, about 1769. Solo. Linley's 'Dramatic Songs of Shakspere.'
DR. COOKE, about 1780. Catch.
*MISS C. A. MACIRONE, 1864. Part Song, S.A.T.B. Novello.

Sonnets.

[Sonnets 5, 6, and 7 are of those in which Shakspere appeals to
his handsome young friend, William Herbert, afterwards (A.D. 1601)
Earl of Pembroke, to marry, and beget children.]

5. "THOSE HOWERS THAT WITH GENTLE WORKE."

Thoſe howers, that with gentle worke did frame
   The louely gaze where euery eye doth dwell,
Will play the tirants to the very ſame,
   And that vnfaire which fairely doth excell;   4

For neuer reſting time leads Summer on
   To hidious winter, and confounds him there;
Sap-checkt with froſt, and luſtie leau's quite gon,
   Beauty ore-ſnow'd, and barenes euery where.   8

Then—were not ſummers diſtillation left,
   A liquid priſoner pent in walls of glaſſe,—
Beauties effect with beauty were bereft,
   Nor it, nor noe remembrance what it was: 12

But flowers diftil'd, though they with winter meete,
Leefe but their fhow; their fubftance ftill liues fweet. 14

*RICHARD SIMPSON, publisht (after his death) April 1878. Solo.
Lucas and Weber, New Bond St. (All Richard Simpson's are of
the same date. He had set all the Sonnets to music, and many
other pieces. Out of them, Mrs. G. A. Macfarren chose a thin folio
volume for publication.)

6. "THEN, LET NOT WINTERS WRAGGED HAND."

Then let not winters wragged hand deface
  In thee, thy fummer, ere thou be diftil'd!
Make fweet fome viall! treafure thou fome place
  With beauties treafure, ere it be felfe kil'd!   4

That vfe is not forbidden vfery,
  Which happies thofe that pay the willing lone;
That's for thy felfe to breed an other thee,
  Or ten times happier, be it ten for one!   8

Ten times thy felfe, were happier then thou art!
  If ten of thine, ten times refigur'd thee:
Then what could Death doe, if thou fhould'ft depart,
  Leauing thee liuing in pofterity?   12

Be not felfe-wild! for thou art much too faire
To be deaths conqueft, and make wormes thine heire. 14

*RICHARD SIMPSON, 1878. Solo. Lucas and Weber, New Bond St.

7. "LOE! IN THE ORIENT, WHEN THE GRACIOUS LIGHT."

Loe! in the Orient, when the gracious light
  Lifts vp his burning head, each vnder eye
Doth homage to his new appearing fight,
  Seruing with lookes his facred maiefty;   4

And hauing climb'd the fteepe vp heauenly hill,
  Refembling ftrong youth in his middle age,
Yet mortall lookes adore his beauty ftill,
  Attending on his goulden pilgrimage;   8

But when from high-moft pich, with wery car,
  Like feeble age, he reeleth from the day,
The eyes (fore dutious) now conuerted are
  From his low tract, and looke an other way: 12

So thou, thy felfe out-going in thy noon,
Vnlok'd-on dieſt, vnleſſe thou get a ſonne.   14

SIR HENRY BISHOP, 1824.   Glee and Chorus, l. 1-8 in *As You Like It.*
*RICHARD SIMPSON, 1878.   Solo.   Lucas and Weber, New Bond St.

18. "SHALL I COMPARE THEE TO A SUMMERS DAY?"

[Shakspere assures his friend William Herbert of eternal life
through his (Sh.'s) Sonnets to him.   See nos. 54, 63, and 81 below.]

Shall I compare thee to a Summers day?
  Thou art more louely and more temperate:
Rough windes do ſhake the darling buds of Maie,
  And Summers leaſe hath all too ſhort a date: 4

Sometime, too hot the eye of heauen ſhines,
  And often is his gold complexion dimm'd;
And euery faire, from faire ſome-time declines,
  By chance, or natures changing courſe, vntrim'd;   8

But thy eternall Sommer ſhall not fade,
  Nor looſe poſſeſſion of that faire thou ow'ſt;
Nor ſhall Death brag thou wandr'ſt in his ſhade,
  When, in eternall lines, to time thou grow'ſt: 12

  So long as men can breath, or eyes can ſee,
  So long liues this, and this giues life to thee.   14

CHARLES HORN, 1821.   Duet, S.C.   It was sung in the *Tempeſt.*
E. J. LODER, 1841.   Duet, S.S.   No. 3 of 'Six new vocal Duets.'—Part
  of a work called *The Melophon.*
J. REEKES, about 1850.   The three first and ninth lines have been used.
  'Six Shakspere Songs.'
*ROBERT HOAR, 1876.   Song.   Hutchins and Romer, 9, Conduit St.
*LADY RAMSEY OF BANFF.   Czerny, 211, Oxford St.

Sonnet 25.   Lines 1—4.

[Shakspere contrasts his lowly ſtate with that of Fortune's
favourites.   Yet they may feel her fickle change, while he is sure of
his Friend's constant Love.]

Let thoſe who are in fauour with their ſtars,
  Of publike honour and proud titles boſt,
Whilſt I, whome Fortune of ſuch tryumph bars,
  Vnlookt for, ioy in that I honour moſt.   4

Great Princes fauorites, their faire leaues ſpread
  But as the Marygold at the ſuns eye,
And in them-ſelues their pride lies buried,
  For, at a frowne, they in their glory die.   6

The painefull warrier, famoſëd for worth,
　After a thouſand victories once foild,
Is from the Booke of Honour raſëd quite,
　And all the reſt forgot, for which he toild.　　　　12

　Then happy I, that loue, and am beloued
　　Where I may not remoue, nor be remoued!　　　14

*SIR HENRY R. BISHOP, 1821. In his operatiſed *Two Gentlemen of
Verona*, he has introduced the first 4 lines as a sequel to the Chorus
from *As you like it* 'Good Duke, receive thy Daughter', which is
preceded by the first 4 lines of *Sonnet* 97. He makes Julia and
Sylvia sing a duet, Julia singing Sonnet 25, and Sylvia, Sonnet 97,
the first 4 lines of each—both at the same time.

---

27. "WEARY WITH TOYLE."

[Shakspere, away from his young friend, cannot sleep on his
weary bed, for thinking of him.]

Weary with toyle, I haſt me to my bed,
　(The deare repoſe for lims with trauaill tired,)
But then begins a iourny in my head,
　To worke my mind, when boddies work's expired:　　　4

For then my thoughts (from far where I abide)
　Intend a zelous pilgrimage to thee,
And keepe my drooping eye-lids open wide,
　Looking on darknes which the blind doe ſee　　　8

Saue that my ſoules imaginary ſight
　Preſents their ſhaddoe to my ſightles view,
Which, (like a iewell hunge in gaſtly night),
　Makes blacke night beautious, and her old face new.　　　12

　Loe! thus, by day my lims, by night my mind,
　For thee, and for my ſelfe, noe quiet finde.　　　14

*RICHARD SIMPSON, 1878. Solo. Lucas and Weber, New Bond St.

---

29. "WHEN IN DISGRACE WITH FORTUNE AND MENS EYES."

[Shakspere, when forlorn and sad, has but to think of his Friend,
and then is lifted into bliss.]

When, in diſgrace with Fortune and mens eyes,
　I all alone beweepe my out-caſt ſtate,
And trouble deafe heauen with my bootleſſe cries,
　And looke vpon my ſelfe, and curſe my fate,　　　4

G

Wishing me like to one more rich in hope,
　Featur'd like him, like him with friends possest,
Desiring this mans art, and that mans skope,—
　With what I most injoy, contented least,—　　8

Yet, in these thoughts my selfe almost despising,
　Haplye I thinke on thee; and then my state,
(Like to the Larke, at breake of daye arising,
　From sullen earth) sings himns at Heauens gate!　12

　For, thy sweet loue remembred, such welth brings,
　That then I skorne to change my state with Kings.　14

SIR HENRY BISHOP, 1821.　Solo brillante.　Sung by Miss M. Tree in
Two Gentlemen of Verona: 2 movements, 1. andante, 2. allegro

30. "WHEN TO THE SESSIONS OF SWEET SILENT THOUGHT."

[Shakspere so loves his Friend, that even when he thinks over all
the losses he has suffered during his life, yet the vision of his Friend
makes up for all these losses and brings him joy.]

When to the Sessions of sweet silent thought
　I summon vp remembrance of things past,
I sigh the lacke of many a thing I sought,
　And, with old woes, new waile my deare times wast;　4

Then can I drowne an eye (vn-vs'd to flow)
　For precious friends hid in Deaths datels night,
And weepe a-fresh, Loues long since canceld woe,
　And mone th' expence of many a vanisht sight.　8

Then can I greeue at greeuances fore-gon,
　And heauily, from woe to woe, tell ore
The sad account of fore-bemonèd mone,
　Which I new pay, as if not payd before:　12

　But if, the while, I thinke on thee (deare Friend,)
　All losses are restord, and sorrowes end.　14

H. M. CORBETT, 1879.　Song entitled 'Remembrance.'　Compass from
lower B to upper A.

33. "FULL MANY A GLORIOUS MORNING HAVE I SEENE."

[Shakspere excuses his young Friend's neglect of him, and complains not of it.]

Full many a glorious morning haue I seene,
　Flatter the mountaine tops with soueraine eie,
Kissing with golden face the meddowes greene,
　Guilding pale streames with heauenly alcumy;　4

Anon permit the bafeſt cloudes to ride,
　With ougly rack, on his celeſtiall face,
And from the fór-lorne world his viſage hide,
　Stealing vnſeene to weſt with this diſgrace :　　3

Euen ſo my Sunne one early morne did ſhine,
　With all triumphant ſplendor on my brow;
But, out, alack ! he was but one houre mine;
　The region cloude hath maſk'd him from me now !　12

　　Yet, him for this, my loue no whit diſdaineth :
　　Suns of the world may ſtaine, when heauens ſun ſtaineth.

J. REEKES, about 1850. Solo. 'Six Shakſpere Songs.' Eight lines :
　1-4, 9-12. Two octaves, lower to upper C.
SIR H. BISHOP. 1820. Soprano Song. Sung by Miss M. Tree. Opera,
　Twelfth Night.

---

40. "TAKE ALL MY LOVES, MY LOVE! YEA, TAKE THEM ALL!"

[Shakſpere says he is willing to give up his dark Lady-love (? Mrs.
Fytton[1]) to his young Friend, William Herbert, later, Earl of Pembroke. Whatever she does, the Poet and Earl must not quarrel.]

Take all my loues, my Loue ! yea, take them all !
　What haſt thou then more then thou hadſt before ?
No loue, my Loue, that thou maiſt 'true loue' call :
　All mine was thine, before thou hadſt this more :　4

Then, if for my loue, thou my Loue receiueſt,
　I cannot blame thee, for my loue thou vſeſt;
But yet be blam'd, if thou this ſelfe deceaueſt
　By willfull taſte of what thy ſelfe refuſeſt.　8

I doe forgiue thy robb'rie, gentle Theefe,
　Although thou ſteale thee all my pouerty;
And yet, loue knowes, it is a greater griefe
　To beare loues wrong, then hates knowne iniury.　12

　　Laſciuious Grace, in whom all ill, wel ſhowes,
　　Kill me with ſpights ! yet we muſt not be foes.　14

SIR HENRY BISHOP, 1820. Solo, Soprano. Sung by Miss Greene in
　Twelfth Night.
CHARLES HORN, 1821. Solo, Tenor or Baſs. Sung by him in the
　Tempeſt.

---

[1] See Mr. T. Tyler's letters in the *Academy* of March 8, March 22, and
April 19, 1884. Mrs. Fytton was Lord Pembroke's 'cause', and had a child
by him.

44. "IF THE DULL SUBSTANCE OF MY FLESH WERE THOUGHT."

[Shakspere says that if his body were Thought, he'd spring to his friend Lord W. Herbert from the greatest distance. As it isn't, he must wait and weep.]

If the dull substance of my flesh were Thought,
  Iniurious Distance should not stop my way;
For then, dispight of space, I would be brought
  From limits farre remote, where thou doost stay.   4

No matter, then although my foote did stand
  Vpon the farthest earth remoou'd from thee;
For nimble thought can iumpe both sea and land,
  As soone as thinke the place where he would be.   8

But, ah! Thought kills me that I am not Thought,
  To leape large lengths of miles when thou art gone,
But that, so much of earth and water wrought,
  I must attend Times leisure with my mone;   12

    Receiuing nought by elements so sloe,
    But heauie teares, badges of eithers woe.   14

*CHARLES KENSINGTON SALAMAN, 1880. Song entitled 'Thought.'
Lucas and Weber.

---

54. "OH, HOW MUCH MORE DOTH BEAUTIE, BEAUTIOUS SEEME!"

[Shakspere assures his young Friend that when his youth fades, his Truth shall liue for euer in Shakspere's verse. Compare Sonnet 15 above, and 63 and 81 below.]

Oh, how much more doth Beautie, beautious seeme,
  By that sweet ornament which Truth doth giue!
The Rose lookes faire; but fairer we it deeme,
  For that sweet odor, which doth in it liue: 4

The Canker bloomes haue full as deepe a die,
  As the perfumed tincture of the Roses;
Hang on such thornes, and play as wantonly,
  When sommers breath their masked buds disclofes: 8

But, for their vertue only is their show,
  They liue vnwoo'd, and vnrespected fade,
Die to themselues. Sweet Roses doe not so:
  Of their sweet deaths, are sweetest odors made: 12

    And so of you, beautious and louely youth,
    When that shall vade, by[1] verse distils your truth.   14

    [1] by, generally emended to my.

SIR HENRY BISHOP, 1820. First 4 lines. Solo, Soprano. Sung by
Miss Greene in *Twelfth Night.*
*EARL BEAUCHAMP, 1866. Glee. Gaind the 2nd prize at the Noblemen's
and Gentlemen's Catch Club. Novello.
GEORGE BARKER, 1870. Solo. Composed for, and printed in, the
'Ballad Album.'

---

57. "BEING YOUR SLAVE, WHAT SHOULD I DOE?"

[Shakspere is so devoted to his Friend, that when he is away, the
poet can only wait and watch, and long for him, and think how
happy those are with whom he is.]

Being your flaue, what fhould I doe, but tend
  Vpon the houres, and times of your defire?
I haue no precious time at al to fpend;
  Nor feruices to doe til you require.   4

Nor dare I chide the world-without-end houre,
  Whilft I (my Soueraine) watch the clock for you,
Nor thinke the bitternelfe of abfence fowre,
  When you haue bid your feruant once ' Adieue.'   8

Nor dare I queftion with my iealious thought,
  Where you may be, or your affaires fuppofe:
But, like a fad flaue, ftay and thinke of nought,
  Saue, where you are, how happy you make thofe!   12

So true a foole is loue, that in your Will,
  (Though you doe anything), he thinkes no ill.   14

*CHARLES E. HORN, 1826. Song, T. or B. Sung in the operatized
Tempest.

---

58. "THAT GOD FORBID."

[Shakspere will not presume to blame his young Friend for ill
spending of his time or neglecting Shakspere.]

That God forbid, that made me firft your flaue,
  I fhould in thought controule your times of pleafure,
Or at your hand th' account of houres to craue,
  Being your vaffail, bound to ftaie your leifure!   4

Oh, let me fuffer (being at your beck)
  Th' imprifon'd abfence of your libertie;
And patience, tame to fufferance, bide each check,
  Without accufing you of iniury!   8

Be where you lift! your charter is fo ftrong,
  That you your felfe may priuiledge your time
To what you will; to you it doth belong,
  Your felfe to pardon of felfe-doing crime.   12

I am to waite, (though waiting fo be hell;)
Not blame your pleafure; be it ill or well.   14

*RICHARD SIMPSON, 1878. Solo. Lucas and Weber, New Bond St.

59. "IF THERE BEE NOTHING NEW."

[Shakspere wishes he could see old records, to find whether any
one has ever been so handsome as his young Friend, Wm. Herbert.]

If their bee nothing new; but that which is,
    Hath beene before; how are our braines beguild,
Which, laboring for inuention, beare amiffe
    The fecond burthen of a former child!   4

Oh that record could (with a back-ward looke,
    Euen of fiue hundreth courfes of the Sunne,)
Show me your image in fome antique booke,
    Since minde at firft in carrecter was done,   6

That I might fee what the old world could fay,
    To this compofed wonder of your frame;
Whether we are mended, or where[1] better they,
    Or whether reuolution be the fame.   12

    Oh, fure I am, the wits of former daies,
    To fubiects worfe, haue giuen admiring praife!   14

*RICHARD SIMPSON, 1878. Song. Lucas and Weber, New Bond St.

63. "AGAINST MY LOVE."

[Shakspere declares his Friend's beauty shall, when it fades, live in
his (Sh.'s) lines. Compare Sonnets 18 and 54, above, and 81, below.]

Againft my Loue fhall be, as I am now,
    (With Times iniurious hand chrufht and ore-worne,)
When houres haue dreind his blood, and fild his brow
    With lines and wrincles; when his youthfull morne   4

Hath trauaild on to Ages fteepie night;
    And all thofe beauties, whereof now he's King,
Are vanifhing, or vanifht out of fight,
    Stealing away the treafure of his Spring;—   8

For fuch a time do I now fortifie
    Againft confounding Ages cruell knife,
That he fhall neuer cut from memory
    My fweet Loues beauty, though my louers life.   12

    His beautie fhall in thefe blacke lines be feene:
    And they fhall liue; and he in them ftill greene.   14

*RICHARD SIMPSON, 1878. Solo. Lucas and Weber, New Bond St.

                    1 where, whether.

64. "WHEN I HAVE SEENE THE HUNGRY OCEAN."

[Looking at the destruction wrought by Time, Shakspere sees that it will some day take his young Friend from him.]

When I haue seene, by Times fell hand defaced
  The rich proud coft of outworne buried age;
When fometime loftie towers, I fee downe rafed,
  And braffe, eternall flaue to mortall rage;   4

When I haue feene the hungry Ocean gaine
  Aduantage on the Kingdome of the fhoare,
And the firme foile win of the watry maine,
  Increafing ftore with loffe, and loffe with ftore;   8

When I haue feene fuch interchange of ftate,
  Or ftate it felfe confounded, to decay,
Ruine hath taught me thus to ruminate:
  That Time will come, and take my loue away.   12

    This thought is as a death which cannot choofe,
    But weepe to haue, that which it feares to loofe.   14

SIR HENRY BISHOP, 1821. Solo. Sung by Master Longhurst in *Two Gentlemen of Verona*. Begins, "When I have seen the hungry ocean," line 5.

71. "NOE LONGER MOURNE."

[Shakspere begs his Friend not to mourn for him when he dies, and not even to love his memory, lest the World should mock his friend for so doing.]

Noe Longer mourne for me when I am dead!
  Then you fhall heare the furly fullen bell
Giue warning to the world, that I am fled
  From this vile world, with vildeft wormes to dwell: 4

Nay, if you read this line, remember not,
  The hand that writ it! for I loue you fo,
That I in your fweet thoughts would be forgot,
  If thinking on me then fhould make you woe.   8

O! if (I fay) you looke vpon this verfe,
  When I (perhaps) compounded am with clay,
Do not fo much as my poore name reherfe;
  But let your loue, euen with my life decay,   12

    Leaft the wife world fhould looke into your mone,
    And mocke you with me, after I am gon.   14

*E. J. LODER, 1841. Duet for two Sopranos. No. 5 of 'Six new vocal duets.' Part of *The Melophon*.
*RICHARD SIMPSON, 1878. Solo. Lucas and Weber, New Bond St.

73. "THAT TIME OF YEEARE THOU MAIST IN ME BEHOLD."

[Shakspere is growing old (? 34),[1] and this, his young Friend sees, and therefore values him the more, as he may lose him soon.]

That time of yeeare thou maift in me behold,
  When yellow leaues, or none or few, doe hange
Vpon thofe boughes which fhake againft the could,
  Bare ruin'd quiers, where late the fweet birds fang.   4
In me thou feeft the twi-light of fuch day,
  As after Sun-fet fadeth in the Weft,
Which by and by blacke night doth take away,
  Deaths fecond felfe that feals vp all in reft.   8
In me thou feeft the glowing of fuch fire,
  That on the afhes of his youth doth lye,
As the death-bed, whereon it muft expire,
  Confum'd with that which it was nurrifht by.   12
    This thou perceu'ft, which makes thy loue more ftrong,
    To loue that well, which thou muft leaue ere long.   14

SIR HENRY BISHOP, 1821. Lines 1-8 only. Cavatina, sung by Miss
  M. Tree in *Two Gentlemen of Verona.*
*RICHARD SIMPSON, 1878. Solo. Lucas and Weber.

---

81. "OR SHALL I LIVE."

[Shakspere assures his young Friend of future life in his (S.'s) verse. Compare Sonnets 18, 54, and 63, above.]

Or I fhall liue, your Epitaph to make,
  Or you furuiue when I in earth am rotten :
From hence, your memory Death cannot take,
  Although in me each part will be forgotten.   4
Your name from hence, immortall life fhall haue,
  Though I (once gone) to all the world muft dye :
The earth can yeeld me but a common graue,
  When you intombèd in mens eyes fhall lye :   8
Your monument fhall be my gentle verfe,
  Which eyes not yet created, fhall ore-read,
And toungs to be, your beeing fhall rehearfe,
  When all the breathers of this world are dead,   12
    You ftill fhall liue (fuch vertue hath my Pen)
    Where breath moft breaths, euen in the mouths of men. 14

*RICHARD SIMPSON, 1878. Solo. Lucas and Weber.

---

[1] The *Sonnets* were publifht in 1609, when Shakspere was 45. Meres
spoke of some of them in 1598, when Shakspere was 34. That he considerd
a man quite old at 40, we know from *Sonnet* II.

87. "FAREWELL! THOU ART TOO DEARE FOR MY POSSESSING."

[Shakspere, thinking his Friend (Lord W. Herbert) has withdrawn
his friendship from him, acquiesces in the fact.]

Farewell! thou art too deare for my poſſeſſing!
And, like enough, thou knowſt thy eſtimate:
The Charter of thy worth giues thee releaſing;
My bonds in thee are all determinate.   4

For how do I hold thee, but by thy granting?
And for that ritches, where is that deſeruing?
The cauſe of this faire guiſt in me is wanting,
And ſo my pattent back againe is ſweruing.   8

Thy ſelfe thou gau'ſt, thy owne worth then not knowing,
Or mee to whom thou gau'ſt it, elſe miſtaking;
So thy great guift, vpon miſpriſion growing,
Comes home againe, on better iudgement making.   12

Thus haue I had thee, as a dreame doth flatter:
In ſleepe a King; but waking, no ſuch matter.   14

J. REEKES, about 1850.   Solo.   'Six Shakspere Songs.'   Lines 1-4.
*L. CARACCIOLO, 1879.   Solo.   Ricordi.

92. "SAY THO' YOU STRIVE TO STEAL YOURSELF AWAY."

[Shakspere so loves his Friend, that if that Friend withdraws his
love from him, he will die, and be happy in his death. But even if
his Friend is false to him, he may not know it.]

Bvt doe thy worſt to ſteale thy ſelfe away,
For tearme of life thou art aſſurëd mine;
And life no longer then thy loue will ſtay,
For it depends vpon that loue of thine.   4

Then need I not to feare the worſt of wrongs,
When in the leaſt of them my life hath end;
I ſee, a better ſtate to me belongs,
Then that which on thy humor doth depend: 8

Thou canſt not vex me with inconſtant minde,
Since that my life on thy reuolt doth lie:
Oh! what a happy title do I finde!
Happy to haue thy loue; happy to die!   12

But whats ſo bleſſed faire, that feares no blot?
Thou maiſt be falce, and yet I know it not.   14

*Sir Henry R. Bishop, 1821. Duet, S.A., in the Operatised *Two Gentlemen of Verona.* No. 3, p. 11. Line 1 is alterd to 'Say tho' you strive to steal yourself away.'

96. "SOME SAY THY FAULT IS YOUTH."

[Shakspere's Friend has committed faults. Though these, in him, look graces, Shakspere prays him to abstain from them, for his good name is Shakspere's too.]

Some say thy fault is youth; some, wantoneffe;
Some say thy grace is youth and gentle fport:
Both grace and faults are lou'd of more and leffe:
Thou makft faults graces, that to thee refort: 4

As on the finger of a thron'd Queene,
The bafeft Iewell will be well efteem'd,
So are thofe errors that in thee are feene,
To truths tranflated, and for true things deem'd. 8

How many Lambs might the fterne Wolfe betray,
If, like a Lambe, he could his lookes tranflate?
How many gazers might thou lead away,
If thou wouldft vfe the ftrength of all thy ftate? 12

But doe not fo! I loue thee in fuch fort,
As thou, being mine, mine is thy good report. 14

*Richard Simpson, 1878. Solo. Lucas and Weber.

97. "HOW LIKE A WINTER HATH MY ABSENCE BEEN."

[Shakspere has been away from his Friend; and tho' he has been prosperous, yet his gain has seemd lofs, for all his joy is in his Friend.]

How like a Winter, hath my abfence beene
From thee, the pleafure of the fleeting yeare!
What freezings haue I felt! what darke daies feene!
What old Decembers barenefle euery where! 4

And yet this time remou'd, was Sommers time,
The teeming Autumne big with ritch increafe,
Bearing the wanton burthen of the prime,
Like widdowed wombes, after their Lords deceafe. 8

Yet this aboundant iffue feem'd to me,
But hope of Orphans, and vn-fathered fruite;
For Sommer, and his pleafures, waite on thee;
And thou away, the very birds are mute; 12

Or if they fing, tis with fo dull a cheere,
That leaues looke pale, dreading the Winters neere. 14

SIR HENRY BISHOP, 1821. Concerted Piece, in the operatised *Two
Gentlemen of Verona*. Some lines only.

---

109. "O, NEVER SAY THAT I WAS FALSE OF HEART."

[Shakspere declares that his abfence never leffend his love for
his Friend. He is the poet's Rose of the World.]

O, neuer fay that I was falfe of heart,
  Though abfence feem'd my flame to quallifie:
As eafie might I from my felfe depart,
  As from my foule, which in thy breft doth lye: 4

That is my home of loue. If I haue rang'd,
  Like him that trauels, I returne againe,
Iuft to the time, not with the time exchang'd,
  So that my felfe bring water for my ftaine.   8

Neuer beleeue, though in my nature raign'd
  All frailties that befiege all kindes of blood,
That it could fo prepofterouflie be ftain'd,
  To leaue for nothing all thy fumme of good;   12

    For 'nothing', this wide Vniuerfe I call,
    Saue thou my Rofe! in it, thou art my all.   14

M. P. KING. Glee or Trio with an accompaniment.
SIR HENRY BISHOP, 1821. Bravura Song. Sung by Miss Hallande
  as Sylvia in *Two Gentlemen of Verona*, p. 19. Only lines 1-4, 13-14.
*C. ARNOLD, 1835. Song, Soprano. Sung by Miss Adelaide Kemble.
*ALBERTO RANDEGGER, 1869. Song, Contralto. Entitled *The Un-
  changeable*. Sung by Madame Patey. Compass, E to lower A.

---

110. "ALAS! 'TIS TRUE I HAVE GONE HERE AND THERE."

[Shakspere confesses that he has made himself cheap to other
men. But he prays his Friend—next to God, his Best—to love him
again.]

    Alas! 'tis true I haue gone here and there,
      And made my felfe a motley to the view,
    Gor'd mine own thoughts, fold cheap what is moft deare,
      Made old offences of affections new.   4

Moſt true it is, that I haue lookt on truth
  Aſconce and ſtrangely : But, by all aboue,
Theſe blenches gaue my heart an other youth ;
  And worſe eſſaies, prou'd thee my beſt of loue.   8

Now all is done,—haue what ſhall haue no end,—
  Mine appetite I neuer more will grin'de
On newer proofe, to trie an older friend,
  A God in loue, to whom I am confin'd.   12

    Then giue me welcome, next my heauen the beſt,
    Euen to thy pure, and moſt, moſt louing breſt!   14

*RICHARD SIMPSON, 1878.   Solo.   Lucas and Weber.

---

116. "LET ME NOT TO THE MARRIAGE OF TRUE MINDS ADMIT IMPEDIMENTS."

[Shakſpere aſſures his Friend that Love lasts thro' all changes and disasters, even to the edge of Doom.]

Let me not to the marriage of true mindes
  Admit impediments. Loue is not loue,
Which alters when it alteration findes,
  Or bends, with the remouer, to remoue.   4

O no! it is an euer fixèd marke,
  That lookes on tempeſts, and is neuer ſhaken ;
It is the ſtar to euery wandring barke,
  Whoſe worths vnknowne, although his higth be taken.   8

Lou's not Times foole, though roſie lips and cheeks
  Within his bending ſickles compaſſe come !
Loue alters not with his breefe houres and weekes,
  But beares it out euen to the edge of doome !   12

    If this be error and vpon me proued,
    I neuer writ, nor no man euer loued.   14

JOHN BRAHAM, 1828. Duet : Soprano, Tenor. Sung by himſelf and
  Miss F. Ayton in *Taming of the Shrew*. Called "Love is an ever-
  fixed mark." Lines 5-14.

---

123. "NO! TIME! THOU SHALT NOT BOST THAT I DOE CHANGE."

[Shakspere fears not Time, or its works. He will be true to his Friend for ever.]

No! Time! thou fhalt not boft that I doe change!
Thy Pyramyds, buylt vp with newer might,
To me are nothing nouell, nothing ftrange:
They are but dreflings of a former fight.   4

Our dates are breefe; and therefor we admire
What thou doft foyft vpon vs that is ould,
And rather make them borne to our defire,
Then thinke that we before haue heard them tould.   8

Thy Regifters and Thee, I both defie,
Not wondring at the Prefent, nor the Paft;
For thy Records, and what we fee, doth lye,
Made more or les by thy continuall haft.   12

This I doe vow, and this fhall euer be:
I will be true, difpight thy Syeth and Thee.   14

SIR HENRY R. BISHOP, 1824. Solo, S. In the operatised *As you like
it.* Opens with a *largo*, and closes with an *allegro.* Roffe, p. 107.
Only lines 1—4, and 13—4, are set.

---

148. "O ME! WHAT EYES HATH LOVE PUT
IN MY HEAD."

[Shakfpere asks himself how he can think his plain dark Miftress
(? Mrs. Fytton) fair, when she is foul. It is, because she keeps him
tearful, anxious for her love, and thus blind.]

O me! what eyes hath loue put in my head,
Which haue no correfpondence with true fight?
Or, if they haue, where is my iudgment fled,
That cenfures falfely what they fee aright?   4

If that be faire whereon my falfe eyes dote,
What meanes the world to fay it is not fo?
If it be not, then loue doth well denote,
Loues eye is not fo true as all mens: No!   8

How can it? O, how can loues eye be true,
That is fo vext with watching and with teares?
No maruaile then though I miftake my view:
The funne it felfe fees not, till heauen cleeres.   12

O cunning loue, with teares thou keepft me blinde,
Leaft eyes well feeing, thy foule faults fhould finde. 14

SIR HENRY BISHOP, 1824. Song, Soprano. Sung by Miss M. Tree as
Rofalind, in *As You Like It.* Roffe, p. 107.

Venus and Adonis.

STANZA I. "EVEN AS THE SUN, WITH PURPLE-COLOURED FACE."

[Venus comes to woo Adonis, bent on hunting.]

(1)

E Ven as the funne, with purple-colourd face, 1
 Had tane his laft leaue of the weeping morne,
Rofe-cheekt *Adonis* hied him to the chace :
 Hunting he lou'd ; but loue, he laught to fcorne : 4
 Sick-thoughted *Venus* makes amaine vnto him,
 And like a bold-fac'd futer ginnes to woo him. 6

CHARLES EDWARD HORN, 1823. Hunting Song, Soprano. Sung by
Anne Page in the operatiſed *Merry Wives.* In 'Shakspere Vo. al
Mag,' No. 15, 1864, &c.
SIR HENRY BISHOP, 1824. Glee, A.T.T.B. Operatised *As You Like It.*

Venus and Adonis, Stanza 24, lines 145—150.

"BID ME DISCOURSE, I WILL ENCHANT THINE EAR."

[Venus is rehearsing her charms, in order to tempt Adonis.]

(25)

Bid me difcourfe I will inchaunt thine eare ; 145
 Or like a Fairie, trip vpon the greens ;
Or, like a Nimph, with long difheueled heare,
 Daunce on the fands, and yet no footing feene. 148
 Loue is a fpirit all compact of fire,
 Not groffe to finke, but light, and will afpire. 150

SIR HENRY BISHOP, 1820. Solo. Soprano. Sung by Miss M. Tree s
Viola in the operatised *Twelfth Night.* Roffe, p. 110.

Venus and Adonis, Stanza 34, lines 169—174.

"ART THOU OBDURATE, FLINTIE, HARD AS STEELE."

[Adonis has refuzed Venus's advances. She remonstrates with him, and asks for one kiss.]

(34)

Art thou obdurate, flintie, hard as fteele ? 169
Nay more then flint, for ftone at raine relenteth,
Art thou a womans fonne, and canft not feele
What t s to loue, how want of loue tormenteth ? 172

O, had thy mother borne fo bad a mind,
She had not brought foorth thee, but dyed vnkind.   174

(35)

What am I, that thou fhouldft contemne me this[1]?   175
Or what great danger dwels vpon my fate?
What were thy lips the worfe, for one poore kiffe?
Speake, Faire: but fpeake faire words or elfe bee mute.   178
Giue me one kiffe, Ile giue it thee again;
And one for int'reft, if thou wilt haue twaine.   180

SIR HENRY BISHOP, 1824.   Song : Soprano or Tenor.   Sung in *As You Like It.*

Venus and Adonis, Stanza 130, lines 775—780.

"IF LOVE HATII LENT YOU TWENTIE THOUSAND TONGUES."

[Adonis refuzes Venus's preffing offers of love.]

(130)

If Loue haue lent you twentie thoufand tongues,   775
And euerie tongue more mouing then your owne,
(Bewitching like the wanton Marmaides Songs,)
Yet from mine eare the tempting tune is blowne.   778
For know, my heart ftands armed in my eare,
And will not let a falfe found enter there,   780

(131)

Left the deceiuing harmony fhould runne   781
Into the quiet clofure of my breft,
And then my little heart were quite vndone,
In his bed-chamber to be bard of reft: 784
No Lady, no: my heart longs not to grone,
But foundly fleeps, while now it fleeps alone.   786

SIR HENRY BISHOP, 1824.   Song, Soprano.   Sung by Miss Tree in the operatized *As You Like It.*
G. REEKES, ab. 1850.   Solo, Alto or Bass.   J. Reekes, 'Six Songs of Shakspere.'

Venus and Adonis, Stanza 143, lines 753-8.

"LO, HERE THE GENTLE LARKE, WEARIE OF REST."

[Adonis has run from Venus.   She laments all night; and in the dawning, greets the Lark, and Sun.]

[1] *this* = thus.

(143)

Loe here the gentle Larke, wearie of reft,   753
From his moift cabinet mounts vp on high,
And wakes the morning, from whofe filuer breft,
The Sunne arifeth in his Maieftie;   756
·Who doth the World fo glorioufly behold,
That Cedar tops and hils feeme burnifht Gold.   758

(144)

Venus falutes him with this faire good morrow;   759
O thou cleere God, and Patron of all light,
From whom each lamp & fhining ftar doth borrow
The beautious influence that makes him bright.   762
There liues a Son, that fuckt an earthly mother,
May lend thee light as thou doft lend to other.   764

SIR HENRY BISHOP, 1819. Song, Soprano. Flute Obbligato. Sung by Miss Stephens in Comedy of Errors (p. 88, ed. 1819). Only stanza 143 is set.

Venus and Adonis, Stanza 180, lines 1075-80.

"ALAS, POORE WORLD, WHAT TREASURE HAST THOU LOST."

[Adonis being dead—kild by the Boar he was hunting—Venus laments: What is now worth looking at or hearing or thinking of? All Beauty died with Adonis.]

(180)

Alas, poore world what treafure haft thou loft,   1075
What face remains aliue that's worth the viewing?
Whofe toong is mufick now? what canft thou boaft,
Of things long fince, or anything infuing?
The floures are fweet, their colours frefh & trim,
But true fweete beautie liu'd, and di de with him.   1080

*A. R. GAUL, 1876. Part-Song, S.A.T.B. Novello. (Entitled, The death of Adonis.)

Venus and Adonis, Stanza 183, lines 1093—8.

183. "TO SEE HIS FACE, THE LION WALKT ALONG."

(st. 183 only, set)

[Venus defcribes the gentlenefs of Adonis, and the love of all other animals for him. Even the Boar who kild him, did fo becaufe it wanted to kifs him.]

(183)

To fee his[1] face, the Lion walkt along,   1093
Behind fome hedge, becaufe hee would not fear[2] him ;
To recreate himfelfe when he hath fong,
The Tygre would be tame, and gently heare him :   1096
  If he had fpoke, the Wolfe would leaue his prey,
  And neuer fright the filly Lambe that day.   1098

(184)

When he beheld his fhadow in a Brooke,   1099
The filhes fpred on it their golden gils :
When he was by, the birds fuch pleafure tooke,
That fome would fing fome other in their bils,   1102
  Would bring him Mulberies, and ripe red Cherries :
  He fed them with his fight, they him with berries.   1104

(185)

But this foule, grim and vrchinfnouted Boare,   1105
Whofe downward eye ftill looketh for a graue,
Ne're faw the beauteous liuery that he wore ;
Witneffe the entertainment that he gaue :   1108
  If he did fee his face, why then, I know,
  He thought to kiffe him, and hath kild him fo.   1110

(186)

Tis true, true, true, thus was *Adonis* flaine,   1111
He ran vpon the Boare with his fharpe fpeare,
Who would not whet his teeth at him againe,
But by a kiffe thought to perfwade him there :   1114
  And noufling in his flanke, the louing Swine,
  Sheath'd vnaware the tuske in his foft groine.   1116

(187)

Had I been tooth'd like him, I muft confeffe,   1117
With kiffing him I fhould haue kild him firft :
But he is dead and neuer did he bleffe
My youth with his : the more am I accurft :   1120
  With this fhe[3] falleth in the place fhe ftood,
  And ftaines her face with his congealed bloud.   1122

SIR HENRY BISHOP, 1821.   Round for four **male** voices.   In the
operatised *Two Gentlemen of Verona*, p. 41 ; also publisht
separately by Novello.   Only the first 4 lines of stanza 183 are set.

        [1] Adonis's.   [2] frighten.
                    [3] each. Qo. 1.

                                                              H

𝔗𝔥𝔢 𝔓𝔞𝔰𝔰𝔦𝔬𝔫𝔞𝔱𝔢 𝔓𝔦𝔩𝔤𝔯𝔦𝔪.

7. "FAIRE IS MY LOVE, BUT NOT SO FAIRE AS FICKLE."

[None of the following pieces from this mi-cellaneous Collection is certainly Shakspere's. Most are certainly not his. "Crabbed age and youth" may perhaps be his.]

VII.

[A jilted lover describes his false Love's beauty and untruth.]

Faire is my loue, but not so faire as fickle.   1
Milde as a Doue, but neither true nor truftie ;
Brighter then glasse, and yet, as glasse is, brittle ;
Softer then waxe, and yet, as Iron, rusty :   4
  A lilly pale, with damaske die to grace her ;
  None fairer, nor none falfer to deface her.   6

Her lips to mine, how often hath she ioyned.   7
Betweene each kiffe, her othes of true loue fwearing :
How many tales to pleafe me hath she coyned,
Dreading my loue, the losse whereof still fearing.   10
  Yet in the mids of all her pure proteftings,
  Her faith, her othes, her teares, and all were ieaftings. 12

She burnt with loue, as straw with fire flameth ;   13
She burnt out loue, as soone as straw out burneth :
She fram'd the loue, and yet she foyld the framing ;
She bad loue last, and yet she fell a turning.   16
  Was this a louer, or a Letcher whether ?
  Bad in the best, though excellent in neither.   18

*Name unknown. Madrigal.
SIR HENRY BISHOP, 1824. Song. Sung by Mr. Fawcett in *As You Like It.*
*RICHARD SIMPSON, 1878. Solo. Lucas and Weber.

Passionate Pilgrim. No. 8. RICHARD BARNFIELD'S Sonnet to a Lover of Music.

8. "IF MUSICKE AND SWEET POETRIE AGREE."

VIII.

[A lover of Poetry and Spenser, shows how natural is his love for a friend who is devoted to Music, and Dowland.]

If Muficke and fweet Poetrie agree,
As they muft needs (the Sifter and the brother,)
Then muft the loue be great twixt thee and me,
Becaufe thou lou'ft the one, and I the other.)   4
Dowland[1] to thee is deere, whofe heauenly tuch
Vpon the Lute, dooth rauifh humane fenfe :
Spenfer to me, whofe deepe Conceit is fuch,
As paffing all conceit, needs no defence.   8
Thou lou'ft to heare the fweet melodious found,
That *Phœbus* Lute (the Queene of Muficke) makes :
And I in deepe Delight am chiefly drownd,
When-as himfelfe to finging he betakes.   12
   One God is God of both (as Poets faine) ;
   One Knight loues Both, and both in thee remaine.   14

JOHN BRAHAM, 1828.   Song.   Sung by himfelf in the *Taming of the Shrew*, and printed in the operatifed version of that play.

Passionate Pilgrim, No. 10.   To a fair one dead.

10.   "SWEET ROSE, FAIRE FLOWER, VN-TIMELY PLUCKT, SOON VADED."

X.

Sweet Rofe, faire flower, vntimely pluckt, foon vaded,   1
Pluckt in the bud, and vaded in the fpring !
Bright orient pearle, alacke, too timely fhaded !
Faire creature kilde too foon by Deaths fharpe fting !   4
   Like a greene plumbe that hangs vpon a tree,
   And fals (through winde) before the fall fhould be.   6

I weepe for thee ; and yet no caufe I haue ;   7
For why[2] thou lefts me nothing in thy will :
And yet thou lefts me more then I did craue ;
For why I craued nothing of thee ftill :   10
   O yes, (deare friend,) I pardon craue of thee :
   Thy difcontent thou didft bequeath to me.   12

WM. SHIELD, 1790.   Elegy, in four vocal Parts.   Accompaniments for Muffled Drums, Trumpet, Bells with Sordini and Flute.   In 'A Collection of Canzonets, and an Elegy,' by Wm. Shield, p. 27 : called "Shakspears Love's Lost, an Elegy sung at the Tomb of a young Virgin."
SIR HENRY BISHOP, 1819.   Cavatina.   Sung by Miss M. Tree in the operatised *Comedy of Errors*.

---

[1] John Dowland, musician, 15-16.
[2] *For why* = because.

H 2

12. "CRABBED AGE AND YOUTH."

[A Girl sings how she hates her old lover, and loves her young
one, whom she bids hie to her soon.]

XII.

Crabbèd age and youth cannot liue together,
Youth is full of pleasance, Age is full of care;
Youth like summer morne, Age like winter weather,
Youth like summer braue, Age like winter bare.   4

Youth is full of sport; Ages breath is short;
Youth is nimble; Age is lame;
Youth is hot and bold; Age is weake and cold;
Youth is wild, and Age is tame.   8

Age, I doe abhor thee! Youth, I doe adore thee!
O, my loue, my loue is young!
Age, I doe defie thee! Oh sweet Shepheard, hie thee!
For me thinks thou staies too long.   12

G. GIORDANI, 1782. Duet: S.S. or T.T.
R. J. S. STEVENS, 1790. Glee for four male voices, A.T.T.B.
SIR HENRY R. BISHOP, 1820. Song. Sung by Miss Greene in Opera
    Twelfth Night.
*CHARLES E. HORN, 1823. Song in the operatized *Merry Wives of
    Windsor.*
SIR HENRY R. BISHOP, 1824. Dramatic Trio, S.C.B. In *his Vow
    Like It.*
EARL OF WESTMORELAND, 1833. Solo.
*MRS. MOUNSEY BARTHOLOMEW, February 6, 1882. Song, Soprano or
    Tenor. 'Six Songs.' No. 1. Lucas and Weber.

---

13. "BEAUTY IS BUT A VAINE AND DOUBTFULL GOOD."

XIII.

(1)

Beauty is but a vaine and doubtfull good;
A shining glosse, that vadeth sodainly;
A flower that dies, when first it gins to bud,
A brittle glasse, that's broken presently.   4
    A doubtfull good, a glosse, a glasse, a flower,
    Lost, vaded, broken, dead within an houre.   6

(2)

And, as goods loſt, are feld or neuer found ;   7
As vaded glotſe, no rubbing will refreſh ;
As flowers dead, lie withered on the ground ;
As broken glaſſe, no ſymant can redreſſe ;   10
So, beauty blemiſht once, for euer's¹ loſt,
In ſpite of phiſicke, painting, paine and coſt.   12

*SIR HENRY R. BISHOP, 1819. Solo, Bass. 'Beauty's Valuation.'
Sung by Mr. Durusett in Shakspeare's *Comedy of Errors*, at the
Theatre Royal, Covent Garden.

Passionate Pilgrim. No. 14.

14. "GOOD NIGHT, GOOD REST."

XIV.

(1)

'Good night, good reſt'! Ah! neither be my ſhare :
She bad good night : that kept my reſt away,
And daſt me to a cabben hangde with care,
To deſcant on the doubts of my decay.   4
    'Farewell (quoth ſhe) and come againe to morrow'!
    'Fare well' I could not, for I ſupt with ſorrow.   6

(2)

Yet at my parting, ſweetly did ſhe ſmile,   7
In ſcorne or friendſhip, nill I conſier whether :
'T' may be, ſhe joyd to ieaſt at my exile ;
'T' may be, againe to make me wander thither,   10
    'Wander,' a word for ſhadowes like my ſelfe,
    As take the paine, but cannot plucke the pelfe.   12

*SIR HENRY BISHOP, 1821. Glee, S.A.T.B. In the Operatised *Two
Gentlemen of Verona*, p. 25.
*WALTER MACFARREN, 1863. Part Song for S.A.T.B.
*RICHARD SIMPSON, 1878. Song, Baritone. Lucas and Weber.
K. J. PYE, 1879. Solo, Tenor. In "Two little Songs." First stanza
only used.

Sonnets to Sundry Notes of Musicke.

Passionate Pilgrim. No. 15.

15. "IT WAS A LORDINGS DAUGHTER."

[A Girl hesitates between a Learned man and a Knight, and then
chooses the Learned man. (Right and wise of her !)]

¹ euer. Qo. 1.   H*

XV.[1]

It was a Lordings daughter, the faireſt one of three,
That liked of her maiſter, as well as well might be,
Till looking on an Engliſhman, the faireſt that eie could ſee,
    Her fancie fell a turning.   4

Long was the combat doubtfull, that loue with loue did fight,
To leaue the maiſter loueleſſe, or kill the gallant knight;
To put in practiſe either, alas it was a ſpite
    Vnto the ſilly damſell.   8

But one muſt be refuſed: more mickle was the paine,
That nothing could be vſed, to turne them both to gaine;
For of the two, the truſty knight was wounded with diſdaine:
    Alas, ſhe could not helpe it.   12

Thus Art with Armes contending, was victor of the day,
Which, by a gift of learning, did beare the maid away.
Then lullaby! the learned man hath got the Lady gay;
    For now my ſong is ended.   16

WM. SHIELD, 1796. Song. Sung by Madame Vestris. 'Shakspere
    Vocal Album,' 1864. No. 22.
CHARLES EDWARD HORN, 1823. Song, Soprano. Sung in the opera-
    tized *Merry Wives of Windsor.* 'Shakspere Vocal Album,' 1864.
STEPHEN GLOVER, 1846. Song.

[For No. 16, "On a day, alacke the day!" See *Love's Labour's
Lost.* IV. iii. 99-118. p. 20-21 above.]

Passionate Pilgrim. No. 17, in 3 Parts.

PART 17. "MY FLOCKES FEEDE NOT."

[The Shepherd Coridon laments his woes (in three outbursts),
now that his Love has jilted him, and he must live alone.]

XVII. PART I.

My flocks feede not, my Ewes breed not,
    My Rams ſpeed not, all is amis!
Loue is[2] dying, Faithes defying,
    Harts[3] denying, cauſer of this.   4
All my merry Iigges are quite forgot;
All my Ladies loue is loſt (God wot!)   6
Where her faith was firmely fixt in loue,
There a nay is plact without remoue.   8

---

[1] The poem usually numbered XV. is but a Continuation of XIV.
'The Lover's Night of Waiting.' See Prof. Dowden's Introduction to the
forthcoming Facsimile of the little Quarto of the P. P.
[2] Loue is = Loues, Love's.   [3] nenying, Q². 1.

One filly croſſe, wrought all my loſſe!
O frowning fortune! curſed fickle dame!
For now I ſee, inconſtancy,
More in women[1] then in men remaine.[2]   12

2nd PART. "IN BLACKE MORNE I."

In blacke morne I, all feares ſcorne I;   13
Loue hath forlorne me, liuing in thrall:
Hart is bleeding, all helpe needing;
O cruell ſpeeding, froughted with gall!   16
My ſhepheards pipe can found no deale;
My weathers bell rings dolefull knell;   18
My curtaile dogge that wont to haue plaid,
Plaies not at all, but ſeemes afraid;   20
My[3] ſighes ſo deepe, procures to weepe,
In howling wiſe, to ſee my dolefull plight.
How ſighes reſound through hartles ground,
Like a thouſand vanquiſht men in blodie fight.   24

3rd PART. "CLEARE WELS SPRING NOT."

Cleare wels ſpring not, ſweete birds ſing not,   25
Greene plants bring not forth their die;
Heards ſtands weeping, flocks all ſleeping,
Nimphs backe[4] peeping fearefully: 28
All our pleaſure knowne to vs poore ſwaines,
All our merrie meetings on the plaines,   30
All our euening ſport from vs is fled!
All our loue is loſt, for loue is dead.   32
Farewell, ſweet loue[5]! thy like nere was,
For a ſweet content, the cauſe of all my woe.[6]
Poore Coridon muſt liue alone!
Other helpe for him, I ſee that there is none.   36

THOMAS WEELKES, 1597.   Three Madrigals, all for S.S.T.   'Book of
Madrigals,' by Thomas Weelkes.   (Mus. Antiquarian Soc. 1843.)
*CHARLES EDWARD HORN, 1830(?).   'In black mourn I,' Cald 'Poor
Corydon.'   Lines 19—28, 52-3; 27-8, 53-6, slightly alterd.

Paſſionate Pilgrim.   No. 19, by KIT MARLOWE.

"COME LIVE WITH ME, AND BE MY LOVE."

[The lover recites the pleasures of the Country, and asks his Love
to ſhare them with him.   She doubts.]

[1] wowen, Qo. 1.
[2] Signed *Ignoto*, in *England's Helicon*, 1600.   It is also in Weelkeses
Madrigals, 1597.
[3] With, Qo. 1.   'My'—Weelkeses *Madrigals*.
[4] backe (creeping).— Weelkeses *Madrigals*, 'blacke.'   P. P., 1599.
[5] laſſ: Weelkeses *Madrigals*.   [6] moane: *England's Helicon*.

XIX.

Liue with me, and be my Loue;
And we will all the pleaſures proue,   2
That hilles and vallies, dales and fields,
And all the craggy mountaines yeeld.   4
There will we ſit vpon the Rocks,
And ſee the Shepheards feed their flocks,   6
By ſhallow Riuers, by whoſe fals[1]
Melodious birds ſing Madrigals.   8
There will I make thee a bed of Roſes,
With a thouſand fragrant poſes,   10
A cap of flowers, and a Kirtle
Imbrodered all with leaues of Mirtle.   12
A belt of ſtraw and Yuie buds,
With Corall Claſps and Amber ſtuds :   14
And if theſe pleaſures may thee moue,
Then liue with me, and be my Loue !   16

LOUES ANSWERE.

If that the World and Loue were young,
And truth in euery ſhepheards toung.   18
Theſe pretty pleaſures might me moue
To liue with thee, and be thy Loue.   20

*S. ARNOLD, 1774. 'The words by Marlow.' Solo, with accompaniment
   for two Violins, Viola, and Basso. In 'A Third Collection of Songs
   sung at Vauxhall and Marybone Gardens,' p. 21-3.
*G. E. FOX, 1877. Song, Baritone. First four stanzas used.
MALCOLM L. LAWSON, 1879. Song, Bass. Called *The Passionate
   Shepherd*. Lucas and Weber.
S. WEBBE. Glee, A.T.T.B.

Passionate Pilgrim. No. 20, by RICHARD BARNFIELD.

"AS IT FELL UPON A DAY."

[A forlorn man sympathises with a Nightingale who is lamenting
the loss of her mate. When troubles come, false friends fly. But
the true Friend helps in need, and shares all one's sorrows.]

XX.

As it fell vpon a Day,
In the merry Month of May,   2
Sitting in a pleaſant ſhade
Which a groue of Myrtles made,   4

[1] For the settings of the lines 'By shallow rivers,' see *Merry Wives of
Windsor* above, p. 32.

Beaftes did leape, and Birds did fing.
Trees did grow, and Plants did fpring;   6
Euery thing did banifh mone,
Saue the Nightingale alone.   8
Shee (poore Bird) as all forlorne,
Leand her breaft vp-till a thorne,   10
And there fung the dolefulft Ditty,
That, to heare it was great Pitty :   12
Fie, fie, fie, now would fhe cry;
Teru, Teru, by and by :   14
That, to heare her fo complaine,
Scarce I could from teares retraine :   16
For her griefes, fo liuely fhowne,
Made me thinke vpon mine owne.   18
Ah (thought I) thou mournft in vaine!
None takes pitty on thy paine :   20
Senflefse Trees, they cannot heare thee ;
Ruthlefse Beares,[1] they will not cheere thee.   22
King Pandion,[2] he is dead :
All thy friends are lapt in Lead :   24
All thy fellow Birds doe fing,
Carelefse of thy forrowing.[3]   26
Whilft as fickle Fortune fmilde,
Thou and I, were both beguild.   28
Euery one that flatters thee,
Is no friend in miferie :   30
Words are eafie, like the wind;
Faithfull friends are hard to find :   32
Euery man will be thy friend,
Whilft thou haft wherewith to fpend :   34
But if ftore of Crownes be fcant,
No man vill fupply thy want.   36
If that one be prodigall,
Bountifull they will him call :   38
And with fuch-like flattering,
Pitty but he were a King !   40
If he be addict to vice,
Quickly him, they will intice.   42
If to Women hee be bent,
They haue at Commaundement :   44
But if Fortune once doe frowne,
Then farewell his great renowne :   46

[1] beasts : *England's Helicon.*
[2] Father of Philomela, the nightingale.
[3] *England's Helicon* adds the lines—
          Euen so, poore Bird, like thee,
          None aliue will pitty me.

They that fawnd on him before,
Vfe his company no more.   48
Hee that is thy friend indeede,
Hee will helpe thee in thy neede :   50
If thou forrow, he will weepe ;
If thou wake, hee cannot fleepe :   52
Thus of euery griefe, in hart
Hee, with thee, doeth beare a part.   54
Thefe are certaine fignes, to know
Faithfull friend, from flatt'ring foe.   56

EARL OF MORNINGTON, ob. 1770.   Four-Part Madrigal.   S.A.T.B.
WILLIAM KNYVETT, about 1812.   Three-Part Madrigal for A.T.B.
SIR HENRY BISHOP, 1819.   Duet.   Sung by Miss Stephens and Miss
    Tree in the operatised *Comedy of Errors.*
*JOHN PARRY, 1820 (?).   Duet, T.B.   Begins, "Words are ease, &c."
    (lines 31—36).
*T. COOKE, 1832.   Glee, A.T.T.B.
*JAMES COWARD, July 28, 1856.   Prize Glee.
*S. REAY, 1862.   Part Song. S.A.T.B.   Novello.
*CHARLES GARDNER, 1872.   Song.

𝕿𝖍𝖊 𝕽𝖆𝖕𝖊 𝖔𝖋 𝕷𝖚𝖈𝖗𝖊𝖈𝖊.

Stanza 56, lines 386—390. (Qo. 1 1594. sign. D 2.)

"ONE OF HER HANDS, ONE ROSY CHEEK LAY UNDER."[1]

[Shakspere describes Lucrece asleep in bed, as Tarquin sees her.]

[St. 56]

Her lillie hand, her rofie cheeke lies vnder,   386
  Coofning the pillow of a lawfull kiffe,
VVho therefore angrie feemes, to part in funder,
  Swelling on either fide to want his bliffe;
Betweene whofe hils her head intombed is,   390
  VVhere, like a vertuous Monument, fhee lies,
  To be admir'd of lewd vnhallowed eyes.   392

[St. 57]

VVithout the bed her other faire hand was,   393
  On the greene coucrlet, whofe perfect white
Showed like an Aprill dazie on the graffe,
  VVith pearlie fwet refembling dew of night.
Her eyes like Marigolds had fheath'd their light,   397
  And canopied in darkeneffe fweetly lay,
  Till they might open to adorne the day.   399

*Dr. T. A. Arne, 1745. Song. *Lyric Harmony*. Vol. II, p. 197.

Rape of Lucrece, Stanza 160, lines 1114-1120. (Qo. 1, 1594, sign. H 3.)

"TIS DOUBLE DEATH, TO DROWNE IN KEN OF SHORE."

[After Tarquin's rape of her, Lucrece laments.]

[St. 158]

So fhee, deepe drenchèd in a Sea of care,   1100
  Holds difputation with ech thing fhee vewes,
And to her felfe, all forrow doth compare;
  No obiect, but her paffions ftrength renewes,
  And as one fhifies, another ftraight infewes: 1104
    Somtime her griefe is dumbe, and hath no words;
    Sometime tis mad, and too much talke affords.   1106

[1] Song entitled: "On Cloë sleeping." Shakspere's words altered. Begins, "One of her Hands one rosy Cheek lay under."

[St. 159]

The little birds that tune their mornings ioy,   1107
  Make her mones mad, with their sweet melodie;
" For mirth doth search the bottome of annoy;
  " Sad foules are slaine in merrie companie;
  " Griefe best is pleas'd with griefes societie;   1111
    " True sorrow then is feelinglie suffiz'd,
  " When with like semblance it is sympathiz'd.   1113

[St. 160]

" Tis double death to drowne in ken of shore: 1114
  " He ten times pines, that pines beholding food:
" To see the salue, doth make the wound ake more:
  " Great griefe greeues most at that wold do it good:
  " Deepe woes roll forward like a gentle flood,   1118
    VVho being stopt, the bounding banks oreflowes:
  Griefe dallied with, nor law nor limit knowes.   1120

RICHARD SIMPSON (the late), published 1878. Song. (" The above
are in the original print; they are often put before maxims.")

Clay and Taylor, Printers, Bungay, Suffolk.

INDEX OF FIRST LINES.

SHA. VIII s

SHAKSPERE'S SONGS.

ADDENDA AND CORRIGENDA FOR SECOND EDITION.

p. 3, l. 5. *For* (d. 1828) *read* (d. 1826).

p. 3, l. 6. *After* English *insert* Litolff, x 83.

p. 4. *Between ll.* 9 *and* 10 *insert*, *Henry Hugo Pierson. 1864. Chorus for male voices. Written for the Shakspere Tercentenary.

p. 7, l. 10 *from bottom. For* 704 *read* 774. *For* Wilbey *read* Wilbye.

p. 7, l. 11 *from bottom. After* Solo. *insert* ("First booke of Ayres or Little short songs to sing and play to the lute, with the Base Viole"). *Dele* In *and insert* See

p. 10, l. 22. *For* (d. 1828) *read* 1826. *After* Solo *insert* Litolff, vii 40.

p. 13, l. 16 *from bottom. After* Virginal Book *add* Page 235. Set by Giles Farnaby.

p. 26, l. 7 *from bottom. For* Welden *read* Weldon.

p. 26, *at foot. For* Sacred, &c. *read* Royal College of Music.

p. 33, l. 3 *from bottom. For* Dr. *read* Sir William.

p. 34, l. 10 *from bottom. For* C. Addison *read* John Addison.

p. 50, l. 24. *For* Tenor Solo *read* Solo, Tenor.—*and dele* Composed . . . Allen.

p. 52, l. 16. *Dele* (* Pelham . . . . . . 1812), *and insert it instead on p.* 53, *between lines* 22 *and* 23 *immediately before* G. Giordani.

p. 53, l. 22. *For* Signor *read* G.

p. 58, l. 3 *from bottom. For* C. H. Hubert *read* C. Hubert H.

p. 64, l. 22. *Dele* Dr. . . . MS.

p. 74, l. 19. *Add* (2). *At foot add Note*. Schubert's settings of Shakspere's Songs were written at Währing in July 1826. Cf. the interesting anecdote as to "Hark the Lark!" &c., in Grove's *Dictionary of Music*, vol. iii. p. 327 a.

p. 74, l. 34. *After* Winter's Tale *dele* (2) *and insert* (3).

p. 74 (*footnote*), l. 4 *from bottom, before* Composed *insert* (1).

p. 74 (*footnote*), l. 2 *from bottom, dele* (2) *and insert* (3).

p. 80, l. 12 *from foot. For* Sonnet 25, Lines 1—4 *read* 25. LET THOSE WHO ARE IN FAVOUR WITH THEIR STARS.

p. 108, last 2 lines. *Read* (The above " " (overline commas) are in the original, &c.).

4

New Shakspere Society.

———•———

CRITICAL AND HISTORICAL PROGRAM

OF THE

𝕸𝖆𝖉𝖗𝖎𝖌𝖆𝖑𝖘, 𝕲𝖑𝖊𝖊𝖘, 𝖆𝖓𝖉 𝕾𝖔𝖓𝖌𝖘

TO BE GIVEN AT

𝕿𝖍𝖊 𝕾𝖊𝖈𝖔𝖓𝖉 𝕬𝖓𝖓𝖚𝖆𝖑 𝕸𝖚𝖘𝖎𝖈𝖆𝖑 𝕰𝖓𝖙𝖊𝖗𝖙𝖆𝖎𝖓𝖒𝖊𝖓𝖙

AT

UNIVERSITY COLLEGE, LONDON,

ON

FRIDAY, 9TH MAY, 1884, AT 8 P.M.

———◇———

𝕻𝖗𝖎𝖓𝖙𝖊𝖉 𝖋𝖔𝖗 𝖙𝖍𝖊 𝕾𝖔𝖈𝖎𝖊𝖙𝖞 𝖇𝖞

CLAY AND TAYLOR.

MDCCCLXXXIV.

CONTENTS.

FIRST PERIOD. EARLY CONTRAPUNTAL.

TO MIDDLE OF SEVENTEENTH CENTURY.

THE vocal pieces which are included in this program are arranged not in strict chronological order, but so as to illustrate, to some extent, the artistic development of the different schools of music. As illustrations, however, they cannot all be considered typical and complete. Shakspere music forms but a small part of music in general, the great composers having usually been satisfied with texts of inferior literary value. English musicians, indeed, have not neglected the capabilities of our best poetry; but then English music is not a very important element in European art. Our composers have seldom exercised much influence abroad; while they, on the other hand, have often been indebted to continental masters. It is true that in the Tudor period England produced a native and original school of music, but this school does not present many peculiarly English features. Distinctions of national style could not become marked until music had reached a more advanced age.

At the Renascence almost every species of art had already acquired elaborate technical resources, and was capable of expressing the energetic thought and vivid feeling of that creative time. Music alone was in a backward state. It did not possess the material means of raising itself to the level of other arts. The form of the scale was still unsettled; few appropriate and connected successions of chords had been discovered; keyrelationship and modulation were only half understood; and instrumental accompaniment was in its infancy. In part-music the treatment of the voices was

3   *

contrapuntal : *i. e.* each part was of equal importance in producing the general effect, but was not always of a melodious character if taken separately. The absence of marked accent and definite phrase often causes the rhythm of the old contrapuntists to appear vague to modern ears. *Imitation* was the chief structural principle, and was worked out in many species of fugue and canon, the different voices taking up the same theme one after the other, in different parts of the scale, so that the latter portion of the theme often formed a harmony to the beginning. The *genres* of composition were comparatively few and rudimentary, Church music being usually founded on the form of the motet, poetic on that of the madrigal. Extended pieces, whether solo or concerted, vocal or instrumental, were as yet unthought of.

The graphic means then at the musician's disposal were very defective. Till the middle of the seventeenth century, barring was not usual in English music, and the text often did not show even where accidental flats, naturals, and sharps were to be used. All these the singer had to supply mentally according to traditional rules. Indications of speed, loudness, phrasing, style, and expression, were likewise absent.

These difficulties have not prevented modern musicians from appreciating the esthetic value of the early school, its sustained style of grandeur and pathos, its liturgical solemnity. Sacred themes engrossed the best talents of a large number of English composers ; and as the Church was then the only school of technical music, its style pervaded other branches of the art, where subjects of merely poetic interest were dealt with. Many of the cathedral services and anthems of Tallis, Farrant, Byrd, Bull, and Orlando Gibbons are still kept alive by their merits ; while only a few of the songs and madrigals of Ward, Wilbye, and Weelkes are now sung, except for their historic interest.

But while the learned musicians had been laboring at heavy counterpoint, the natural, untrained talent of the people found expression in an endless number of gay dance-tunes and expressive songs. Something of this gift of melodious invention appears in the works of Dowland, Ford, and Morley. But the union between

4

the popular and the technical elements was hardly accomplished till the eighteenth century, when every available form of dance tune was eagerly caught up by composers, and worked into the Suite, from which sprang the great designs of later instrumental music.

1. MADRIGAL. In black mourn I. *Passionate Pilgrim*, xvi. b. By THOMAS WEELKES.

The date of this composer's birth and that of his death are unknown. In 1600 he was organist of Winchester College, and in 1608 organist of Chichester Cathedral. In 1597 he published three sets of madrigals, of which the second begins our program. The words are taken from the *Passionate Pilgrim*, a collection of poems published by one Jaggard, with Shakspere's name as author; though most of them, including nos. 1, 17, and 18 in the present program, were by other writers.

Weelkes composed two more sets of madrigals between 1597 and 1608.

This madrigal is a good example of the style, being full of ingenious contrapuntal imitation. The omission of the third in several chords, and the use of the triad of Eb in the key of F, are noteworthy.

The derivation of the word *madrigal* has been much disputed. Passing by the conjectures of unscientific writers, it will be enough to quote the opinion of Diez (dhts). He gives an earlier form of the word as *mandriale*, and considers that it is 'not improbably' descended from Latin *mandra*, a flock, or a shepherd's song.

2. SONG. It was a lover and his lass. *As You Like It*, V. iii. By THOMAS MORLEY (born about 1550, died 1604).

In 1591 he was organist of S. Paul's Cathedral, and in 1592 Gentleman of the Chapel Royal. His compositions were more melodious than those of most of his predecessors, and many of his madrigals and 'ballets' have obtained lasting popularity. This song (No. 2) was printed in 'The first book of ayres or little songs to play on the lute,' 1600. A copy in MS. of at least as early a date is preserved in the Advocate's Library, Edinburgh.

5

3. HARMONIZED AYRE. **Full fathom five.** *Tempest*, I. ii.
By ROBERT JOHNSON.
Arranged for three voices by Dr. John Wilson.

Robert Johnson, in 1573-4, was a retainer in the household
of Sir Thomas Kytson of Hengrave Hall, Suffolk.   He subsequently
came to London, and became a composer for the theatres.   In 1611
he was in the service of Prince Henry, eldest son of James I., at
an annual salary of £40.   In 1612 he composed music for *The
Tempest*, from which we take ' Full fathom five,' afterwards arranged
for three voices by Dr. John Wilson (born 1597, died 1673).

A special interest attaches to the first three pieces in our
program, as they were all composed in Shakspere's life-time.
Dr. Burney, indeed, does not attribute the melody of ' Full fathom
five' to Robert Johnson, but considers the whole to be the composition of Dr. Wilson.   But in Wilson's work, ' Cheerful Ayres or
Ballads, first composed for single voice, and since set for three
voices,' it is printed under Johnson's name.   Wilson's statement
that 'some few of these ayres were originally composed by those
whose names are affixed to them, but are here placed as being new
set by the author of this work,' appears to mean that he did not
invent the melody, but only harmonized one already existing.   The
use of the word *set* in this sense is peculiar, and may easily have
misled Burney.   See Rofie's ' Handbook of Shakspere Music.'

At this time part-music was frequently printed on one sheet in
such a manner, that when three, four, or five singers sat round
a table, the music-sheet would present to the eyes of each vocalist
his or her own part.   A specimen of a five-part piece of ' Table
Music,' as it was called, is given on the next page.

Dr. Wilson's three-voice arrangement of ' Full fathom five,' by
Robert Johnson, is printed in this way, and our musicians will
endeavor to sing it as it would have been sung in a drawing-
room in the reign of Queen Elizabeth.

Example of Score of Table-Music.

SECOND PERIOD. LATE CONTRAPUNTAL.

FROM MIDDLE OF SEVENTEENTH TO MIDDLE OF EIGHTEENTH CENTURY.

THE influence of the Puritans, though unfavorable, was not fatal to English music. The quires were dispersed, the training of singers and players interrupted, cathedral scores lost, and organs destroyed; yet private cultivation did not cease, and there was no break in the history of composition. Many who had been brought up in the traditions of the early school, were able to resume the exercise of their art on the fall of the Commonwealth. Among these were Henry Lawes, Christopher Gibbons, William Child, John Jenkins, and Benjamin Rogers, whose lives extended through the greater part of the seventeenth century. But with Charles II. a new taste came in, which transformed first the style of performance and then that of composition. Evelyn thus describes the service at the Chapel Royal on Dec. 21, 1663:—

'One of his Majesty's Chaplains preached; after which, instead of the ancient, grave, and solemn wind-music accompanying the organ, was introduced a concert of twenty-four violins between every pause, after the French fantastical, light way, better suiting a tavern or play

7

house than a church. This was the *first* time of change, and now we no more heard the cornet which gave life to the organ; that instrument quite left off in which the English were so skilful!'

Of the older composers Henry Lawes was the most successful in adopting the new style. But he, like the rest, had soon to give place to the rising talent of Pelham Humfrey, Michael Wise, and John Blow, choristers in the Chapel Royal. Humfrey was sent by the King to study in Italy and France. On his return he brought an important element into English music, viz. declamatory power. The forcible expression of the words, the careful observance of quantity and stress, and the discovery of dramatic effects in progressions and modulations, fascinated and absorbed this fresh and vigorous school. Their productive time was destined soon to end, for Humfrey died in 1674, and Purcell, who imitated and excelled him, died in 1695. Each showed, even in a short career, remarkable creative powers, attended of course with some defects as regards continuity and design, since these qualities are usually absent at the beginning of a new period in music, and only reappear when the style arrives at maturity. This stage the later contrapuntal school did not reach in England. Purcell left no equal, and the prospects of native music were not improved by the introduction of Italian opera, and the advent of Hændel. This composer almost fills up the musical history of England till the middle of the eighteenth century. In his oratorios the contrapuntal style received its highest development, the most artificial devices of imitation being used with admirable effect in many styles, epic, lyric, and dramatic. Many of Milton's finest passages form the foundation of his works. We must regret that he was not also attracted to Shakspere.

4. SONG. *Come unto these yellow sands. Tempest*, I. ii.

By JOHN BANISTER; born 1630: died 1679.

His father, one of the Waitts of the parish of S. Giles-in-the-Field, was his instructor in the rudiments of music. Having become a good violinist, he was sent by the King to France, and in 1663 was appointed 'chief of his Majesty's violins.' It is said that he was dismissed from this post for saying, in the King's

S

hearing, that the English violinists were superior to the French.
He gave afternoon concerts at his house in White Friars every day
during the last seven years of his life. He was buried in the
cloisters of Westminster Abbey. A MS. copy of the 1st act of
Banister's music to 'Circe,' a tragedy, performed in 1676, is still
preserved. In the same year was also performed Banister's and
Pelham Humfrey's setting of the *Tempest*, from which the above
song is taken.

5. Song. **Where the bee sucks.** *Tempest*, V. i.
   By PELHAM HUMFREY; born 1647; died 1674.

He was one of the Children of the Chapel Royal, re-established
at the Restoration. His talent for composition was early displayed,
and when about 17 years of age, he was sent by Charles II. to the
Continent to study the new style of music brought in by Carissimi
and Lulli. During his travels, which lasted three years, he received
£450 from the Secret Service fund. We find the following description of Humfrey on his return, in the diary of Mr. Samuel Pepys:—

15th Nov. 1667 . . . . . 'Home, and there find, as I expected,
Mr. Caesar and little Pelham Humfrey, lately returned from France,
and is an absolute Monsieur, as full of form and confidence and
vanity, and disparages everything and everybody's skill but his own.
But to hear how he laughs at all the King's musick here, as Blagrave
[Gentleman of the Chapel of Charles II.] and others, that they
cannot keep time nor tune, nor understand anything; and that
Grebus the Frenchman, the King's master of the musick, [= Louis
Grabu, defined in Grove's Dictionary as an 'impudent pretender']
how he understands nothing, nor can play on any instrument, and
so cannot compose: and that he will give him a lift out of his
place, and that he and the King are mighty great! I had a good
dinner for them, as a venison pasty and some fowl, and after dinner
we did play, he on the theorbo, Mr. Caesar on his French lute, and
I on the viol, and I see that this Frenchman do so much wonders
on the theorbo, that without question he is a good musician, but
his vanity do offend me.'

Humfrey was appointed 'Master of the Children,' and 'Composer in Ordinary for the Violins to his Majesty' in 1672. He
died two years later, aged 27, and was buried in the cloisters of
Westminster Abbey.

His works consist mostly of anthems and songs.

9

THIRD PERIOD. EARLY HARMONIC.

SECOND HALF OF EIGHTEENTH AND BEGINNING OF NINETEENTH CENTURY.

THE periods of musical history cannot be defined exactly by dates. Before the contrapuntal style had even reached perfection, another style, the harmonic, began to appear; and when the latter became predominant the former did not die out, but has lasted, in certain branches of the art, down to our own time. Although the different schools overlap in this way, there is a marked distinction between the style characteristic of the earlier part of the eighteenth century, and that which afterwards prevailed.

The change was connected with the rise of the great solo singers and solo violinists, who then appeared in many countries, but principally in Italy. Their powers could not be exhibited to advantage in contrapuntal music, for this was essentially a *choral* style, without contrast or variety between one vocal part and another. The melodic interest now became concentrated in a single part, to which the rest merely supplied a harmony. In this way the prominence of the soloist was secured; and a style of melody far more brilliant and ornate than any previously known, came into fashion.

The growth of instrumental accompaniment also helped forward the new school. In the contrapuntal system, the different capabilities and resources of the various orchestral instruments were but slightly studied or utilized. The same kind of treatment was applied to the accompaniment as to the voice, although many passages, too difficult to be sung, might be safely assigned to the violin and oboe; while, on the other hand, the trumpet and horn were not at all adapted for playing contrapuntal themes, but chiefly for sustaining single notes in the harmony. Thus a complete transformation was brought about, when composers began to discover the endless effects of ornament and expression which could be obtained from orchestral coloring.

It is unfortunate that there is no accurate and popular name for the style of music that succeeded counterpoint. The terms

'Homophonic' and 'Monodic,' besides being pedantic, are incorrect, as they imply that the new compositions were all in unison, or for a single voice. To speak of counterpoint as 'Strict,' and the new style as 'Free,' is equally inappropriate. Every rising composer is supposed to violate rules, until his methods are understood and systematically defined. The name 'Massive,' again, is often opposed to 'Contrapuntal,' because the harmony was now arranged in prolonged masses supporting the melody, instead of incessantly changing with the movement of each voice. But this name, as well as that of 'Harmonic,' which we here employ as the most familiar, is inaccurate if it leads to the supposition that the contrapuntal period was distinguished by solos and not by part-music. The contrary was the case.

The most suitable names yet found for the two styles are 'Horizontal' and 'Vertical.' The contrapuntist regards music as an affair of themes; he fixes on the subject and countersubject beforehand, and only uses such chords as can arise from their combination. The harmonist starts with the conception of chords; often he takes a chord in arpeggio as theme, and gives the accompanying parts only as much melody as is compatible with the harmony he has designed. However, it is not yet usual to talk of the 'horizontal' and 'vertical' styles in music, though every one knows the 'perpendicular' style in architecture.

The treatment of Form also underwent a great change at this time. In counterpoint, variety was obtained chiefly by making one part imitate another at a greater or a less distance of time, or in notes of twice or half the length. Often the theme was treated first direct and then inverted, moving down where it had formerly moved up, and conversely. Again it might be reversed, the end being taken as a beginning. Mechanical devices like these could be carried out by a deaf-mute, provided that he could read and write. When the contrapuntists, while obeying these rules, succeeded in producing music that the world cared to hear, it was not by reason of their training.

The new structural principle was that of *Variation*. At each repetition, new ornament was added to the theme, or the harmony was changed, or one particular phrase was taken as a suggestion for a long development through many keys. In this way arose what is called the 'Sonata form,' which, however, only applies to the *first* movement of the Sonata, Quartet, Symphony, &c. The opening theme is soon followed by a second and contrasting theme. Then both are varied or 'developed' in the 'free fantasia.' Next the first two themes reappear, and lastly comes the 'coda.' Between each of the main features, episodes were usually introduced. The analogy of this procedure with that of oratory and poetry, has often been pointed out.

The Early Harmonic period is sometimes called, in the restricted sense, 'Classical.' It was the period when most of the designs of pure music, such as the Symphony, Concerto, Overture, became recognizable. The best works of that time are distinguished to modern ears by moderation, sanity, and perfection within limits: the inferior works have no worse quality than florid conventionality; all well-known characteristics of 'Classical' art.

Since the decay of the Madrigal style in the first quarter of the seventeenth century, no form of poetic part-music for unaccompanied voices was cultivated in England till the beginning of the eighteenth century, when the 'Glee' arose. The characteristic of the Glee is the succession of several short melodies, often in different keys and different metres, never contrapuntally treated, but only harmonized in the modern manner. These repeated changes often produce a disconnected impression, which, in comparison with the later contrapuntal music, must have made the Glee appear a rather rudimentary form of art. The best effects in this form of composition are obtained by sustained or contrasted chords, always beautiful when rendered by well-trained and unaccompanied voices. The Madrigal, on the other hand, was founded on a few themes elaborately combined in imitation, making little use of the progression known as the 'perfect cadence,' and being generally independent of modern ideas of harmony.

The Glee style was founded and most successfully practised by Samuel Webbe, who gained twenty-seven prizes for his works. Other writers of Glees were Stevens, Calcott, Horsley, Attwood,

Battishill, Cooke, Lord Mornington, Spofforth, Stafford Smith, and Sir Henry Bishop.

6. SONG. 𝕭𝖑𝖔𝖜, blow, thou 𝖜𝖎𝖓𝖙𝖊𝖗 𝖜𝖎𝖓𝖉. *As You Like It*, II. vii.

7. SONG. 𝕯𝖑𝖍𝖊𝖓 𝖉𝖆𝖎𝖘𝖎𝖊𝖘 𝖕𝖎𝖊𝖉. *Love's Labour's Lost*, V. ii.

8. SONG. 𝖀𝖓𝖉𝖊𝖗 𝖙𝖍𝖊 𝖌𝖗𝖊𝖊𝖓𝖜𝖔𝖔𝖉 𝖙𝖗𝖊𝖊. *As You Like It*, II. v.

By THOMAS AUGUSTUS ARNE; born 1710, died 1778.

Arne was intended by his father for the profession of the law, and on leaving Eton College was placed in a solicitor's office for three years. But his love for music prevailed, and instead of applying himself to legal studies, he secretly conveyed a spinet to his bed-room, and by muffling the strings with a handkerchief, contrived to practise during the night undetected.

He took lessons on the violin from Festing, and would occasionally borrow a livery in order to gain admission to the servants' gallery at the opera. He made such progress as to be able to lead a chamber band at the house of an amateur, who gave private concerts. There he was accidentally discovered by his father, who made fruitless efforts to induce him to become a lawyer, but at last gave up the attempt. Being free to practise openly, he charmed the whole family by his skill on the violin.

In 1738 he established his reputation as a lyric composer by the capital manner in which he set Milton's 'Comus.' In this he introduced a light, original, and pleasing melody, wholly different from that of Purcell or of Hændel, whom all English composers had hitherto either borrowed from or imitated. Till a more modern Italian style was introduced in the *pasticcio* English operas of Bickerstaff and Cumberland, Arne's melody was the standard of all perfection at our theatres and public gardens. (See Burney's 'History,' vol. iv. p. 659, &c.) In 1746 Arne set several of Shakspere's songs, from which we select the above.

On July 6, 1759, the University of Oxford created Arne a Doctor of Music. He was the first who introduced female voices into oratorio choruses. This he did at Covent Garden Theatre, Feb. 26, 1773, in a work of his own, *Judith*.

13

9. Song. **Full fathom five.** *Tempest*, I. ii.

By JOHN CHRISTOPHER SMITH ; born 1712, died 1795.

His father, a German named Schmidt, acted as Hændel's treasurer.
He himself was Hændel's amanuensis during the blindness of the
great composer. Smith's style often resembles that of his master,
but in the present song it belongs to the more modern harmonic
period. He composed two Shaksperian Operas, 'The Tempest,'
and ' The Fairies,' which is the *Midsummer Night's Dream* alterd.

The compositions of Christopher Smith and Purcell have sometimes been confounded : for instance, in an arrangement by Loder
of Smith's 'Full fathom five,' Purcell's chorus has been added
without any remark as to the real authorship ; while Smith's 'No
more dams,' has been twice reprinted with the name of Purcell
attached to it. Dr. Clarke in his 'Beauties of Purcell' has made
this mistake.

10. Glee. **The cloud capt towers.** *Tempest*, I. ii.

By RICHARD JAMES SAMUEL STEVENS ; born about 1753, died
1837.

Stevens was a Londoner, and was educated in St. Paul's
Cathedral. His first appointment was as organist to the Temple
Church. In 1795 he became organist of the Charter House, and in
1801 was elected Professor of Music at Gresham College. His
glees speedily obtained public favor, and have retained it till
now.—' English Cyclopaedia,' vol. v. p. 718.

11. Song. **When that I was and a little tiny boy.** *Twelfth
Night*, V. i.

By J. VERNON.

William Linley in his ' Dramatic Songs of Shakspere' attributes
this song to Fielding, but Dr. Rimbault states that it was really
composed by J. Vernon, a well-known tenor singer at the theatres
and concerts, about 1760–80.

12. Glee. **Tell me where is fancy bred.** *Merchant of Venice*,
III. ii.

By R. J. S. STEVENS. (See above, No. 10.)

13. SONG. 𝕸illo𝖜 𝕾ong. *Othello*, IV. iii.

By JAMES HOOK ; born at Norwich 1746, died at Boulogne 1827.

He was for many years organist of S. John's, Horseley Down. From 1774 to 1820 he was organist and composer at Vauxhall Gardens, and wrote a large number of glees, catches, and songs. He published an oratorio, the 'Ascension,' in 1776. His 'Lass of Richmond Hill,' ''Twas within a mile,' and 'A little farm well tilled,' continue to be popular ; and many of his other pieces, such as 'Sweet Lilies of the Valley,' 'The Maid of the Green,' only require to be revived to gain equal favor.

14. GLEE. 𝕳ark, hark, the lark. *Cymbeline*, II. iii.

By DR. BENJAMIN COOKE ; born 1734, died 1793.

At twelve years of age he became deputy-organist of Westminster Abbey, in 1757 was appointed master of the choristers there, in 1758 lay vicar, and in 1762 organist of the Abbey. In 1775 he passed as Doctor of Music at Cambridge, and in 1782 was admitted to the same degree at Oxford. Dr. Cooke's compositions, which are voluminous, are for the Church, concert-room, and chamber. The works by which he is best known, and which will hand down his name to posterity, are his numerous and beautiful glees and canons, for seven of which he gained prizes. Apart from his eminence as a practical musician, Dr. Cooke was one of the most learned theorists of his time. He died September 14th, 1793, and was buried in the cloisters of Westminster Abbey, where a mural tablet recounts his merits and exhibits one of his canons in three parts by augmentation and diminution.

15. DUET. 𝕴 kno𝖜 a bank. *Midsummer Night's Dream*, II. ii.

By CHARLES EDWARD HORN ; born 1786, died 1849.

Horn was a singer. His voice was poor, but of such extensive compass that he was able to take baritone as well as tenor parts. He also displayed considerable ability as an actor. He composed many small operas, in which some of the songs remain popular to the present time ; as, for instance, 'Cherry ripe!' 'I've been roaming,' and 'Thro' the wood.'

16. Song. **Should he upbraid.** *Taming of the Shrew*, II. i. (alterd).

17. Song. **Fair is my love.** *Passionate Pilgrim*, VII.

18. Duet. **As it fell upon a day.** *Passionate Pilgrim*, XX.

By Sir Henry Rowley Bishop; born 1786, died 1855.

He early showed a talent for dramatic composition, and when he was eighteen years old wrote his first work, which was performed at Margate. He became Bachelor of Music in 1839, and was knighted in 1842.

Bishop wrote more music to Shakspere's words than any other composer before or since. His pieces show capital spirit and character. His 'Home, sweet home' and 'Mynheer Van Dunck' are not likely to be soon forgotten.

Intermezzo.

In Memoriam Miss Teena Rochfort-Smith.

Part Song. **Fear no more the heat of the sun.** *Cymbeline*, IV. ii.
  By James Greenhill.

Miss Rochfort-Smith planned a Four-Text edition of *Hamlet*, which she intended to give to the New Shakspere Society. She hoped also to compile for the Society a fresh Concordance to all Shakspere's works, giving references to lines, as well as Acts and Scenes. Her death, after a week's severe suffering, took place on Sept. 4, 1883. The Committee of the New Shakspere Society, at its first meeting last October, passed a Resolution expressing their sense of the great loss which the Society and the progress of Shakspere study had suffered by the sad death of their gifted helper. Mr. Greenhill has composed this elegy for the present occasion.

FOURTH PERIOD.   LATE HARMONIC.

NINETEENTH CENTURY.

EARLY in the present century, music passed entirely out of the preparatory stages, in which it had so long remained, and made a fresh start, less to discover new kinds of technical resource, than to apply in detail those already known. Instruments of all the necessary types having been invented and improved, the time was ripe for an immense growth of orchestral writing. As a means of pure expression, every instrument was obviously inferior to the voice ; but this defect could be compensated by the endless contrasts of orchestral tones ; by great varieties of speed ; by the continual use of chromatic chords, very distantly related to the key ; and by a similar freedom of modulation. The forms of accompaniment reached a degree of elaboration never before known, and not seldom surpassing in importance the melody itself. Thus the reaction from the method of two centuries before, was complete. Instead of treating instruments as if they were voices, it now became the practice to write for voices as if they were instruments. The influence of the Italian style, formerly so powerful on the side of vocal melody, had grown too feeble and trivial to resist these modern tendencies.

From a more general point of view, the present period seems characterized by an entire disregard of the authority of the past. Traditional rules, however ancient, are never observed, if they interfere with any effect which the composer desires, in order to increase the attractiveness of his work. Banished from living art, these rules may yet be discovered in the divergent creeds of teachers, theorists, or critics.

Of Church music according to the established pattern, little has been produced in the nineteenth century, and that little rather as an imitative archaism than a free invention. Sacred works which represent modern tendencies, like Beethoven's 'Missa Solennis,' deviate from every ecclesiastical type. The faithful transmission of stereotyped forms has ceased to be the aim of composers, and has given place to the forcible rendering of new poetic conceptions.

Music, indeed, is no longer dependent for subject-matter on either liturgy or drama. Instead of being a decorative adjunct, a translation of literary ideas, music has become an original structure, an independent creation. It presents itself as a new language for thought and emotion; not possessing the definiteness of speech, but far surpassing it in range and power. The first composer who thus drew his inspiration direct from life was Beethoven; and he has so familiarized the world with what is called 'poetic music,' that one can hardly now realize how startling must have been its first apparition, eighty years ago.

Released from so many conventional trammels, music could not fail to be soon transformed by the 'Romantic movement.' Every phase of this influence, long ago recognized in other arts, had its analogue in music. 'Local color' was closely studied, with a new and deeper feeling for the characteristics of folk-song. The Bohemian, Suabian, and Spanish elements were brought into cultivated music by Weber, the Hungarian Gipsy by Schubert, the Highland Keltic by Mendelssohn in his Scotch Symphony and his Overture, 'Fingal's Cave.' The Slavonic temperament has also arrived at artistic expression, seeming to promise a renewal of European music now that the decay of German originality has followed the decay of Italian. In the study of dramatic appropriateness, even savage music has not been neglected. One of the first successes in this branch was the Chorus of Dervishes in Beethoven's 'Ruins of Athens.' A native Arabic melody is taken as the foundation of an elaborate finale in Weber's 'Oberon,' and the same opera contains an unsurpassable picture of Islamite truculence, in the chorus, 'Glory to the Khalif.' If the plot of a new work is laid in Japan, and the composer does not produce some eccentric effects, capable of being interpreted as 'local color,' he is at once denounced by the critics.

Weber, again, was the first in music to adventure into the realms of diablerie and fairyland, and to call up the forms of fiend, wizard, sprite and mermaid, with the living and fascinating reality of folk-lore. Mendelssohn, whose *Midsummer Night's Dream* is also inspired by the magical style, was perhaps too classical an artist to

18

meet with such perfect success in this purely 'barbarian' mystery. Later composers have often followed in the steps of these two, and the manufacture of the supernatural is now a well-understood and formulated process. While the nineteenth century has seen an untiring search after every possible or impossible beauty, after every kind of ornate or picturesque material, it has also been marked by a strong taste for the sombre and the grotesque. The exciting and exhausting effects of romantic art necessitate the use of violence and ugliness as means of contrast and relief. Philosophical exposition of this method may be found in Vischer's '.Æsthetik der Hæsslichen.' To Mendelssohn, this aspect of the romantic movement appears to have been repulsive. But the nervous excitability of his style, its fanciful elegance, elaboration of detail, and breathless speed, mark it clearly enough as an offspring of the nineteenth century. Possibly, future music may go so much farther in the same direction, as to make the works of the present day seem colourless and pedantic by the side of the more drastic and original effects which then may be discovered.

18. Song. Hark, hark, the Lark. Cymbeline, II. iii.
By FRANZ PETER SCHUBERT ; born Jan. 31, 1797 ; died Nov. 19, 1828.

Lichtenthal, near Vienna, was Schubert's birth-place, but his ancestors came from Moravia. Beginning to compose when only thirteen, his progress as a musician was interrupted by his turning school-teacher, in order to avoid the conscription. When seventeen, his first mass attracted the attention of Salieri, an old Italian composer, long resident in Vienna, who took him up and gave him lessons. Schubert lived for many years in great poverty, supported sometimes by the friends he had made by his music. He attracted little public notice till about 1816, when Vogl, a Viennese Opera singer, made his acquaintance, and was fascinated by his songs. In 1818 he became teacher of music in the family of Count Johann Esterhazy ; and retained this situation for seven years. The summers were passed at the Count's Hungarian country-seat ; the

19

winters in Vienna. His stay **in** Hungary made **Schubert acquainted** with the remarkable dances and songs **of the Magyars,** which he turned to account in many of his best instrumental works.

Schubert was by far the most prolific of composers. He **wrote several operas,** masses, symphonies, string quartets, and a multi-**tude of pianoforte** pieces and songs. Few, however, were published during his life, and these were miserably paid for. He sent three of his songs to Goethe in 1819, but the poet took no notice of the composer, who was afterwards to give **some of** his songs a wider popularity than they could otherwise have enjoyed. Though Beethoven's stay in Vienna coincided for so many years with Schubert's lifetime, they only met twice. On the first occasion, Schubert's **nervousness** overcame him, and he rushed out of the room before he **had written** a word for the deaf Beethoven **to read.** On **the second, Beethoven** was hardly conscious, being then in his last illness. **But some days** before he had become acquainted **with a selection of Schubert's** songs. These excited his admiration, **and caused him to say,** 'Truly, Schubert has the divine fire.'

Though Schubert's name was now becoming more widely known, he was still in poverty; sometimes on **the** brink of starvation. He died of typhus fever at the age of thirty-one. Of his many works only a small proportion was publicly performed during his life. **Schumann** was the first to force the world to listen to the treasures they had disregarded. **Liszt also aided the success** of other **works of** Schubert; and **in England a similar service has been rendered** by Sir George Grove.

Schubert set only three **of** Shakspere's songs. '**Come, thou** monarch **of the** Vine,' 'Who **is** Sylvia?' and 'Hark, **hark, the** Lark!' The last is **included in** our program. **In this song a** happy use is made of the dominant pedal, **and of the modulation into** the key a major Third below.

'The isolated songs of Schubert, from their beauty, fitness, freshness, **and** number, place him in general estimation, and deservedly, **at** the head of all song-writers of whatever age or country. As **a** practitioner **on** a more extended scale, a composer of symphonies and chamber-music symphonic in its scope and character, his **place is** lower. He is rich in—nay, replete with—

ideas of which he is rather the slave than the master. . . . He is diffuse to an extent far beyond the practice of any composer of like power. . . . If ever Schubert's reputation as a symphony writer dies, it will be of the plethora of invention exhibited in ' his works. (Hullah, ' Lectures on Musical History.')

The best account yet published of Schubert's life and works is by Sir George Grove in his ' Dictionary of Music and Musicians,' Parts XV, XVI, pp. 319 to 381.

PART SONG. **Tell me where is fancy bred.** *Merchant of Venice*, III. ii.

By IL CAVALIERE CIRO PINSUTI; born May 9, 1829.

He is a native of Sinalunga, Siena. He came to England in 1830, and remained here fifteen years, carrying on his musical studies. In 1845 he returned to Italy and became a pupil of Rossini. Three years later he again came to England, and started as a teacher of singing, sometimes residing in London, sometimes in Newcastle. Many eminent singers, including Grisi, Bosio, Patti, Mario, have come to him for direction. Several of his operas, of which one is founded upon *The Merchant of Venice*, have been produced with success in Italy. His part songs are melodious, spirited, and popular. The present one, in the key of G, starts in a modern and striking manner with the chord of D♯, A, F♯, C.

SONG. **Willow Song.** *Othello*, IV. iii.

By SIR ARTHUR SEYMOUR SULLIVAN; born May 13, 1842.

He was a chorister in the Chapel Royal till 1857. He was elected Mendelssohn scholar at the Royal Academy in 1856, and was the first to hold that distinction. Goss and Sterndale Bennett were his teachers. Two years later he went to Leipzig, returning to London at the end of 1861, and bringing his music to Shakspere's *Tempest*, by which his first public success was obtained.

An Overture, ' In Memoriam,' written in 1866 on the death of his father, is still often heard. In 1873 he composed an Oratorio, ' The Light of the World ; ' and in 1880 another, ' The Martyr of Antioch,' received with applause at the Birmingham and Leeds Festivals respectively.

Of late years the names of Gilbert and Sullivan have become fixed in the public mind as author and composer of a series of comic operettas, 'Trial by Jury,' the 'Sorcerer,' 'H.M.S. Pinafore,' the 'Pirates of Penzance,' 'Patience,' 'Iolanthe,' 'Princess Ida.' The farcical absurdity of the words and the pretty ingenuity of the tunes have led to the most successful runs in English and American theatres.

Sir Arthur Sullivan is also universally known as the favourite composer, almost the creator, of the modern English drawing-room ballad. His part songs, hymns, and anthems are of equal merit.

He was knighted on May 15, 1883.

23. Song. 𝕎hen that 𝕀 was and a little tiny boy. *Twelfth Night*, V. i.

By John Liphot Hatton; born at Liverpool, 1809.

He was almost entirely a self-taught musician. His songs and part songs have become very popular. In 1844 he went to Vienna to bring out his Opera 'Pascal Bruno.' On his return to England he took the pseudonym of 'Czapek,' meaning 'hat on' in Hungarian, and published under it several of his works. He was director of the music at the Princess's Theatre under Charles Kean, and during this engagement produced settings of *Macbeth, Henry VIII., Richard II., Lear, The Merchant of Venice, Much Ado about Nothing*, etc. In 1877 his sacred drama, 'Hezekiah,' was performed at the Crystal Palace.

24. Trio. "How sweet the moonlight." *Merchant of Venice*, V. i.

By John George Callcott; born 1821.

Organist at Teddington. For twenty-four years he was accompanyist to Henry Leslie's choir. He has published two cantatas, 'The Golden Harvest' and 'Halloween,' as well as many part songs and pieces of dance-music.

25. Song. **Orpheus with his lute.** *Henry VIII.*, III. i.

26. Song. **O Mistress mine.** *Twelfth Night*, II. iii.

By Sir A. Sullivan. (See No. 22.)

27. PART SONG. **Will you buy?** *Winter's Tale*, IV. iii.

By CLARA ANGELA MACIRONE ; born in London, 1821.

Miss Macirone is of Roman descent.   She received her musical education at the Royal Academy, where she was afterwards appointed to a 'professorship.'   Her 'Te Deum' was the first composition by a woman which was performed in the Church service.   Her setting of the ' Benedictus ' obtained the admiration of Mendelssohn.   But she is chiefly known by her part songs, many of which have been sung with success by various London choirs.   Of late years Miss Macirone has organized a school of musical instruction.

The accounts given of the lives and works of composers are compiled from Baptie's ' Biographical Dictionary,' by permission of the publishers, Messrs. Morley and Co., Regent Street ; also from Grove's ' Dictionary of Music and Musicians,' published by Messrs. Macmillan and Co., Bedford Street.

www.ingramcontent.com/pod-product-compliance
Lightning Source LLC
Chambersburg PA
CBHW031410270326
41929CB00010BA/1400